C000176523

IMMIGRATION SERVICE
★ - 4 OCT 2001 ★
DEPARTED
(1095)
HONG KONG

DEPARTMENT OF IMMIGRATION
PERMITTED TO ENTER
AUSTRALIA.
on 24 APR 1996
For stay of 12 Month
SYDNEY AIRPORT 54

IMMIGRATION DIVISION BANGKOK THAILAND
A
72
DEPARTED
- 6 FEB 1998
SIGNED

IMMIGRATION ETHNIC AFFAIRS
...... Person
30 OCT 1999
DEPARTED
AUSTRALIA
SYDNEY 32

T R A V E L E R' S
HONG KONG
C O M P A N I O N

上陸許可
ADMITTED
15. FEB. 1996
Status: 4-1- 4
Duration: 90 days
NARITA(N)
Immigration Inspector
日本国

ADMITTED
20 OCT. 1998
Status: 4-1-16
Duration 180 days
Port: HANEDA
Signature

Nº 011278
THE UNITED STATES
OF AMERICA
NONIMMIGRANT VISA
ISSUED AT
U.S. IMMIGRATION
170 HHW 1710
JUL 20 1998

SSED
Air Port

HONG KONG
(1038)
- 7 JUN 1998
IMMIGRATION
OFFICER

The 2001–2002 Traveler's Companions
ARGENTINA • AUSTRALIA • BALI • CALIFORNIA • CANADA • CHILE • CHINA •
COSTA RICA • CUBA • EASTERN CANADA • ECUADOR • FLORIDA • HAWAII • HONG KONG •
INDIA • INDONESIA • JAPAN • KENYA • MALAYSIA & SINGAPORE • MEDITERRANEAN
FRANCE • MEXICO • NEPAL • NEW ENGLAND • NEW ZEALAND • PERU • PHILIPPINES •
PORTUGAL • RUSSIA • SOUTH AFRICA • SOUTHERN ENGLAND • SPAIN • THAILAND •
TURKEY • VENEZUELA • VIETNAM, LAOS AND CAMBODIA • WESTERN CANADA

Traveler's HONG KONG Companion

First published 1998
Second Edition 2001
The Globe Pequot Press
246 Goose Lane, PO Box 480
Guilford, CT 06437 USA
www.globe-pequot.com

© 2001 by The Globe Pequot Press, Guilford CT, USA

ISBN: 07627-1007-1

Distributed in the European Union by
World Leisure Marketing Ltd, Unit 11
Newmarket Court, Newmarket Drive,
Derby, DE24 8NW, United Kingdom
www.map-guides.com

Created, edited and produced by
Allan Amsel Publishing, 53, rue Beaudouin
27700 Les Andelys, France.
E-mail: AAmsel@aol.com
Editor in Chief: Allan Amsel
Editor: Anne Trager
Picture editor and book designer: Roberto Rossi
Original design concept: Hon Bing-wah

Printed by Samwha Printing Co. Ltd., Seoul, South Korea

TRAVELER'S
HONG KONG
COMPANION

by Derek Maitland and Chris Taylor

photographs by Nik Wheeler

Second Edition

The
Globe
Pequot
Press

GUILFORD
CONNECTICUT

Contents

Lok Ma Chau

San Tin

Mai Po
Marshes

Lau Fau Shan

2

Lam Tsuen North
Country Park ▲
585 m

Wang Chau

HONG
(SPECIAL ADMIN

Ngau Hom Sha

Yuen Long

Pat Heung

Ful Sha Wai

Walled •
Village

Kam Tin

Nim Wan

Shui Tsiu
San Tsuen

Yuen Kong

• Miu Fat
Monastery

Chin Chung Koon •

New Territories

Tai Lam Pat Heung
▲ Country Park
507 m

Chuen Lun

Castle
Peak
583 m

Tuen Mun

MacLehose Trail

Tai Lam Chung
Country Park

Tai Lam
Chung
Reservoir

Sham Tseng

Castle
Peak
Bay

PILLAR
POINT

to Macau

2

BROTHERS
POINT

Tsing Ma
Bridge

Ma Wan

The Brothers

Kap Shui
Mun Bridge

Tsing Yi

⊗ MASS TRANSIT RAILWAY

TSUEN WAN LINE	KWUN TONG LINE	ISLAND LINE	KOWLOON, CANTON RAILWAY
▪ CENTRAL	▪ QUARRY BAY	▪ SHEUNG WAN	⟷
▪ ADMIRALTY	▪ LAM TIN	▪ CENTRAL	
▪ TSIM SHA TSUI	▪ KWUN TONG	▪ ADMIRALTY	▪ LO WU
▪ JORDAN	▪ NGAU TAU KOK	▪ WAN CHAI	▪ SHEUNG SHUI
▪ YAU MA TEI	▪ KOWLOON BAY	▪ CAUSEWAY BAY	▪ FANLING
▪ MONG KOK	▪ CHOI HUNG	▪ TIN HAU	▪ TAI WO
▪ PRINCE EDWARD	▪ DIAMOND HILL	▪ FORTRESS HILL	▪ TAI PO MARKET
▪ SHAM SHUI PO	▪ WONG TAI SAN	▪ NORTH POINT	▪ UNIVERSITY
▪ CHEUNG SHA WAN	▪ LOK FU	▪ QUARRY BAY	▪ FO TAN
▪ LAI CHI KOK	▪ KOWLOON TONG	▪ TAI KOO	▪ RACECOURSE
▪ MEI FOO	▪ SHEK KIP MEI	▪ SAI WAN HO	▪ SHA TIN
▪ LAI KING	▪ PRINCE EDWARD	▪ SHAUKEI WAN	▪ TAI WAI
▪ KWAI FONG	▪ MONG KOK	▪ HENG FA CHUEN	▪ KOWLOON TONG
▪ KWAI HING	▪ YAU MA TEI	▪ CHAI WAN	▪ MONG KOK
▪ TAI WO HAU			▪ KOWLOON
▪ TSUEN WAN			

RUSSIA

JAPAN

CHINA

**HONG
KONG**

INDIA

TAIWAN

VIETNAM

Chek Lap Kok
Hong Kong
International Airport ✈

Airport Express

Pak Mong

Discovery Bay

Discovery
Bay

Peng
Chau

Kau Yi
Chau

Lantau Trail

Tung Chung

Lantau Island

Mui Wo

Silver
Mine
Bay

Sunshine
Island

Lantau North
Country Park

Ngong Ping

Sunset
▲ Peak
869 m

Tai O

▲ Lantau
Peak
933 m

Lantau South
Country Park

Hei Ling Chau

Lantau Trail

Shek Pik
Reservoir

*Chi Ma Wan
Peninsula*

Fan Lau

Cheung
Chau

Shek Kwu Chau

N

Lantau Channel

Outlying Islands

Soko Islands

0	2	4	6	8	10km

0		3		6 miles

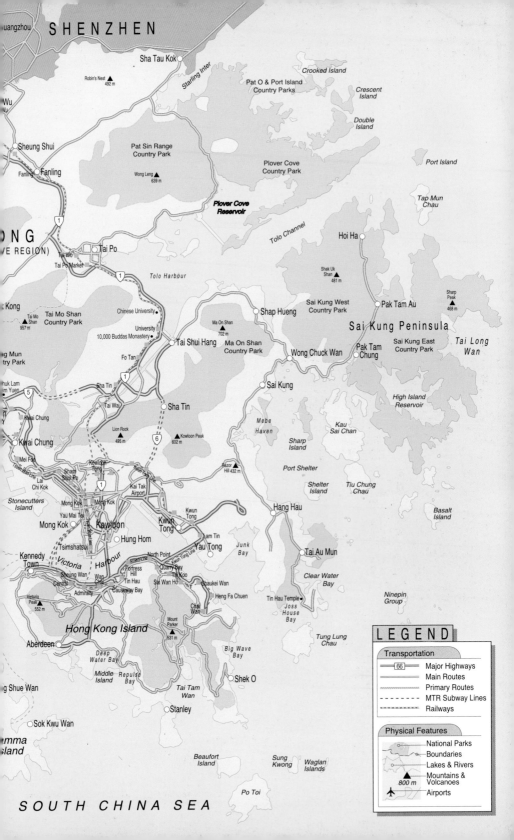

TOP SPOTS

Brace Yourself for the Peak

IN 1885, WHEN PHINEAS KYRIE AND WILLIAM KERFOOT HUGHES ANNOUNCED THAT THEY INTENDED TO BUILD A TRAMWAY TO THE TOP OF VICTORIA PEAK — early Hong Kong's exclusive residential area for colonial Brits — they were ridiculed. No one, it was thought, could possibly engineer a tram to tackle the steep and forested 554-m-high (1,817-ft) peak on Hong Kong Island. Indeed, no one anywhere in the region had ever attempted such a thing. And besides, what was wrong with sedan chairs, the then current mode of transport to the elite eyrie?

Three years later, the impossible became reality and two trams (strictly speaking, it's a "double reversible funicular railway," in which one tram goes down as the other goes up) started trundling up the Peak, starting from Garden Road and finishing 373 m (1,224 ft) higher, just below the summit. During the first year of operation they carried some 150,000 people.

The Peak Tram has been going strong ever since, carrying more than four million passengers in 2000. It has seen some changes. In 1926 the coal-powered hauling system was replaced with an electrically powered system. In 1956 and 1989, the tram cars were upgraded. In 1996 the summit terminal was torn down and rebuilt. But fundamentally, the operating system and the route itself haven't changed — the trams still run on the same tracks that were laid down in 1888. And it has run almost without interruptions. The only times service stopped were during World War II and during a ferocious 1966 typhoon which washed away some of the hillside.

Today's passengers are mostly tourists (Peak residents tend to prefer their chauffeur-driven limousines), although many Mid-Level residents (those living in the lower reaches of the Peak) still use it to commute to and from work: the four stops en route are at Kennedy, MacDonnell, May and Barker Roads.

Don't even think, however, about getting off before reaching the top: on a clear day, the eight-minute journey is

OPPOSITE: A panoramic view of Hong Kong Island and Kowloon. ABOVE: The bright lights of Hong Kong Harbor at night.

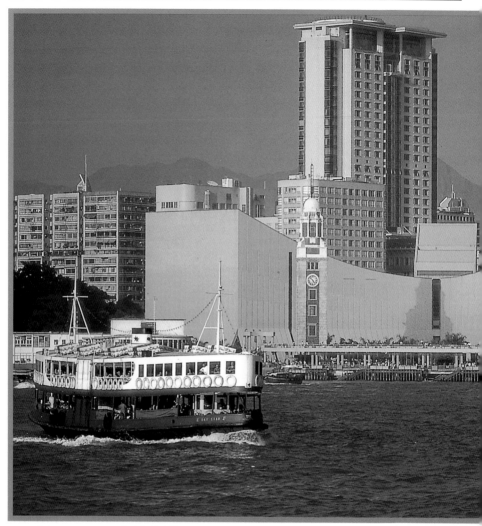

one of the most remarkable in Hong Kong. Pick a right-hand seat and fantastic views unfold as the tram slowly glides uphill: the tower blocks of Central and Mid-Levels far below, the rooftop penthouses and swimming pools, and the stunning harbor beyond. Nearby, almost close enough to touch, the untamed greenery and banyan creepers are full of chattering birds. Keep an eye out also for some of Hong Kong's older buildings — the whitewashed Helena May Boarding House and St. Paul's Church. As the gradient increases, the buildings below seem to tilt and passengers are almost laid flat, as if in a G-force experiment.

At the top is the Peak Tower, a seven-story extravaganza that opened in 1997. It incorporates not only the tram terminus but also shops, restaurants and entertainment including a motion-simulated ride called the Peak Explorer and a computer-operated ride, the Rise of the Dragon, which makes a journey through the history of Hong Kong. On a tackier note is the Ripley's Believe it or Not! Museum, with 500 oddities from around the world.

But the real attraction is the Peak's spectacular views. Spread out below is Hong Kong Island, Central, Quarry Bay, the harbor, Kowloon and many of the outlying islands. It's hard to say which

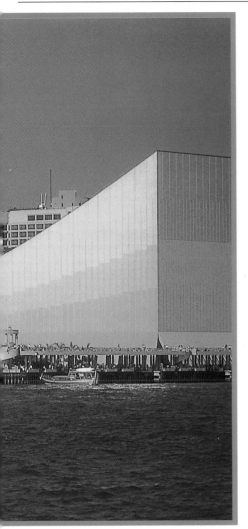

Take the World's Cheapest Cruise

THERE ARE FEW CONSTANTS IN A CITY LIKE HONG KONG, WHERE TRADITION HABITUALLY DEFERS TO THE IMPERATIVES OF PROGRESS. Even the harbor itself yields before the never-ending reclamation projects that satisfy Hong Kong's hunger for space. But, as long is there *is* a harbor, one constant is the Star Ferry.

The first report of a regular ferry service running between Tsimshatsui in Kowloon and Hong Kong Island dates from December 28, 1888, the same year the Peak Tram started operation. The ferry was a steam-powered shuttle called the *Morning Star*, with departures every 40 minutes. Take a look at the sepia print on the wall just beyond the Tsimshatsui Ferry Terminal ticket turnstile for an idea of what the ferry looked like: a floating bucket, with seemingly barely enough room for 20 passengers.

Little is known of these early days. The ferry services were started by an affluent Parsee, Dorabjee Nowrojee, under the name of the Kowloon Ferry Company. Some time around the turn of the last century he was bought out by a company that inherited what was a small flotilla of four coal-burner-powered boats all bearing the word "star" in their names — *Morning Star*, *Night Star* being two that have been handed down to this day. By extension, the service became the Star Ferry, and the boats have stuck to the "star" theme — the *Golden Star* and the *World Star* are two of the most recent additions to the fleet.

Like the Peak Tram, the Star Ferry has had its interruptions. In 1906, a typhoon destroyed two ferries and swept away the Kowloon-side ferry terminus. From December 12, 1941, when the ferries were brought into action to evacuate

is the more dramatic time to be up here — at night or during the day. It's worth taking in both.

And the Peak offers more. Opposite the terminus, Harlech and Lugard roads provide a delightful one-hour walk encircling the Peak, a cool escape in summer and great for jogging at any time. When hunger calls, the Peak Tower and the adjacent Peak Galleria both have restaurants, including the exquisite Café Deco Bar & Grill, a must for art deco buffs. Gazing out at the view, raise a glass in honor of those determined Gentlemen, Mr. Kyrie and Mr. Hughes, without whom the Peak might still be the exclusive domain of the Hong Kong rich.

The Star Ferry — the proposal to hike up the fares led to civil unrest in Hong Kong in 1966 — is still probably the cheapest sightseeing ride in the world.

civilians and key personnel from Kowloon, the Japanese occupation saw a 44-month hiatus in the ferry service.

But for the most part, come rain, come shine, the ferries have puttered across the narrow channel between Tsimshatsui and Central, providing passengers with one of the world's most scenic boat rides at a price that started at five cents and is still today an extremely inexpensive HK$2.20 first-class.

Take some time out on the Tsimshatsui side to peruse the sepia prints on the wall that document the history of the service. There are not many, but they are fascinating all the same. There are also several prints of Hong Kong from the early twentieth century, intriguing street scenes with not a vehicle in sight, rickshaw men waiting in the shadows of colonnaded buildings, an odd pedestrian in coolie attire carrying parcels on bamboo poles.

Be sure to travel on the second-floor, first-class section of the boat. With its parquet flooring, reversible chairs, the backs all imprinted with the "star" emblem, and the quaint old signs urging passengers to refrain from spitting and to watch for pick-pockets (which the Cantonese call "little hands"), it's usually a more peaceful place to enjoy the ride — at only eight minutes, as a tourist it's easy to wish it lasted longer.

It's fun to watch the old ferry hands at work. Dressed in navy-blue tunics and matching pants, often with cigarettes hanging from their mouths, they pole the mooring ropes to the boat as it grunts its way into a position at the end of the short journey, before the whistle blows and the gangplank is lowered, initiating a brief busy moment as everyone files off board.

To be sure a few things have changed: the skylines on either side of the harbor for one; the introduction of diesel powered boats in 1933 for two. But, despite the fact that today's Star Ferries have room for 750 passengers each, there's still an Old World air about the service that makes it one of Hong Kong's smallest but most enjoyable treats.

Do You *Dim Sum?*

FOR THOSE WITH THE MONEY TO SPEND, THERE'S NO DOUBT ABOUT IT, HONG KONG HAS THE BEST CHINESE FOOD IN THE WORLD. But even those who can't afford a splurge in one of Hong Kong's name restaurants can at least enjoy a *dim sum* brunch. The tiny snacks, wheeled around on trolleys and accompanied by tea, are one of the high points of Cantonese cuisine and can hardly be accused of breaking anyone's budget.

Dim sum — it means "little heart" — is the collective name for Cantonese snacks — savory or sweet, steamed or fried — and while other parts of China have equivalents (called *dian xin* in Mandarin) the sheer range of more than 2,000 varieties by some counts makes the Cantonese the most innovative. Not that Cantonese say they are going to "*dim sum*"; they go to *yum cha* — "drink tea." Indeed the snacks are considered as only an accompaniment to gossip and conversation held over innumerable tiny cups of oolong or jasmine tea — naturally, eat enough snacks and you have a meal; filling up at a *yum cha* session is never a problem.

OPPOSITE: A lavish display of specialties including Peking duck as the centerpiece at a Central District restaurant. ABOVE: Duck, crab, squid and sausage, Chiu Chow style.

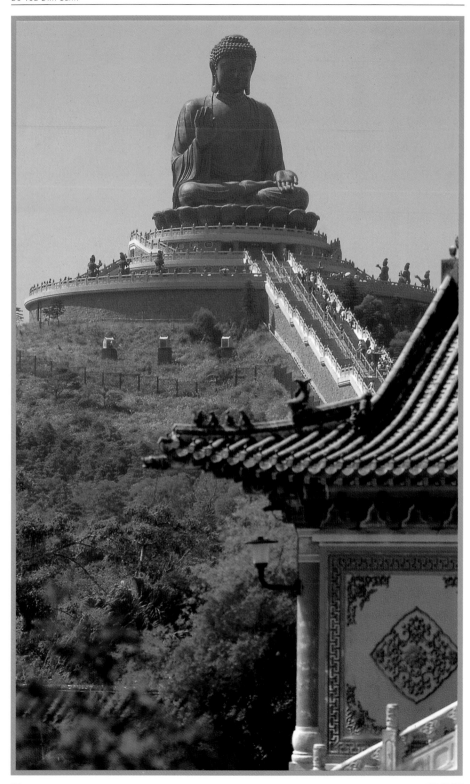

As for those 2,000 varieties, even the most ambitious *dim sum* restaurants limit their repertoire to around 100, and most of those are obscure compared to a handful of famous *dim sum* that will be dutifully trotted out by every Hong Kong *yum cha* venue.

Probably the two most famous are *ha gao* (in Mandarin *xia jiao*) and *siu mai* (*shao mai*). Both are steamed. The former is a shrimp filling wrapped in a triangular translucent rice skin. The latter is round and made from pork. Like most *dim sum* they come in a set of three in a small bamboo steamer. The wait staff offering these snacks are the most frequently heard in the restaurant, as they wander with carts amongst the diners crying "Ha gao! Siu mai!"

China's most famous *dim sum* export — the spring roll — also makes an appearance, though it usually will make the rounds with a selection of other fried, and sometimes roasted, items on plates, and it is rare to hear serving staff calling out the Cantonese name: *chun kuen* (*chun juan*). They should be very like the spring rolls at home, unless home is far from the nearest Chinatown.

Rather more filling are the steamed buns that appear at almost all *dim sum* restaurants. Steamed buns (*baozi*) are a northern specialty, and in Beijing and further north tend to be filling lumps of steamed bread that accompany soups and other savories. The Cantonese variety, on the other hand — *cha siu bao* (*cha sha bao*) — is light and fluffy and has a delicious savory-sweet filling of roast pork. The downside: eat more than one and little room remains to enjoy more of the *dim sum* range.

For those who want to be a little more adventurous — and only a little — try the *luo mei gai* (*nuo mi ji*), a delicious parcel of sticky rice, dried mushrooms, chicken, and sometimes an egg yolk and some pork, wrapped in a lotus leaf. They come, usually two at a time, in a bamboo steamer.

More of an acquired taste is *cheong fun* (*chang fen*), a steamed rice-flour "pastry" that comes in strips filled with

barbecued pork, prawns or beef and accompanied by soy sauce. And to take a further daring step, try the famous steamed chicken feet (*feng zhua*), or "phoenix talons." They're actually very tasty, though no one could accuse of them of being filling — there is not much meat on a chicken foot.

To top it all off, the eponymous *dan tart*, a Cantonese-Western hybrid, is one of the few local sweets that foreigners take to immediately — a sweet egg custard in a flaky-pastry tart. It's difficult to stop at one.

See the World's Biggest Outdoor Buddha

ON HONG KONG ISLAND AND IN TSIMSHATSUI, KOWLOON, THE TEMPLES OF COMMERCE DOMINATE THE SKYLINE; ON LANTAU ISLAND IT'S THE WORLD'S BIGGEST SEATED BUDDHA. Of course, China and Southeast Asia have their fair share of giant Buddhas, but very few have been built with modern money, and few impress like this one in the wilds of Lantau Island. Add the adjacent monastery, easily one of Hong Kong's most picturesque temple sights and the setting for countless Hong Kong kung fu action films, and it's easy to see why Lantau gets more tourist traffic than any other outlying island.

For anyone who is overwhelmed by Hong Kong's getting and spending, city stress melts away on the hour-long ferry ride to Lantau, the largest of Hong Kong's 235 outlying islands and long a haven for Buddhist retreats. Tucked away in the island's central range of hills are several nunneries and monasteries. But the most famous of them all is Po Lin (Precious Lotus) Monastery, situated high on Ngong Ping plateau. Po Lin, first established in 1905, has undergone considerable renovation and extension. The latest addition to the now huge complex of temples, halls and dormitories was the huge 34-m-high (112-ft) Buddha

The world's biggest outdoor Buddha, at Po Lin Monastery on Lantau Island.

statue that dominates the complex from an adjacent plateau. Oddly enough, it was forged in Nanjing, China, by the China Space Agency. The funding came from wealthy Hong Kong Buddhists.

The 275-ton Tian Tan Buddha, his palm raised as in greeting, was opened to the public at the end of 1993 and has become Lantau's foremost attraction. If possible, avoid weekends, when the souvenir stalls around the statue do a roaring trade in Buddhist trinkets, medallions and photos, and the area becomes more like a theme park than a place of worship. During the week, on the other hand, it is possible to climb up the more than 260 steps in relative solitude and enjoy the majestic sight of the Buddha on its hilltop site without the distraction of bustling crowds. It's difficult not to think that should it outlast the skyscrapers, the Buddha will give archeologists of future centuries a somewhat skewed view of twentieth-century Hong Kong.

The best time to visit is mid-morning, which leaves plenty of time to explore the temple complex, photograph the Buddha, and be in time for an excellent vegetarian lunch provided in the temple grounds. After lunch, take the superb walk west towards the coastal village of Tai O. The downhill walk along the mountain ridge passes several other smaller monasteries before arriving at Tai O, from where buses do the 45-minute run back to Mui Wo and ferries leave for Central.

Hike the Trails of Hidden Hong Kong

DAWN AT THE SUMMIT OF FUNG WONG SHAN, A 934-M-HIGH (3,063-FT) PEAK, MELTS AWAY THE MIST TO REVEAL A LANDSCAPE OF HILLS MARCHING INTO THE DISTANCE. Far below are lush valleys, resonant with birdsong; in the distance the sparkling sea. No cars or buildings mar the view, nor even a road or a village. If not for the subtropical heat, this might well be a landscape snatched from a remote

corner of Scotland. Welcome, instead, to Hong Kong's biggest surprise: wilderness.

Lantau Island's Fung Wong Shan (more commonly called Lantau Peak) is Hong Kong's second highest, after the 958-m (3,142-ft) Tai Mo Shan in the New Territories, and is one of the most popular peaks to climb in the territory, largely because of its accessibility from the Po Lin Monastery. You will need to spend a Spartan night at the nearby youth hostel, however, if you want to arrive at the summit for sunrise. Many

do. Such outdoor adventures have become increasingly popular in recent years with Hong Kong's young generation: so much so that weekends, when the mountain is invaded by camera-clicking hordes, are best avoided. On weekdays, the wilderness lives up to its name.

Over 70 percent of all Hong Kong's territory is rural, left untouched by the developers thanks to its remoteness from the city or to its mountainous, rugged terrain. Since the 1970s, about 30 percent of Hong Kong's land has been classified into 21 country parks or specially protected areas. Clearly marked trails wriggle their way across many of the parks, up hill and down dale, past reservoirs and woodlands, along coastlines and beaches. Many of them have sections that would challenge the most determined hiker (and there are designated camping sites if you're keen to do an overnight stint), but there are also shorter, gentler "family walks" at many of the parks' entrances if you only want a simple stroll.

splendid climbs up Lantau or Sunset peaks or a coastal dawdle along the southern shore to Tai O.

A popular segment, and one that isn't too demanding, follows the northern coast, from Tung Chung (accessible by bus from the ferry terminal of Mui Wo and right opposite the new Chek Lap Kok Airport) westwards to surprisingly unspoiled Tai O — a four-hour walk which can be done in either direction, though the bus connections at the end of the day (and the restaurant choices) are

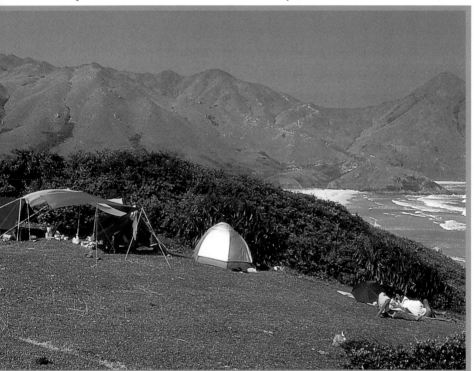

The most easily accessible trail is the Hong Kong Trail on Hong Kong Island: it starts at the Peak and ends at Shek O, right at the other side of the island, though a couple of hours downhill to Aberdeen is usually enough for most people. For a sense of real countryside, though, Lantau Island takes the cake, with not only Lantau Peak, but also the 70-km (44-mile) Lantau Trail. Few manage the entire trail, but any segment of it is feasible as a day trip, and the mountaintop trail doubles back along the coast, providing a choice of scenically

best at Tai O. From Tai O it is also possible to hike up to Po Lin Monastery in around one hour.

For a hike to really make those leg muscles ache, consider the 100-km (63-mile) Maclehose Trail in the New Territories or the newest and perhaps toughest trail of all, the 78-km (49-mile) Wilson Trail which, unique among Hong Kong's trails, runs south–north (across Hong Kong Island into the New Territories) instead of east–west.

Hiking and camping are popular in Sai Kung.

Don't be deceived by the easy accessibility of most of these trails: on a blustery peak or a deserted beach, the sense of remoteness is very real indeed. Be sure to take a map (excellent ones are available at the Government Publications Center in Queensway, Central) and plenty of water. And be prepared for the shock of returning to the noise and crowds of the city after the birdsong, breezes and wilderness of Hong Kong's hidden hills.

Ride the Museum Shuttle

FEW PEOPLE THINK OF MUSEUMS IN THE CONTEXT OF HONG KONG, BUT IT'S WORTH DOING THE ROUNDS. The best of Hong Kong's museums, which are mostly modest in scale, are conveniently grouped together and can be visited in a leisurely morning or afternoon of sightseeing. And, conveniently, the Hong Kong Tourism Association (HKTA) makes it even easier with the Museum Shuttle, which makes regular stops on the Kowloon museum trail every 45 minutes between 10 AM and 5:30 PM. All that's required is a HK$80 Museum Monthly Pass, which can be bought at HKTA offices and which provides shuttle transport as well as entry to the museums.

The distinctive buses — emblazoned with scenes from Hong Kong — set out from the Kowloon Hotel, 19-21 Nathan Road. Their first stop is the Hong Kong Museum of History and the Hong Kong Science Museum. The former may not look particularly promising from the outside, but with 17,500 sq m (188,000 sq ft) of exhibition space, the new building will easily be the most comprehensive introduction to Hong Kong. The major attraction was in the final stages of completion at the time of writing — a 6,000-year overview of Hong Kong's history that promises to be one of the region's best historical exhibitions. The Hong Kong Science Museum is a hands-on experience with galleries devoted to everything from "water and wave"

to "light." A curious section covers mathematics, which sounds distinctly dull but ends up being fascinating. There's a special children's section, but children should find most of the museum a good diversion, especially the Light Gallery, which has an interesting "anti-gravity mirror" that creates the illusion that you are floating in mid-air.

The next stop is the Hong Kong Heritage Museum in Shatin, New Territories. Opened in December 2000, the five-story museum built in the classical Chinese style around a central courtyard is easily one of Hong Kong's best cultural attractions. The first-floor

Cantonese Opera exhibit is worth the trip alone, but there are numerous other things to see, including a good section on contemporary art and design.

From here, the shuttle backtracks to Kowloon, where it stops at the Tsimshatsui waterfront to take in the Hong Kong Museum of Art and the Hong Kong Space Museum. At the former, the visiting exhibitions, many on loan from elsewhere in China, often provide the best attraction, but the permanent exhibition of Chinese Fine Art is a must-see, even for those with only a passing interest in Chinese art. Another popular gallery is the one

devoted to historical art with pictures not just from historical Hong Kong but also Macau and Shanghai. There are scenes from daily life — a Cantonese opera, a blacksmith and a shoemaker at work — a memorable "City of Victoria" still life among others and portraits, all of them collectively making an unparalleled composite of early Western contact with China. The largest collection is of Chinese antiquities, but for those without a particular interest it's less

Looking across from the sphere of the Space Museum's Planetarium to the luxurious Peninsula Hotel. The perfect way to round off a museum shuttle tour.

compelling than the paintings. The items displayed are mostly from Guangdong.

The Hong Kong Space Museum is the perfect way to round off a museum tour and a great place to take kids. The Planetarium, known as the Sky Show, is one of the world's largest and also has an Omnimax theater, usually showing a feature with an astronomical orientation.

Raise a Glass to Suzy

SUZY WONG MAY BE LITTLE MORE THAN THE EPONYMOUS HEROINE OF AN OBSCURE NOVEL, BUT SHE HAS ACHIEVED ICONIC STATUS IN HONG KONG. She represents a bygone era. Never mind that it's an era Hong Kong is glad to have left behind — Suzy represents the carefree days of wine, song and quick fortunes won and lost. And her spiritual heartland is Wanchai, once ground zero for the R&R hordes seeking solace and escape from a war the United States still frets about having entered.

The truth is, such days are long gone. Suzy was respectably married decades ago. Today she's clucking over grandchildren. And as for Wanchai, well, the "golden days" linger on in a somewhat tawdry strip of over-priced hostess bars catering to the expense-account tribe: while Richard Mason's 1957 bestseller, *The World of Suzy Wong* is still a great read, Wanchai isn't all that raunchy these days. Instead of brothels there are office blocks, and in place of the topless bars stand art galleries, conference centers and five-star hotels. True, there's still a scattering of garish neon here and there, but the new beats in Wanchai are a lot more upmarket and in tune with Hong Kong's glitzy international image.

To see how the tide has turned, first pop into Delaney's, an Irish-style pub at 18 Luard Road with Guinness on tap, live Irish music on Tuesdays, Fridays and Saturdays and Irish stews on the menu. The clientele on weekdays is predominantly Suits (the territory's successful young businessmen seem to be everywhere these days), who don't think twice about paying over the odds for Delaney's exclusive "designer" ale, specially brewed for the pub by Hong Kong's very own micro-brewery.

Delaney's, however, is positively Old World compared to Tango Martini, on the third floor of the Empire Land

Commercial Center, 81-85 Lockhart Road. The drink of choice is, of course, the martini, and the setting is pure James Bond, with zebra-skin upholstery and an atmosphere of high-class debauch — with prices, needless to say, to match. The Grand Hyatt Hotel, at 1 Harbor Road, is another class act, offering the glamorous Champagne Bar, which prides itself on stocking Hong Kong's widest range of champagne along with understated live music — it's hard to image anything further from the rowdy Suzy Wong days than this.

But that's not to say that the "Wanch," as the area is still affectionately called, can't provide some good old-fashioned fun, too. Many of the drinkers in Central's Lan Kwai Fong roll down here for late-night dancing. At the lower end of the sophistication spectrum, the Big Apple Pub & Disco, at 20 Luard Road, is reliable if a little tired these days. The Wanch, at 54 Jaffe Road, is another long-runner and a friendly place that is home to Hong Kong's underground rock and folk scene; it's also memorable for the nostalgic old Hong Kong decor. Meanwhile, bravely upholding Wanchai's reputation for notoriety is Joe Bananas, at 23 Luard Road, which has a happy hour lasting an incredible 11 hours (from 11 AM to 10 PM daily) and a crowd of inebriated dancers packing the place every weekend — it's not for the faint hearted.

But the classiest of Wanchai's clubs is the Grand Hyatt Hotel's immensely popular (and expensive) JJ's. Don't even think about "dressing down" unless you're the kind of person that makes dressing down hip. It's a place to see and be seen, consistently Hong Kong's "in" nightspot.

If JJ's is just a wee bit too pretentious, there is always that long-runner, the Old China Hand, at 104 Lockhart Road. The decor has the pedigree — aged, to put it politely — but it's celebrated for its regular pub atmosphere and greasy breakfasts, lunches and dinners: British pub food at its best, or worst, depending on how you look at it.

Gaze into the Crystal Ball

IT MAY BE A GET-AHEAD, MODERN CITY, BUT FOR MANY, HONG KONG'S FUTURE IS ALL IN THE STARS, THE PALMS, THE YI JING, THE STICKS — OR IS THAT THE BUDGERIGARS? In a city where geomancers influence billion-dollar building projects, what lies around the next corner is a serious business. Indeed, there are four choices when it comes to choosing a method of fortune-telling in Hong Kong: palm, face, cards or sticks. Five, to be precise, counting the budgies.

OPPOSITE: Pockets of neon are all that remain of Wanchai's glitzy past. ABOVE LEFT: A fortune teller awaits clients while a palmist RIGHT reads hands at Temple Street night market in Kowloon.

Fortune-tellers of all varieties can be found in Hong Kong's temples (their fees help with the temple upkeep), and their services are widely sought after, even by the younger generation of Hong Kong Chinese, who may be more highly educated than their parents but are often just as superstitious. It's tempting to dismiss it all as so much hocus-pocus, but confronted with the long, earnest queues at the stands of the most popular fortune-tellers and the devotion of worshippers casting fortune sticks at a Chinese temple it's easy to become infected.

The most widely practiced method of Chinese fortune-telling may seem somewhat arbitrary, but it is at least noisy and fun. Fortune sticks — or *chim* — can be found at many of Hong Kong's temples. Casting them involves kneeling before the temple god and shaking a bamboo container of numbered *chim* until one falls out. The number corresponds to a book of fortunes, which the resident fortune-teller (often just the temple caretaker) will interpret. Often three sticks are shaken out to be sure of getting a full interpretation. There's no set fee for using the *chim* in the temple but a small donation is expected. For those who get hooked on the practice, personal sets of *chim* (complete with instructions in English) are on sale for around US$12 from places such as the China Arts & Crafts Store (several locations) or the Welfare Handicraft shop in the basement of Jardine House (next to the HKTA Information & Gift Center).

More popular with foreign visitors are the card-, palm- and face-readers. They can be found in large numbers on the route to Wong Tai Sin Temple and at Yau Ma Tei's Tin Hau Temple and Temple Street. Face-reading has been a Chinese tradition for nearly 3,000 years, and it recognizes eight to ten facial types, depending on the school, and a complex array of eye, nose and ear shapes — thick ear lobes, for example, can mean affluence. And where there are face-readers, there are palm-readers (in fact, many combine both practices).

They will usually ask for your date of birth, and the more accurate this is (as in the hour), the better. Finding English-speaking palm- and face-readers is no problem. At Wong Tai Sin, for example, of nearly 200 fortune-tellers some 30 offer fortunes in English as well as Cantonese.

The most mysterious technique is the *I Ching* (*Yi Jing*), the ancient Chinese *Book of Changes*, which employs the hexagram and arcane methods known as the *bakgwa* (*bagua* in Mandarin) to divine the future. Many Chinese swear by it, using it among other things to play the stockmarket — sometimes with disastrous results, sometimes with great success.

That leaves the budgies, which of all the mirrors on the future has to be the most suspect. Popular in the night-time Temple Street market, the bird (a small parakeet or finch) picks out a card from those displayed by his master, which is then "interpreted" appropriately. The birds, however, are sparing to the point of being niggardly with bad omens. For those in need of some good news, it can be highly recommended.

Catch a Lion Dance

DRUMS THUMPING, THE HIGH-DECIBEL RAT-A-TAT-TAT OF FIRECRACKERS FILLING THE AIR, THE BOOM-CRASH OF CYMBALS AND GONGS, A DRAGON DANCE IS ONE OF HONG KONG'S MOST EXCITING SCENES. Come Chinese New Year, the Tin Hau Festival (see FESTIVE FLINGS, page 73 in YOUR CHOICE), or should some grand new civic building or business be flinging open its doors for the first time, the boisterous beast can be seen charging, posturing and shaking its head in a staccato parody of fierceness. Not that the Chinese dancing lion — a gaudy creature — looks anything like a real lion. But then, given China's absence of the real thing, this can perhaps be forgiven.

A dancing lion walks the plank at a temple in Shau Kei Wan at Tin Hau Festival.

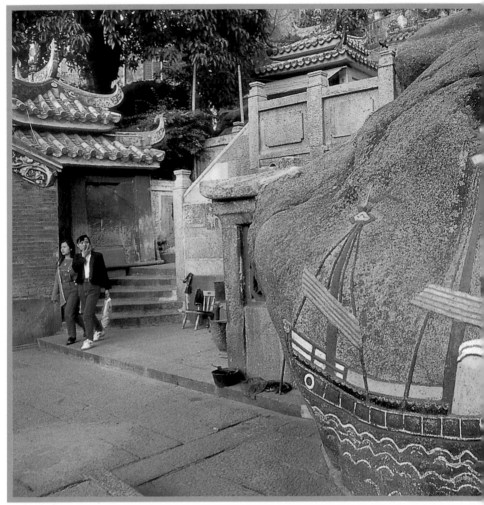

Myths about the origin of the lion dance abound — everything from the dream of a Tang-dynasty (AD 716–907) emperor to a visiting acrobatic troupe from India in ancient times — but the most likely explanation is that the dance derives from actual lions presented to Han dynasty (205 BC–AD 220) emperors by kings from Afghanistan and Iran. Whatever its precise origins, by the Tang dynasty the lion dance is thought to have been firmly established as an accompaniment to festive events. Fierce and wise, the lion drives away evil spirits and brings good luck to whomever he dances for.

Many people who see a lion dance think it's a dragon, and indeed, with its trailing tail it's an easy mistake to make. But if there are two performers (look for two pairs of feet), it's a lion. One dancer operates the head — bamboo levers inside make it possible to control even the eye and mouth movements — and the other the tail. The movements, unlike those of a real lion, are jerky, and are intended that way. The head is often raised high into the air as if in challenge, and the footwork is based on a complex repertoire of kung fu steps. Lion dances are always the provenance of kung fu schools, and were associated with clans who sought to overthrow the Manchu Qing dynasty in the eighteenth and nineteenth centuries.

Although the dance may seem somewhat chaotic, lion dancers act out

set pieces that are familiar to the watchers. In the *shuishi* routine, for example, the lazy lion sits down and nods off before being awoken by fleas, which forces him to attack himself and finally chase himself in circles, much as a dog will do. But, whatever the routine, the highlight is when the dragon realizes he is hungry, and its time to enact the ritual known as "getting the green." Usually a lettuce stuffed with money is used, and it is always put in a place that forces the lion to exert himself with acrobatics of some kind to reach.

The most experienced lion dancers can perform formidable acrobatics — balancing on high poles, jumping from table-tops, rolling on the ground and

prancing in mock-combat with "rival" lions or unicorns (spot the horn to tell the difference). During Cheung Chau's Bun Festival, almost every street association has its own lion dance troupe and the clamor when they encounter one another in the village's narrow streets has to be heard to be believed. This festival is also an ideal time to see the different kinds of lions in action: the shaggy yellow lion originates from north China while the black, yellow or multi-colored lion is a southern beast.

During Chinese New Year, the lion dance is performed not only as part of the public festivities (check with the Hong Kong Tourist Association on likely times and venues) but also to enact a ritual of good-luck blessings on various offices and organizations (who have paid for this service, naturally). The lion begins such ceremonies with a bow before the doorway to the rumble of rolling drums, before jumping up to "get the green." Lions that appear at the opening of new buildings or offices or at the start of an important public event to exorcise any lingering evil spirits and soothe everyone's superstitions will often have their "eyes dotted" by VIP government officials to symbolically give them life — another curious ritual which is still faithfully followed, revealing Hong Kong's tenacious grip on Chinese tradition.

Meet East and West in Macau

JUST AN HOUR BY JETFOIL FROM HONG KONG LIES THE OLDEST OF CHINA'S EUROPEAN SETTLEMENTS. Not that Macau, as the former Portuguese colony is known, is all that European anymore. Established by Portuguese traders in 1557, Chinese-run Macau (it reverted to China in 1999), is as Chinese as it is Latin. In the meantime, the once-sleepy retreat for Hong Kong expats homesick for

Macau's A-Ma temple.

European cuisine and ambiance has been swept up in a frenzy of mainly Chinese-funded development that almost matches the pace of concrete renewal in Hong Kong itself. An international airport welcomes flights from China and around the region, office blocks and hotels have drastically altered the skyline, a massive reclamation project has transformed the waterfront Praia Grande, and the city has emerged as the region's preeminent gambling destination for Chinese from all quarters of the globe.

But this is not to say that Macau's celebrated charm has been buried under parking lots and malls. Unlike Hong Kong, where history is all too often put to the wrecking ball in the name of progress, the Macanese have been careful to preserve and restore much of their fine old European architecture. Perhaps most surprisingly of all, particularly now that the Portuguese have packed up and left for home, there are more excellent Portuguese restaurants than ever before, providing a cuisine and ambiance so utterly Portuguese (and a cosmopolitan clientele from all corners) that it comes as a shock to step outside after dinner back into a city in which the Chinese inhabitants are as much at home as the European.

But then it is precisely shocks such as this that make Macau such a joy to explore. Unfortunately, the city's finest colonial-era hotel, the Bela Vista, once the toast of Hong Kong as a weekend getaway retreat, is now the Portuguese consulate, but alternative historic accommodation is available in the Pousada de São Tiago, the only hotel in China that gives its guests the thrill of staying in a converted seventeenth-century fort.

And then there is the food, which no matter how much everything else changes seems to continue to improve. Macau's outlying islands of Taipa and Coloane (joined to the mainland by bridges and a causeway) have become famous for their typical Portuguese fare: try the popular Fernando's in Coloane, where Fernando is well known for

dispensing with the menu to personally deliver a feast of clams, sardines and salads, matched with a perfect Portuguese wine. Two decades ago, the restaurant was a simple beach-side café with graffiti on the walls. The café is still there, but the main restaurant has expanded behind to cater to the growing band of visitors and Fernando-fans. Cacarola is another Coloane restaurant with a legion of fans, as is Alfonso III, in Macau itself.

For a jolt back to the reality of Chinese administered Macau, visit the Lisboa Hotel Casino, ever packed with bustling crowds of Chinese, making — or one suspects mostly losing — their fortunes, or the famous A-Ma Temple, thick with joss-offering crowds. Of course, such Chinese attractions also have their counterpart in the former colony's architectural legacy, such as the ruins of São Paulo, Macau's iconic picture-postcard cathedral, which is often as crowded as Fernando's, the casino and the temple.

To escape those crowds, visit the delightful Lou Lim Ioc Gardens. Perhaps the last word on East-meets-West, they feature a combination of classic Chinese gardens set around a colonial, Western-style villa. Visit early in the morning, when old men walk their birds and small crowds stretch and limber up with qigong, to remember that while Macau may no longer count itself as a member of the colonial club, its charms are as colonial as they ever were.

The ruins of Macau's famous St. Paul's Cathedral.

YOUR CHOICE

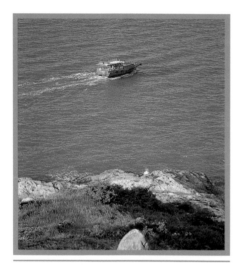

The Great Outdoors

An astonishing 70 percent of Hong Kong's 1,070 sq km (414 sq miles) is rural land, a dramatic combination of wild granite peaks and grassy slopes, bamboo forests and lush, river-fed lowlands. If that is hard to believe — especially in the congested streets of Tsimshatsui or Central — pop into the nearest bookshop to take a look at a couple of photographic books that tell it all: *The Green Dragon* by Martin Williams (Hong Kong: Green Dragon Publishing, 1994), with photographs by wildlife cameraman Michael Pitts, and *Hong Kong's Wild Places* by Edward Stokes (Oxford University Press, 1996) are two fine examples.

Most of their photographs were taken in Hong Kong's 21 **country parks** whose 41,000 ha (101,270 acres) comprise 40 percent of Hong Kong's land. Five of these are on Hong Kong Island, two on Lantau, and 14 in the New Territories. Most are natural wildernesses, although some are forested "green belts," classified as country parks to protect Hong Kong's 17 fresh water supplies and reservoirs. Threading their way through these parks are ancient village trails, linked by new Country Park pathways and **nature trails**. The latter are mostly short, easy rambles (less than five or six kilometers/ three to four miles long) geared for families or school groups, with translated signposts giving information on local plants, animals or geographical features. The trails are easily accessible by public transportation.

But if you're a serious hiker — and determined to discover the real wilderness areas of Hong Kong — you'll need more challenge than this. Consider, instead, Hong Kong's four **long-distance trails,** which have been designed in sections or stages (most accessible by public transportation) so each stage can be completed in a day. The **Country Parks and Marine Parks Authority** (2150-6666, Fifth to Eighth Floor, Cheung Sha Wan Government Offices, 303 Cheung Sha Wan Road, Kowloon, have detailed

Into the arms of mother nature. OPPOSITE: Lamma Island. ABOVE: It is not difficult to get away from it all in a junk.

leaflets and 1:10,000 scale maps for each trail, with information on how to get to the trails' various sections and where to find campsites and youth hostels en route. It's also worth buying the excellent *Exploring Hong Kong's Countryside* book for HK$80; it's available at HKTA offices.

The easiest and shortest trail is the 50-km (31-mile) **Hong Kong Trail**, which traverses Hong Kong Island's high-level country parks, from Victoria Park all the way to Shek O in the southeast. It's a grand walk for city and seascape panoramas, with views out across Victoria Harbor and the outlying islands.

The **Lantau Trail** is considerably more demanding. Stretching for a circular 70 km (42 miles), it runs along the majestic mountainous ridge of the island and then loops back along the southern coast. Few hikers do the whole trail in one stint; better to pick a section for a taste of the trail. The shortest of the stages is just over a couple of kilometers, the longest over 10 km (six miles), and all except one can be reached by bus. For lung-bursting, leg-aching panoramic rewards, the 17.5-km (nearly 11-mile) stretch from Ngong Ping's Po Lin Monastery over the island's two highest peaks, Lantau and Sunset, and all the way down back to the ferry terminal at Mui Wo, is an unbeatable challenge. It's officially estimated to take at least seven hours, though providing you are reasonably fit it should be possible to do it somewhat quicker than this.

For a slightly shorter and all-flat coastal walk, get off the bus at Shek Pik and walk round the southern coast to Tai O. Here it is possible to go for hours without seeing anyone; it includes the ruins of the 1,300-year-old Fan Lau fort, on the southwesternmost headland, and the nearby remains of a mysterious (perhaps Bronze Age) stone circle.

Hong Kong's two newest trails, named after former British governors, offer some of the territory's most challenging and rewarding hikes. The 100-km (60-mile) **Maclehose Trail**, which has been described as "the quintessential Hong Kong outdoor experience," crosses the New Territories in ten stages, from Pak Tam Chung in the Sai Kung Country Park west to Tuen Mun. Seven of the stages are accessible by public transportation. The trail passes through eight country parks, which include some of the grandest mountain scenery in Hong Kong — including the highest peak of all, the 958-m (3,142-ft) Tai Mo Shan. All along the route, you'll be treated to some stunning views of the Kowloon Peninsula and Hong Kong Island — not exactly wilderness views, it's true, but mesmerizing nonetheless. As with the other trails, the stages vary in length and difficulty: the easiest is just over four and a half kilometers (about three miles) and takes less than two hours, while the longer stages require at least five hours each.

Opened in 1995, the 78-km (24-mile) **Wilson Trail** is the only trail to run vertically up the entire territory, from Stanley on the south side of Hong Kong Island to Nam Chung in the northern New Territories. It's also unique in entailing an MTR link to enable hikers to cross the harbor! The trail incorporates the glorious Pat Sin Leng range in the northeast New Territories — a series of eight successive peaks that continually challenge your leg muscles. Information about the Maclehose Trail is available from **Friends of the Country Parks** (2377 2967, Room 701, Ocean Center.

If you're hooked enough on this wilderness scene to want to extend the experience for several days, you'll have to resort to campsites or youth hostels, as there's little else out there on the trail. There are six campsites on the Lantau Trail, and 11 on the Maclehose, plus a couple of youth hostels on each. One of the best places to stock up on camping and hiking supplies is the **Mountaineer Shop** (2397-0585, 395 Portland Street, Kowloon (open 12:30 PM to 10 PM on weekdays and until 7 PM on Saturday). The campsites are simple but usually well maintained and often with excellent washing facilities. But again, avoid weekends if you want to stay clear of the music-playing, barbecue gangs.

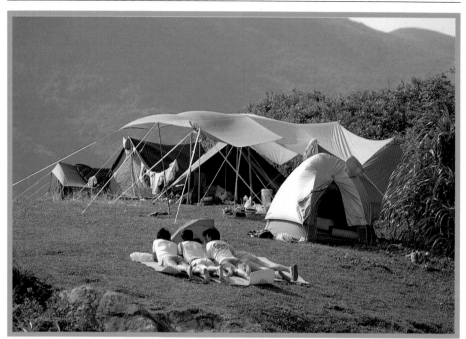

FLORA AND FAUNA

So what are you likely to encounter on the trail of Hong Kong's great outdoors? Not much in the way of wild animals, sadly, since Hong Kong's forests were cleared by early settlers centuries ago. But the flora and the bird and insect life are remarkable. Keen botanists will find booklets on everything from ferns and seaweed to lichen and shrubs at the **Government Publications Center** (2537-1910, Government Offices Low Block, 66 Queensway, Admiralty. Ornithologists might also want to pick up a copy of *Hong Kong Birds* by Karen Phillips & Clive Viney to take along on their hikes. And they'll certainly want to try and visit Hong Kong's most famous bird site — the Mai Po Marshes Nature Reserve, part of one of east Asia's most important wetlands.

Listed under the Ramsar Convention on Wetlands of International Importance, **Mai Po Marshes** cover over 300 ha (741 acres) of shrimp and fish ponds, mudflats and mangrove plants in the northwest corner of Hong Kong, next to the shallow (despite its name) Deep Bay and the mainland Chinese border. One of over 40 Sites of Special Scientific Interest in

Hong Kong, Mai Po is the only extensive area of wetland left in the territory. It is fighting a tough battle against encroaching development and worsening pollution, but the area is still one of Asia's most extraordinary bird-watching sites.

Over half of the 400 species currently known in Hong Kong can be spotted here, including a thriving colony of egrets and herons. Dozens of other species use Mai Po as a vital resting and feeding haven on their migrations between wintering grounds to the south and breeding areas to the north. Among the rarest of Mai Po's visitors are the Saunders' gulls, black-faced spoonbills, Nordmann's greenshanks and oriental white storks — you'll be lucky indeed to spot these — but especially during the winter and spring you'll have a wealth of other birds to spot, including flocks of ducks and sandpipers, buntings, cormorants and black kites.

Since 1981 Mai Po has been managed and funded by the Worldwide Fund for Nature (WWF), Hong Kong (2526-4473 1 Tramway Path, Central, which has

Sai Kung Country Park in the New Territories is rapidly becoming a popular camping and hiking destination.

built an excellent Wildlife Education Center on the site for visitors and school groups and published guides to the marshes' plants and bird life. Unfortunately for tourists, the WWF's necessarily strict protection of the site means that on-the-spot visits are impossible: you have to book and pay for a place on their four daily guided tours in advance (HK$70 per person) and since the tours only take place at weekends and on public holidays you may find they're booked up weeks or months ahead. Still, it's always worth giving WWF a call or popping into their office (next to the Peak Tram entrance) to see if a last-minute space is available.

While the birds of Mai Po are flying into an uncertain future as their habitat is eaten up by development, the **Chinese white dolphins** in Hong Kong's western waters are facing an even more desperate situation. Often called pink dolphins since they are usually more pink than white, there are thought to be no more than 1,000 or so of this Indo-Pacific humpback breed, the *Sousa chinensis*, in the waters around northern Lantau and the mouth of the Pearl River.

Although historical references to Chinese white dolphins date back several centuries, their existence in Hong Kong did not become public knowledge until the reclamation work at Lantau for

a 12-sq-km (130-sq-mile) dolphin sanctuary — the Lung Kwu Chau and Sha Chau Marine Park — in late 1996. But though this will keep out trawlers and recreational water sports it won't affect any of the underwater contaminated waste disposal pits, the construction of the Aviation Fuel Receiving Facility or the offloading of oil tankers.

Hongkong Dolphinwatch (2984-1414, 1528A Star House, 3 Salisbury Road, Tsimshatsui, Kowloon, is a private organization set up in 1995 to raise awareness of the threats the dolphins face. The organization runs morning cruises to the dolphins' usual haunt on Wednesdays, Fridays and Sundays for HK$280 per person (HK$130 per child), during which you can learn all about their sorry fate. Call for bookings, or check out their WEB SITE for more information: www.zianet.com/dolphins. The organization claims a 96 percent success rate in terms of dolphin sightings, and will schedule you on another cruise if the dolphins fail to materialize.

Sporting Spree

The people of Hong Kong may be workaholics, but they've always made time for some physical exercise, whether it's half-an-hour of tai chi ("shadow boxing") in a park at dawn before going to work, a game of basketball in the local playground, or simply a Sunday stroll with the wife and kids.

WINDSURFING

Inspired by local Lee Lai Shan, who won the Olympic gold medal (Hong Kong's first) in 1996, windsurfing has taken off in a big way in Hong Kong. The place where San San (as she's affectionately called) made her first wobbly moves to windsurfing fame is off her home island of Cheung Chau. Her uncle's **Cheung Chau Windsurfing Center** (2981-8316

the new airport got under way. Since the mid-1990s considerable research has been undertaken into the dolphins and their habitat. While pollution and land reclamation are obvious threats to the dolphin (DDT — not banned in China as in other countries — has been found in higher levels in dolphin corpses here than among any other cetaceans anywhere), it is not known with any certainty whether numbers are declining. A recent annual decline in abundance of more than 20 percent is thought by some to be a result of temporary displacement caused by land reclamation at Lantau.

Stirred by growing public outcry, the Hong Kong government declared

You don't have to go out of your way to enjoy windsurfing: Repulse Bay Beach on Hong Kong Island.

FAX 2981-5063, on Tung Wan beach, is now one of the most popular in Hong Kong. Combined with a very pleasant open-air café where you can sit and watch the windsurfers race by, it's a popular weekend spot. It costs around HK$50 to HK$70 an hour to rent a board here (or HK$250 a day) or around HK$550 for a one-day course. Kayaks are also available for rent.

Other good windsurfing spots are Sai Kung in the New Territories — check out the **Windsurfing Center** (2792-5605, at nearby Sha Ha (best if the wind is from north) — and Stanley's **Windsurfing Promotions Center** (2813-2372, on Hong Kong Island (best when there's an easterly or northeasterly wind blowing). Stanley is also where the Hong Kong Open Windsurfing Championship takes place every December (September to December is the ideal windsurfing period), organized by the **Windsurfing Association of Hong Kong** (2504-8255 FAX 2577-7529 WEB SITE www.windsurfing .org.hk/, Room 1001, Sports House, 1 Stadium Path, So Kon Po, Causeway Bay. Incidentally, boardsailors will find Hong Kong a great place to buy sail supplies, since two of the world's leading sail manufacturers are based here.

WATERSKIING
Less popular but still possible is waterskiing. The **Deep Water Bay Speedboat Company** (2812-0391, on the south side of Hong Kong Island, rents out a boat with driver and skis for about HK$520 an hour.

SAILING
A long-established water sport in Hong Kong is, of course, sailing. The Royal Hong Kong Yacht Club (2832-2817 FAX 2572-5399 WEB SITE www.rhkyc.org .hk/ Kellet Island, Causeway Bay, is the biggest of the expatriate yachting organizations and can offer temporary membership if you already belong to a sailing club at home. Other major yacht clubs include Aberdeen Boat Club (2552-8182 WEB SITE www.abclubhk.com, 20 Shum Wan Road, Aberdeen; Discovery Bay Marina Club (2987-9591

E-MAIL bmack@dbgc.com.hk, Discovery Bay, on Lantau; and Hebe Haven Yacht Club (2719-9682, Hiranm's Highway, Pak Sha Wan, Sai Kung, in the New Territories.

If there's a group of you, a cheaper option for taking to the seas and exploring some of Hong Kong's distant hidden bays and beaches is to **rent a junk** for the day — a very popular pastime among local expats. A medium-sized junk, able to take up to 35 people, costs from HK$2,500 for eight hours (more during summer and on weekends). Contact **Charterboats** (2555-7349 FAX 2555-7340, Aberdeen Marina Tower, 8 Shum Wan Road, Aberdeen.

SWIMMING
Swimming has become increasingly popular in recent years in Hong Kong. To be honest, though, unless you are resident in Hong Kong, there are far better places to swim around the region. Hong Kong may well have some charming beaches, but several are now quite dangerously polluted, in particular the beaches between Tsuen Wan and Tuen Mun, and Silvermine Bay on Lantau. The cleanest beaches are those on the south side of Hong Kong Island and in Sai Kung and Clear Water Bay — although the latter two are also occasionally favored by sharks. After a spate of sightings (and a couple of attacks) in 1995 and 1996, special shark nets were installed at many beaches for the safety of swimmers. Warning flags are raised if sharks are seen in the area. Sharks have rarely been spotted in Hong Kong's western waters.

If you're concerned about pollution levels, check with the HKTA about the current situation or find the signboards that are at many of the 42 gazetted public beaches controlled by the Urban Council or Urban Services Department and indicate the level of pollution for the day. Not that danger levels seem to put local people off very much. On weekends and on public holidays during the "official" swimming season (April 1 to October 31) the most popular beaches (for example, at Stanley

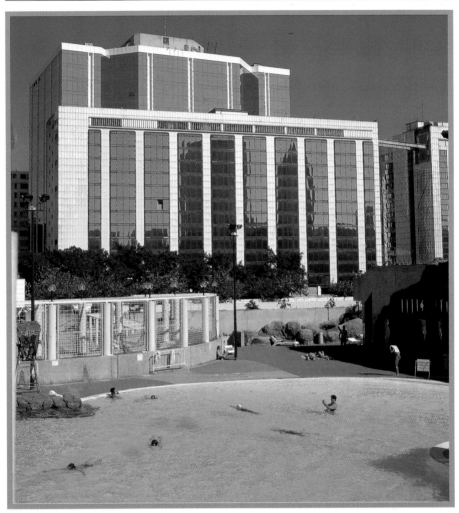

on Hong Kong Island) are packed with swimmers and sunbathers. There are good facilities at these major beaches — lifeguards, warning flags for rough seas, changing rooms and toilets and sometimes even beachside cafés or snack stalls. The biggest and most glorious stretch of beach in Hong Kong is Cheung Sha on Lantau; there are facilities at both ends of the beach, with a couple of Chinese restaurants at its easternmost end (Lower Cheung Sha).

If you prefer to stick to swimming pools, you'll find over a dozen well-maintained pools operated by the urban and regional councils. These tend to be packed during school holidays but practically deserted on weekdays

during school time. Two of the most conveniently located are the outdoor **Victoria Park Swimming Pool** (2570-4682, Causeway Bay, close to Tin Hau MTR station, and **Kowloon Park Indoor Pool** (2724-3577, Tsimshatsui. The **Morrison Hill Swimming Pool** (2575-3028, Wanchai, is a smaller indoor pool, and closes periodically in season for maintenance — call to check that its open before going. Opening hours at all of them are from about 7 AM to 9 PM daily from April through October. For a full listing of Hong Kong's swimming pools, see WEB SITE www.avohk.org/hkpools.html.

The popular outdoor swimming pool at Kowloon Park.

SCUBA DIVING

Granted, Hong Kong is hardly an obvious destination for diving enthusiasts, but diving is not out of the question. Indeed the sport thrives in Hong Kong, with several diving centers offering PADI or NAUI courses. Dive trips take place most weekends to the Sai Kung and Clear Water Bay areas, especially Little Beach and Town Island (popular for novices) and Breakers Reef in Mirs Bay (for experienced divers). Contact the **Underwater Association** (2572-3792, in Queen Elizabeth Stadium, for more information, or one of the following dive centers: **Pro-Dive USA** (2890-5634 FAX 2577-3400; **The Dive Shop HK** (2397-6222 FAX 2398-3199; or the **Scuba Center** (2887-7922 FAX 2887-8680. For a full listing of Hong Kong's dive shops, see the **Hong Kong Scuba Network** WEB SITE www.scuba.net.hk/home.htm

A useful source of information about scuba diving in the Asia region is the excellent *Action Asia* **magazine** WEB SITE www.actionasia.com/, which is packed with sporting tips, feature articles and superb photographs. It's available at most bookstores.

GOLF

Hong Kong has some excellent golf courses and facilities in its private clubs (open to visitors on weekdays only). The most popular is the three-course layout of the **Hong Kong Golf Club** (HKGC) (2670-1211, at Fanling in the New Territories. The green fees for 18 holes cost HK$1,400. The club also has a cheaper nine-hole course at Deep Water Bay (2812-7070 on Hong Kong Island. There's another course (27-hole) high above the Discovery Bay residential development on Lantau Island. Ferries run frequently from Central, and there's a bus to take you up to the course. To contact them in advance, call the **Discovery Bay Golf Club** (2987-7271. The **Clear Water Bay Golf & Country Club** (2719-5936 in Sai Kung charges

The Hong Kong Golf Club at Fanling in the New Territories

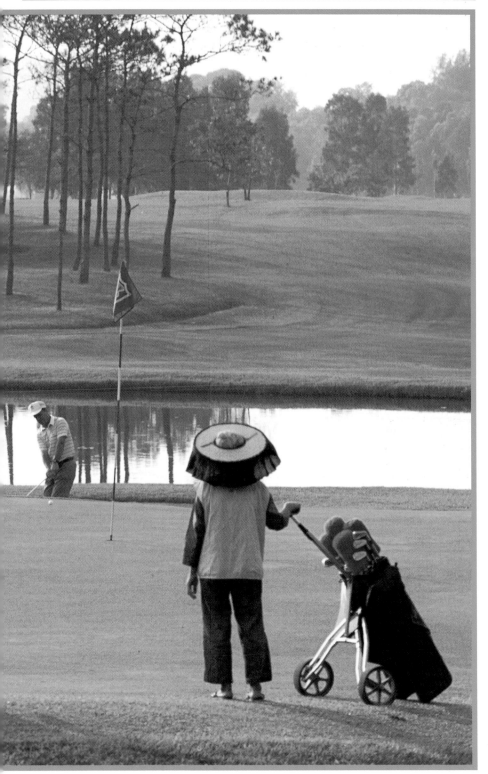

Park (2385-8985 all have courts. For badminton and table tennis, try Queen Elizabeth Stadium, **Sai Wan Ho Complex Indoor Games Hall** (2569-7330, and **South China Athletic Association** (2577-6932, 88 Caroline Hill Road, Causeway Bay. To watch the pros, check with the **Hong Kong Tennis Association** (2890-1132, on the dates for the Hong Kong Open Tennis Championship, held every September.

HORSE RIDING AND RACING

Hong Kong's open countryside may seem ideal for exploring on horseback, but unfortunately opportunities are few. The **Hong Kong Riding Union** (2488-6886, at 76 Waterloo Road, Kowloon Tong, and the **Tai Yuen Riding School** (2471-8492, Castle Peak Road, New Territories, have horses for hire (about HK$500 an hour), and offer riding trails and lessons, but you're unlikely to be able to go far beyond the school boundary. Simply for lessons, try the **Pokfulam Public Riding School** (2550-1359, on Hong Kong Island, and the **Park Lodge Riding School** (2607-3131, in Shatin.

Hong Kong's horse racing industry is operated exclusively by the Hong Kong Jockey Club, which is the largest private employer in Hong Kong. Membership of it is fiercely sought and highly prized. Everything about the Jockey Club's vast domain is bigger, richer and more streamlined than anything like it anywhere else in the world. It operates only two racecourses, one at **Happy Valley** on Hong Kong Island and the other at **Shatin** in the New Territories, but the US$7.6-million Shatin course covers an area of 100 ha (250 acres) — all of it reclaimed land — and has a capacity of 83,000, the biggest on earth. The equipment and facilities at both tracks are pure state-of-the-art, featuring fully computerized betting, closed-circuit television and huge infield video screens which flash late information for punters on the condition of the track, jockey changes and anything else that could possibly shave a half a nose off the anticipated outcome of a race.

Outside the tracks, the club operates more than 100 off-course betting shops and a telephone betting system that covers hundreds of thousands of accounts. There are so many betting combinations available that anyone putting money on a straight win place would be recognized immediately as a rank outsider. There are about 70 race meetings a year — the horses are stood down in the summer months because of the heat, humidity, rainstorms and the threat of typhoons — and the turn-over is enormous. During the 1999 season, for example, punters laid HK$83.4 billion in bets.

The racing season lasts from September through June, and races are held either at the **Happy Valley Race Track** (2966-8111, 1 Sports Road, Happy Valley, or at the **Shatin Racecourse** (2966-6520, Tai Po Road, Shatin. Races are usually held on Saturday or Sundays, and the HKTA runs tours out to the track.

ICE SKATING

Ice-skating enthusiasts should check out the **Cityplaza Ice Palace** (2885-4697, Cityplaza Shopping Center, Taikoo Shing (take exit E at the Taikoo MTR station). It's open from 9:30 AM to 10 PM weekdays, from 7 AM to 10 PM Saturday, and from 12.30 PM to 10 PM Sundays. The cost, including skates, is around HK$50 an hour. In Kowloon, the **Whampoa Super Ice** (2774-4899, Whampoa Gardens Shopping Complex, Hung Hom, also has ice-skating.

MARTIAL ARTS

With advance notice, the **Hong Kong Chinese Martial Arts Association** (2394-4803, Room 1008, Sports House, 1 Stadium Path, So Kon Po, Causeway Bay, will do their best to arrange a demonstration of kung fu, *tai ji chuan* (Chinese tai chi shadow boxing), Thai boxing and other martial art forms, although you can easily see tai chi for yourself any early morning in places such as Kowloon Park in Kowloon and Chater Gardens and Victoria Park on Hong Kong Island.

JOGGING

Despite the heat and the urban crush, Hong Kong is home to armies of joggers and a number of good jogging routes. A spectacular city route is along the waterfront promenade in Tsimshatsui. On the island, popular routes are in Victoria Park, at the Happy Valley Racetrack and, best of all, along the scenic Bowen Road path in the Mid-Levels, which runs for several kilometers above Wanchai and around into Happy Valley to the roundabout at Stubbs and Tai Hang roads. The **Hash House Harriers** (2846-9522 sally forth each week and are remarkable, aside from their stamina, for the considerable amounts of liquid replenishment that they take after each run.

Amateur runners are also welcome to take part in Hong Kong's three annual **marathons**, the Hong Kong to Shenzhen Marathon in February, the Coast of China Marathon on the first Sunday of March, and the International Marathon in Chinese New Year. For details, call the **Hong Kong Amateur Athletics Association** (2504-8215, the **Athletic Veterans of Hong Kong** (2818-4856, or the **Hong Kong Tourist Association** (2807-6177. For full information on Hong Kong's annual running events, see the **Hong Kong Runners** WEB SITE www.hkrunners.com.

ROCK CLIMBING

Recreational climbing is a booming sport in Hong Kong. With its rocky islands and rugged, mountainous terrain, the territory has some ideal locations — most dramatically at the massive, granite 130-m (426-ft) crag of Lion Rock which now offers some 20 different recorded climbing routes; Kowloon Peak, with its overhangs and gullies and vast variety of crags; coastal Shek O, whose rocky point juts into the sea; and Tung Lung Island, south of Clear Water Bay, which perhaps offers the best sports climbing of all in Hong Kong with its many varied routes, from rock walls to 70-m-high (230-ft) cliffs. If you're a novice and fancy getting your first step

up the climbing scene, contact the **Hong Kong Mountaineering Training Center** (2384-8190 FAX 2770-7110, which offers a day's beginner's course for around HK$250. The **Bureaux des Guides** (2791-4269 also has one-day beginners' and advanced courses. Climbing is best done during the "dry" months between October and May. The only climbing wall that can be used by the public on a regular basis is at the **Flora Ho Sports Center** (2904-9661 at the University of Hong Kong on Hong Kong Island.

PARAGLIDING

You will need to be in Hong Kong for several weeks during the dry season to participate in any serious training, but if you're already an experienced flyer, contact the **Hong Kong Paragliding Association** (2543-2901 FAX 2541-7845 WEB SITE www.glink.net.hk/~hkpa/ for free temporary membership, insurance and details on where to fly and not to fly. The Ma On Shan ridge in the New Territories is a popular place for beginners, followed by the horseshoe ridge of Long Ke in Sai Kung, the steep-sided slopes of Lantau Island (especially Sunset Peak) and the dramatic Dragon's Back ridge overlooking Shek O on Hong Kong Island. There are powerful gusts and updrafts around, so be careful.

An opera singer entertains shoppers while ice skaters twirl below in City Plaza, Taikoo Shing.

The Open Road

The bad news: driving in Hong Kong is a recipe for madness. The traffic is too frenetic, the network of roads, tunnels and highways too confusing and parking spaces too frustratingly few. And you'll miss some of the territory's highlights — its outlying islands. The good news: public transportation is so efficient (and taxis so numerous), you won't regret for an instant being away from the wheel. As long as you're equipped with the relevant Hong Kong Tourist Association brochures, maps and information, you'll find getting around by bus, train, tram or boat easy and fun. (Just be sure to have plenty of change in your pocket for the fares.) For serious exploring, you'd be advised to pick up some of the detailed Countryside Series maps (in various scales covering the entire territory) from the **Government Publications Center (** 2537-1910, Government Offices Low Block, 66 Queensway, Admiralty.

Backpacking

Hong Kong might be an expensive destination for backpackers but large numbers pass through all the same. Until the 1997 handover, it was a popular place for overlanders to rest up ˙and make some money before traveling on. With tighter visa regulations and fewer jobs to go around following the collapse of the "Asian miracle," backpackers are not staying as long as they used to. But Hong Kong remains an important port of call for travelers making their way in or out of China, and for overlanders making the epic journey between Europe and Australia.

The good news is that while Hong Kong is one of Asia's most expensive destinations, it is also possible to economize. Public transportation is very inexpensive, particularly if you stick to options such as the Star Ferry and the

Hong Kong Island trams. Getting around on foot is also an option in many areas, given the compact nature of Hong Kong. Inexpensive street food is abundant, and fast-food chains with bargain lunches and dinners abound. The fly in the ointment is accommodation, yet it is possible to economize by heading the backpacker enclave of Tsimshatsui.

Chungking Mansions in Tsimshatsui has long been notorious for its filthy stairwells, its tiny, crowded lifts and its occasional night-time raids by police, but this 17-story complex of five blocks at 30 Nathan Road still offers the cheapest accommodation in town — around HK$200 for a single room or HK$300 to $400 for a double (usually with private bath). Most of Chunking Mansions' guestrooms are on the upper floors of Block A and B. Dormitory accommodation — usually available in the higher floors (see WHERE TO STAY, page 171 under KOWLOON, for details) — starts at around HK$70 per bed.

For all its bad press, Chungking, like the other bargain accommodation centers in Tsimshatsui, has a superb location and is a great place to meet other travelers and find information for traveling farther afield. Tsimshatsui has other backpacker haunts: see WHERE TO STAY, page 171 under KOWLOON, for details.

Once you've got accommodation sorted out, it's possible to survive in Hong Kong quite cheaply with some care. Getting from Tsimshatsui to Central or Wanchai on Hong Kong, for example, costs less than HK$2 on the Star Ferry. On Hong Kong Island, it's possible to get to within striking distance of most of the attractions by tram, which costs a flat HK$2. Ferry fares to the outlying islands, where everything tends to be cheaper than in downtown Hong Kong, are also reasonably priced.

Fresh produce from the Chinese mainland and the New Territories on sale at an open-air market in Wanchai.

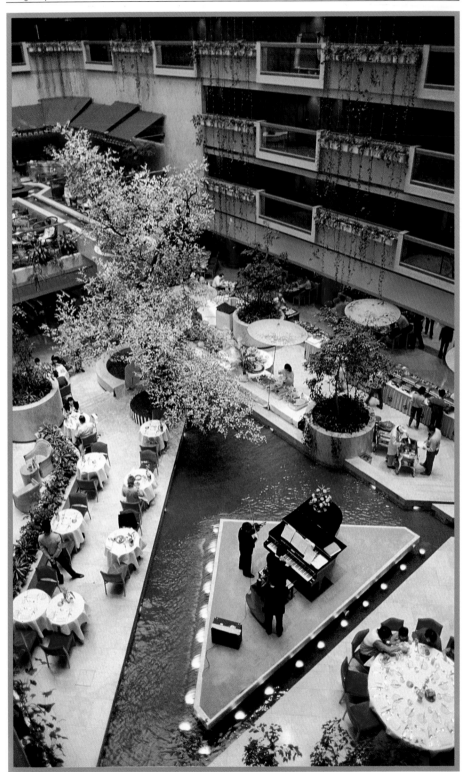

On the dining front, travelers on a budget will be denied the best of Hong Kong's cuisine. But there are many palatable alternatives. Along with the familiar fast-food barns, a branch of one or another is never far away, look out for chains such as **Olivers**, which does excellent sandwiches, and **Café de France**, which is a good place for breakfast. **Maxim's** is a chain that specializes in Cantonese-style fast food such as roast pork and rice, and is a welcome addition to the usual hamburger and French fries format. Also, be sure to check out the food plazas that can be found in all the major shopping complexes of Hong Kong. One of the best — though a little pricier than most — is the one in **Pacific Place**, Admiralty.

Living It Up

For those in search of the good life in Hong Kong, the sky is the limit. Hong Kong has some of Asia's, if not the world's, best hotels and best restaurants.

EXCEPTIONAL HOTELS

Hong Kong has more than its fair share of luxury hotels. Nevertheless, a handful stand out as world-class contenders. Identifying any one of them as the "best," however, is no easy task. Competition is fierce. Identifying the most famous is easier. The **Peninsula**, or the Pen as it's known in some circles, is one of Asia's legendary long-running hotels that, like Raffles in Singapore, has kept up with the times and now attracts guests with both its impeccable standards and a pedigree few other Asian hotels share. Founded in 1928, the Peninsula added a new 30-story tower in 1994 (complete with helipads), but did so in a way that retained the impressive façade and also, if anything, enhanced the tasteful, classically inspired interior. For the ultimate in luxury, ask for one of the corner suites, which sport views of Kowloon and Central across the harbor.

It may not have the Peninsula's history, but the **Mandarin Oriental** is rated as one of the world's best hotels, and has a superb location in the heart of Central. A tasteful Asian theme runs throughout the hotel, with antiquities in the lobby and low-key decor in the rooms. As with the Peninsula, the rooms sport splendid views, and the hotel is home to some of Hong Kong's most highly rated restaurants, notably the French-Asian Vong on the 25th floor.

Close by the Mandarin Oriental is another of Hong Kong's great hotels: the **Ritz-Carlton**. The name — at least in Hong Kong — may not carry quite the clout of either the Peninsula or the Mandarin Oriental, but the Ritz is a close rival in terms of luxury. Rooms have views of either the harbor or Victoria Park, and the hotel has an opulent atmosphere that is heightened by its European antiques and furnishings. It's a good choice for executives, not only for its choice location but also for its state-of-the-art business facilities.

Not far away, in Admiralty, is the **Island Shangri-La**, another top-class hotel with a superb location. The chandeliers (more than 700 in total) are the most obvious distinguishing feature upon entering, which along with the marble floors give the lobby a palatial look. The hotel is also famous for having sponsored the world's biggest Chinese landscape painting — it can be viewed from the elevator between the 39th and 55th floors.

On Harbor Road, Wanchai, and sporting fantastic views of the harbor is the **Grand Hyatt**. Very much a class act, the Hyatt is another rival for top honors in Hong Kong's accommodation stakes. The rooms are almost definitive of understated luxury, and feature winning touches such as the new high-speed, always-on Internet connections available in all rooms — providing you have a network-enabled lap-top. It has some of

Classical musicians entertain diners under the huge atrium of the Royal Garden Hotel in Tsimshatsui East.

Hong Kong's best restaurants, including Grissini and One Harbor Road, and one of the city's most famous nightspots in JJ's.

EXCEPTIONAL RESTAURANTS

As to be expected, some of Hong Kong's best Cantonese dining is to be found in Hong Kong's best hotels. The **Man Wah**, on the top floor of the Mandarin Oriental in Central, is a case in point. With great views of the harbor, the restaurant is famed for its filet of sole in black bean sauce, but its steamed seafood dishes are also excellent. It has an extensive wine list, and the minimalist decor is a treat, especially for those who associate Chinese dining with fluorescent lights and Formica.

The Peninsula, of course, is not without its own top-notch Cantonese restaurant, **Spring Moon**. A meal for two here is even pricier than at the Man Wah, but the 1920s elegance of the decor and the faultless service make it money well spent.

Away from the hotels, in Central the famous Cantonese houses are **Yung Kee Restaurant** and **Luk Yu Tea House**, which is renowned for its *dim sum* — reservations are essential. **Forum**, in Causeway Bay, has been made famous by its chef, who is celebrated in calligraphy on the walls of the restaurant — left by famous patrons. In nearby Wanchai, one of Hong Kong's most famous Cantonese restaurants is **Fook Lam Moon**, which is known for defining dishes such as shark fin and bird's nest soups and braised abalone, along with an extensive wine list. Wanchai is also home to **One Harbor Road**, on the eighth floor of the Grand Hyatt Hotel. The surroundings are less traditional than at many of the name restaurants in Hong Kong, and the superb Cantonese cuisine can be enjoyed over panoramic views of Victoria Harbor.

The hotels are back in the running when it comes to Western cuisine. **Vong**, on the 25th floor of the Mandarin Oriental Hotel, fuses Western with Asian cuisine, and is rated one of Hong Kong's

top dining experiences. On a more traditional front, **Petrus**, in the Island Shangri-La Hotel, is French cuisine as its best and with fabulous 56th-floor views to match.

Not that it's necessary to break the budget when enjoying fine Western dining, even in Central. The SoHo district has an ever-burgeoning number of excellent restaurants where a dinner for two rarely costs more than US$150. **Soho Soho** perhaps sums up the spirit of the area in more than just its name, offering "modern British" cuisine, with surprisingly good results. One of the pioneers in this area, **2 Sardines**, by no means limits its menu to sardines — it is

a homey French restaurant that wins a lot of repeat custom. Also highly recommended, though more for the eyes than for the tastebuds, is the **Peak Café**, with its multi-ethnic cuisine (the Indian is probably the best) and its superlative views — be sure to reserve.

Over in Tsimshatsui, **Felix**, on the 28th floor of the Peninsula Hotel, is justifiably one of Hong Kong's most famous restaurants. The Philippe Starck-designed interior alone is worth the price of a meal — or at least a drink. The "Pacific Rim" cuisine is consistently surprising.

Gaddi's is another Peninsula offering and easily one Hong Kong's top French restaurants, offering impeccable service, decor and cuisine. **Sabatini** has branches in Milan and Tokyo, among other places, and is the perfect place to splurge on Italian at its best — the desserts are much talked about.

Family Fun

Hong Kong's number-one family attraction is **Ocean Park**, Southeast Asia's largest oceanarium and fun park, just half an hour away from Hong Kong

The Luk Yu Tea House is a perennial favorite with local Chinese and expats.

Island's Central district (take bus No. 70 from Central and get off immediately after Aberdeen Tunnel or take the special Ocean Park Citybus service from Admiralty MTR station, which goes directly to the entrance).

Ocean Park was established on the southern slopes of Hong Kong Island in 1977 and has expanded over the years to incorporate some of Asia's greatest thrills: it has Asia's first and largest water play park, Water World (try the 20-m-high (66-ft) Super Slides for a six-second adrenaline splash); the world's largest reef aquarium — Atoll Reef (with 6,000 fish on three levels); and, the biggest thrill of all, one of the world's longest and fastest roller-coasters, a heart-stopping loop-the-loop appropriately called The Dragon. This monster ride takes you soaring up to the sky and back again in a furious two-and-a-half-minute ride which reaches speeds of 48 km/h (77 mph) and has you suspended upside down, on the edge of a cliff. Conquer that one and you're obviously brave enough to tackle some of the other thrill rides here like the Flying Swing, which will lift you in a sea-sickening wave-like motion up to seven meters (23 ft) high; the gravity-defying Eagle Ride; and the Film Fantasia Simulator Ride, whose hydraulically activated seats take you through an "illusionary window" while life-like images are projected on a 15-m-high (50-ft) screen.

There are plenty of less taxing attractions at Ocean Park: after the Atoll Reef, my own favorite is the Ocean Theater, where you can watch a bunch of very talented dolphins, sea lions and a killer whale called Hoi Wai put on a show of incredible aquatic tricks. The Discovery of the Ancient World trail winds through tropical forest enlivened by animated reptiles; and the Dinosaur Trail is popular. And then there are the Aviaries, whose spectacular space-age design offers free-flying room for over

Street theater ranges from traditional opera and dance to remarkable displays of gymnastic skills.

2,000 birds including swans, ducks, cockatoos and hornbills (don't miss the flamingoes, either). There's a special section in the park — Kids' World — just for the younger members of the family, offering carousel and model train rides, a theater with animated shows, and a "Dolphin University," where you can watch the dolphins being trained. Meanwhile, near the Tai Shue Wan (upper level) entrance, the Middle Kingdom recreates 5,000 years of Chinese history through theater, opera, dance and art and craft demonstrations. As you can imagine, you'll need to spend a full day to see just a fraction of Ocean Park's attractions.

The **Space Museum**, with its huge planetarium (featuring Omnimax screenings and Sky shows several times daily) dominating the Tsimshatsui waterfront, has brilliant displays on astronomy and space technology, while the **Science Museum** in Tsimshatsui East is very much a "hands-on" experience and has displays for practically every age range, including robotics, computers, transportation, and virtual reality. The 20-m-high (65-ft) Energy Machine is worth the visit alone. One word of warning: don't come on a Wednesday (free admission day) or you'll be engulfed by crowds of excited local school kids.

Two malls worth checking out are the **Cityplaza Shopping Center** in Taikoo Shing (take the MTR to Tai Koo station) and **Whampoa Gardens** in Kowloon's Hung Hom (easiest to reach by taking a ferry from Central). Both have ice-skating rinks (see SPORTING SPREE, page 35, for details), and the concrete Whampoa gardens mall, which is built in the shape of a ship, has a children's amusement park on the top floor.

But perhaps the best and easiest family outings are those that involve a trip on a tram, train or ferry. The **Peak Tram** is an obvious must (see BRACE YOURSELF FOR THE PEAK, page 11 in TOP SPOTS) and its Peak Tower could keep the kids on a high for hours thanks to its trio of attractions: the Rise of the Dragon

train ride, taking you through the history of Hong Kong; the Peak Explorer motion ride with its individually moveable seats; and a branch of Ripley's Believe it or Not! Museum, with a collection of 500 oddities from around the world. When you come down from the Peak, pop into **Hong Kong Park** (near the tram terminal) to see its fabulous walk-through aviary and three-level children's playground.

Train buffs can make the journey by MTR and KCR to Tai Po Market to visit the **Train Museum**, while the trams trundling from Kennedy Town in the west of Hong Kong Island to Shau Kei Wan in the east are the simplest, cheapest ride of all and a lot of fun for everyone, especially if you can grab the front upper-deck seats. For the best roller-coaster bus ride in Hong Kong, don't miss the No. 6 from Central to **Stanley**, on the south side of Hong Kong Island. One of Hong Kong's best beaches is also near here, at Repulse Bay — a pleasant place to hang out after Stanley's crowded market. Other **beaches** that will suit the kids can be found on Lantau (Cheung Sha is the best), Cheung Chau (you can windsurf here, too) and in the New Territories areas of Sai Kung and Clear Water Bay.

Recommended jaunts by ferry range from the hop across the harbor by the famous **Star Ferry** (dare I mention that there's a Toys 'R Us store in Ocean Center near the Tsimshatsui Star Ferry terminal?) to the hour-long ferry rides to the Outlying Islands of Cheung Chau, Lamma or Lantau — great destinations in themselves for family outings. Lastly, for something with an environmentally educational edge to it, you could consider taking a day-long **Dolphinwatch cruise** to try and spot the last of Hong Kong's Chinese white dolphins — THE GREAT OUTDOORS, page 31 has the details.

Ocean Park is Hong Kong's most popular amusement park. It includes rides, the world's largest aquarium, an enormous Water World with swimming pools and waterslides, an aviary, a forest walk and a display of the acrobatic skills of dolphins, whales and sea lions.

Cultural Kicks

TRADITIONAL CHINESE TEMPLES
Major cultural events in Hong Kong
revolve around its temples, of which
there are no fewer than 600, an amazing
number for so small a place. About half
of these temples are Buddhist, almost
200 are Daoist, and the rest are a mixture
of both.

Where ancient animism endowed
the entire physical world with both
guardian and malignant spirits, Daoism
produced dozens of different gods and
deities, all of them entrusted with the care
and protection of some aspect of moral
life. When Buddhism invaded China in
the fourth century, arriving from India
along the Silk Road, Daoism flexed and
bent like bamboo in its path. In doing so it
survived the challenge. Rather than battle
for supremacy, the two religions adapted
to each other, frequently going so far as to
"borrow" each other's gods. Daoism and
Buddhism have since stood alongside
Confucianism as the paramount Three
Teachings of Chinese culture.

The most common of the gods and
goddesses represented in Hong Kong's
temples are Tin Hau (Goddess of the
Sea), Pak Tai (Emperor of the North),
Kwun Yum (Goddess of Mercy), and
Kwan Kung (God of War). Architecturally,
the temples are often fantastically
ornate and colorful affairs, with curving
roofs (to deter evil spirits), ceramic or
carved wooden friezes depicting deities,
and a series of alcoves or chambers
holding altars to the different gods
and goddesses.

Hong Kong's oldest and most famous
temple is the **Man Mo Temple** on
Hollywood Road, below the island's
Mid-Levels, built within a few years of
the colonial land-grab of 1841. In typical
Daoist style, it's dedicated to the God of
Literature and Civil Servants, known as
Man, and the God of War, Mo. Man Mo
Temple is an ornately decorated old
building, its interior blackened by years
of joss smoke.

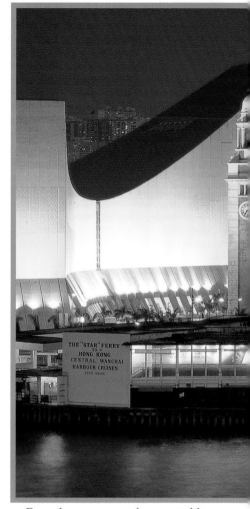

THE "STAR" FERRY
TO
HONG KONG
CENTRAL, WANCHAI
HARBOUR CRUISES
BOOK INSIDE

Even the newer temples — notably,
Kowloon's huge **Wong Tai Sin Temple**,
opened in 1973 — follow traditional
architectural lines. At Chinese New Year,
the Wong Tai Sin complex is packed with
hundreds of thousands of worshippers
praying for a prosperous and happy new
year — an indication of how important
the traditional cultural beliefs still are
among Hong Kong people, despite
modern Western influences.

Another must-see is Shatin's **Temple
of 10,000 Buddhas**, whose statuary
actually numbers closer to 13,000. It's a
steep climb involving nearly 500 steps,
but worth the effort. **Po Lin Monastery**,
on Lantau Island, has Southeast Asia's
biggest Buddha statue.

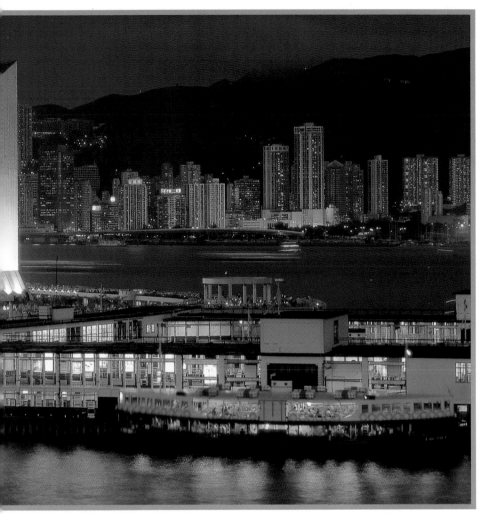

ARCHITECTURE

Colonial architecture has fared poorly in the face of development. As is the case in many other Asian destinations, history is too often swept aside according to the imperatives of modernization. The **Legislative Council** building in Statue Square, the **Clock Tower** in Tsimshatsui, the **Edwardian Helena May Club** on Garden Road, **St. John's Cathedral**, the restored **Western Market**, and the Main Building of the **University of Hong Kong** are among the few examples left that date from the turn of the twentieth century to the early 1920s.

Architectural buffs should perhaps look instead at Hong Kong's soaring modern replacements — notably the Sir Norman Foster-designed **Hongkong Bank** headquarters in Central, and its neighbor, the triangular-shaped **China Bank** building, designed by I.M. Pei. For modern architectural feats on an engineering level, the new **Chek Lap Kok Airport** terminal (also designed by Foster) is also well worth seeing, as are the world's longest suspension bridge, Tsing Ma (linking the airport to Kowloon), and the soaring extension to the **Convention & Exhibition Center** in Wanchai.

The Star Ferry terminus and Hong Kong's Cultural Center almost overwhelm the old railway terminus clock tower. OVERLEAF: Wanchai's Convention and Exhibition Center, where the handover ceremony of Hong Kong to China took place.

THE ARTS

Hong Kong has certainly graduated from its old reputation as a cultural desert — theater, films, ballet, Chinese opera and orchestral concerts and performances by the highly regarded Hong Kong Philharmonic Orchestra are now held on a regular basis.

In January and February each year Hong Kong puts its growing cultural reputation bravely on the line with the **Hong Kong Arts Festival** WEB SITE www.hk.artsfestival.org and the **Fringe Festival** WEB SITE www.hkfringe.com.hk drawing top-class orchestras, soloists, dance troupes, theater companies, movies and fringe events from all over Asia and the West.

In alternate years, in October–November (the last one was held in 2000), there's also the **Festival of Asian Arts**, which concentrates on art forms from all over Asia, including the remotest corners of Central Asia and Mongolia. For film buffs, the annual **International Film Festival** WEB SITE www.hkiff.org.hk, held every April, is well worth trying to catch for its imaginative month-long program of films.

Smaller district art festivals take place throughout the year and often feature excellent local performers. One of the most popular events for both visitors and residents is the trendy **Lan Kwai Fong Street Festival** every August (held around the Central Lan Kwai Fong area),

performances, while the **Fringe Club** (2521-7251, 2 Lower Albert Road, stages more offbeat theater and music shows, and is also a good place to check e-mail and have a drink. The open-air **Hong Kong Stadium** (2895-7895 Eastern Hospital Road, Causeway Bay, stages some of Hong Kong's biggest pop and music shows, as does the indoor **Queen Elizabeth Stadium** (2591-1347, 18 Oi Kwan Road, Wanchai.

In Tsimshatsui, the **Hong Kong Cultural Center** (2734-2010, next to the Star Ferry, terminal, offers a gigantic 2,100-seat concert hall with a 93-stop pipe organ, a Grand Theater with a revolving stage and seating for 1,750, a studio theater for smaller performances and six exhibition galleries, along with restaurants and bars.

In Hung Hom, the 12,500-seat **Hong Kong Coliseum** (2355-7233, 9 Cheong Wan Road, regularly stages massive spectator events — sports meets, ice shows, ballet and pop and rock concerts. Also in Hung Hom, the 2,600-seat amphitheater at the **Ko Shan Theater** (2740-9222, on Ko Shan Road, is the main venue for pop concerts by local underground, and sometimes international, bands. Cantonese opera performances are held at least once a month. For more pop shows and opera, as well as foreign and Chinese films, you can also try the **Academic Community Hall** (2339-5182 at the Baptist College near the Kowloon Tong MTR station. Major classical concerts and Chinese opera performances are often held at the **Tsuen Wan Town Hall** (2414-0144, 72 Tai Ho Road, Tsuen Wan.

For other venues, along with a weekly rundown of events, consult HKTA's monthly *The Official Hong Kong Guide*, the Friday edition of the *South China Morning Post*, or the free weekly *HK Magazine*. The Urban Council also publishes a *City News* digest of events, available free at the City Hall, Cultural Center or HKTA Information Centers.

which is a banquet of food promotions, street entertainment, open-air music performances and other special events.

Visitors in May will likely be surprised to find Hong Kong in the grip of Gallic fever, as the annual **French May Festival of Arts** unfolds. Different events are sponsored each year, and there are always several worth visiting.

PERFORMING ARTS VENUES

Two of Hong Kong's main arts venues can be found in Wanchai: the **Hong Kong Arts Center** (2877-1000, 2 Harbor Road and, next door, the **Hong Kong Academy for Performing Arts** (2584-1500. In Central, **City Hall** (2922-1284, 7 Edinburgh Place, has occasional

Dragon boats prepare for international heats near Tsimshatsui East Promenade.

Or you can check the HKTA web site at www.discoverhongkong.com.

Tickets for events organized by the Urban Council or at Urban Council venues can be booked at URBTIX box office outlets (at nearly all the theaters mentioned above) or by calling the URBTIX number (2734-9009 (daily 10 AM to 9 PM). Tickets can be reserved with an ID card or passport, or paid for by credit card.

CINEMAS

Hong Kongers love going to the movies — even though they probably have the latest VCRs and DVD players at home. There are over 30 cinemas in Hong Kong, the most popular are multi-screen complexes such as UA Queensway (Admiralty), UA Times Square (Causeway Bay), Silvercord (Tsimshatsui), and Golden Gateway (Tsimshatsui). For non-mainstream movies, the best place in Hong Kong is the **Broadway Cinematheque** (2332-9000, Plaza II, Prosperous Garden, 3 Public Square Street, Yau Ma Tei, Kowloon. It has four cinemas, a poster shop, a café, and tickets are just HK$50. The Arts Center's basement **Lim Por Yen Film Theater** (2582-0232 also has screenings of independent movies.

Cinema tickets cost around HK$60 (half price on Tuesdays) and can be booked three days in advance. Phone bookings are often for weekday shows only but with a system called Cityline you can book tickets at most major theaters by calling (2317-6666, paying with a credit card and collecting your tickets from a vending machine outside the theater. There's an additional HK$7.50 charge per ticket for the convenience of this service.

Home-produced Chinese-language films (usually with English subtitles) tend to be violent martial-art movies or slapstick comedies, but Hong Kong cinema has had a serious impact in Hollywood — to learn more about what Hong Kong directors are doing, take a look at the **View from Brooklyn Bridge** WEB SITE www.brns.com.

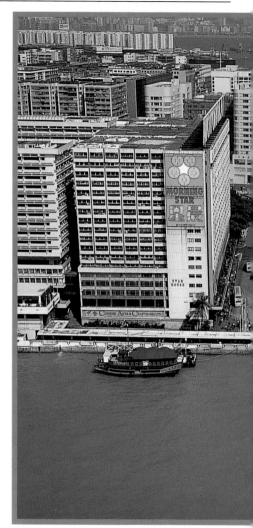

The *South China Morning Post* carries weekend film reviews and a daily listing of current films; even more comprehensive is the free *HK Magazine* (available at many bars, restaurants and bookshops) which unlike the *SCMP* also lists all the cinemas' Chinese names: an essential aid to getting to the theater of your choice by taxi, since few drivers know the theaters' English names.

MUSEUMS

Hong Kong has some 17 museums exhibiting everything from traditional tea ware to 2,000-year-old tombs, and from horseracing to trains. The HKTA has a museums leaflet (available at

their Information Centers) giving full details; they can also provide a special visitor's pass which gives you unlimited admission to four Urban Council museums — Hong Kong Museum of Art, Science Museum, Space Museum and Museum of History — for only HK$50. The pass is valid for one month and includes a 10 percent discount at museum gift shops.

If you've got children in tow, the Science Museum and Space Museum are probably the most appealing (see FAMILY FUN, page 48) but a trio of charming folk museums are also ideal for family visits: the **Law Uk Folk Museum** (2896-7006 is a converted 200-year-old Hakka

village house in the midst of urban development in Chai Wan that reveals what traditional life was once like for rural Hong Kong settlers. The **Sheung Yiu Folk Museum** (2792-6365, way out in the Sai Kung Country Park, makes a very pleasant goal for a day's outing. Once a fortified Hakka village, the museum expands on the Law Uk idea, with displays of typical belongings and furnishings. The **Sam Tung Uk Museum** (2411-2001, in Tsuen Wan, is also a restored 200-year-old rural walled

The Hong Kong Cultural Center in Tsimshatsui includes a concert hall, a theater with a revolving stage and a smaller studio theater, and six exhibition galleries, along with restaurants and bars.

village, now surrounded by the new town of Tsuen Wan. The quirkiest collection of exhibits relating to Hong Kong's heritage can be found at the new **Hong Kong Heritage Museum** (2180-8188, 1 Man Lam Road, Shatin. The 12 galleries cover everything from Cantonese opera to comics, all housed in a northern-style courtyard structure.

Hong Kong's most important art collection is housed in the **Hong Kong Museum of Art** (2734-2167, in the Cultural Center complex in Tsimshatsui. There are seven exhibition galleries, of which four concentrate on Chinese antiquities, fine arts and historical pictures — one of the most comprehensive Chinese art displays in Southeast Asia. Other specialist Chinese art museums include the **University Museum & Art Gallery** (2859-2114 (with the world's largest collection of Yuan Dynasty bronze ware); and the **Tsui Museum of Art** (2868-2688 (with a notable collection of Chinese ceramics).

The museum housing the earliest historical monument in Hong Kong — an early Han Dynasty tomb dating back some 2,000 years — is the **Lei Cheng Uk Museum** (2386-2863, a branch of the Museum of History, at Sham Shui Po. Don't get your hopes up — the tomb isn't actually very exciting and only worth a visit if you're in the area. A favorite for many visitors is the **Flagstaff House Museum of Teaware** (2869-0690, conveniently located in a strikingly handsome nineteenth-century house (once the home of the Commander-in-Chief of the British forces) in Hong Kong Park. Its fascinating exhibits chronicle the history of not just tea-sets but tea itself.

CONCERTS
The **Hong Kong Philharmonic Orchestra** performs a season of classical concerts from September to July at the City Hall Concert Hall, Hong Kong Cultural Center and Tsuen Wan Town Hall. You'll find details of their program at these major venues (or check the *South China Morning Post*).

For a new slant on traditional Chinese music, it's worth inquiring about the **Hong Kong Chinese Orchestra**, the largest of its kind in the world. It combines Chinese instruments and Western orchestrations and gives regular performances at the major venues as well as at district arts festivals. If this unconventional style of Chinese music isn't to your taste, try and track down a performance of traditional **Chinese opera**. This usually takes place to celebrate Chinese festivals (especially major festivals such as the Tin Hau Festival or locally important festivals in honor of a temple god) or as part of the Asian Arts Festival or Hong Kong Arts Festival. The style you're most likely to witness is Cantonese, though the big troupes may well come from the mainland and perform the Peking style. Be prepared for a good deal of clamorous (to Western ears) music and noisy sound effects, and for some fabulous costumes and face makeup. The free monthly *BC Magazine* (available at bars, restaurants and Hong Kong Book Center outlets) keeps tabs on where you can hear a performance.

Music that is more familiar can be heard at the **lunchtime concerts** in St. John's Cathedral in Central every Wednesday. Call (2523-4157 for details or turn up at the door before 1:20 PM.

Shop till You Drop

For a long time Hong Kong was the bargain shopping center of the East. That has changed somewhat over the last five years. Hong Kong's astronomical rents and high standard of living have lifted it out of the bargain bin, though that is not to say that bargains are not to be found — merely that they require some effort to seek out. For a start, if shopping is your main reason for visiting Hong Kong, time your trip with the end-of-season sales in January/February and July/

Hong Kong's commercial extravaganza — the vast atrium of New Town Plaza shopping mall in Shatin.

August, when prices are slashed at the big department stores.

Hong Kong, like most Asian cities, is a place where traditionally certain areas specialize in certain products. Since the 1980s, however, the arrival of mall culture has swept aside tradition. Huge self-contained, climate-controlled, luxury-packed shopping malls have sprung up all over the place revolutionizing the retail industry, many of them featuring multi-story atriums, decorative fountains and regular cultural exhibitions and performances — anything from police brass bands to string quartets or Chinese acrobats — to attract the crowds. Just as the ultra-modern infrastructure of Hong Kong has made the place something of a capitalist fun land, these great retail palaces have made shopping an adventure playground.

Like some kind of living, growing organism, they've also gradually linked up in certain districts, providing environments in which you can browse in air-conditioned comfort for hours, crossing from mall to mall without actually exposing yourself to the outside air — a blessed relief in the sweltering and humid high-summer months.

In **Central District**, for example, you can stroll from Star Ferry to the converted pedestrian overpass between Jardine House and Exchange Square, which gives you the choice of either continuing along the waterfront towards the **Shun Tak Center** shopping arcades (and going across another overpass to the **Wing On** and **Sincere** department stores, giving blissful shelter from rain and the fierce summer heat, not to mention the traffic), or walking straight ahead into the bargain outlets of World-Wide Plaza on your right or to the high-class boutiques in **Swire House** on your left, with access to more shopping floors in St. George's Building and the **Mandarin Hotel** and, via other pedestrian crossovers, **Prince's Building**, **The Landmark** and the posh **Galleria**.

A riot of colored neon competes for the shopper's attention along Nathan Road in Kowloon.

This is the start of the Gucci Trail — alongside Gucci you'll find Chanel, Christian Dior, Lanvin, Hermes, Giorgio Armani, Nina Ricci, Issey Miyake and Salvatore Ferragamo. You'll find Rolex, Seiko, Girard Peregaux and Cartier watches. You'll find heavy 22-carat gold necklaces, bracelets and other high-fashion jewelry, Italian pig-skin shoes and silk ties, French perfumes, fine porcelain, the latest in American and Japanese sports equipment and fashions, Burmese jade, crystal glassware and antique fine arts.

From here, the trail extends past a branch of **Marks & Spencer's**, on the corner of Wyndham Street, to **Lane Crawford** on Queen's Road Central, the traditional home of Harrods-style upper-

drawer British shopping. All along Queen's Road Central are high-class boutiques and jewelry shops. Heading eastwards from the Landmark, take the pedestrian overpass into the walk-through of Queensway hopping plaza that runs between the Far East Finance Center and Admiralty Towers, above the Admiralty MTR station, from where another pedestrian bridge takes you into the glistening shopping mall of Pacific Place.

This vast complex houses a wide range of upmarket boutiques, like **Seibu** (a Japanese department store with a wide range of merchandise and prices that have to be seen to be believed), a **Marks & Spencer's**, specialty shops, restaurants, cinemas and the **Marriott**, **Conrad** and **Island Shangri-La** hotels.

From there it runs down into Wanchai and Causeway Bay, where the accent changes from Western to Japanese high fashion and luxury accessories in the giant Tokyo-style department stores, **Mitsukoshi**, **Daimaru**, **Matsuzakaya** and **Sogo**. Just around the corner from Mitsukoshi, between Russell and Sharp streets, you'll find the spectacular **Times Square** with its soaring glass elevators, upmarket boutiques, huge music store, restaurants and cinemas. There's also another branch of **Lane Crawford** in this district, and the **Excelsior Hotel Shopping Arcade**, with a range of boutiques and shops selling everything from silk scarves to cameras and electronics to Chinese antiques.

Beyond Causeway Bay in the Taikoo Shing housing development at Quarry Bay, you'll find another enormous emporium, **Cityplaza**, which has four towers for upmarket and bargain shopping and a variety of eating places. And if you feel like a little exercise in between window-browsing there's an ice-skating rink in one of the atriums. Cityplaza is easily accessible by MTR — just take the train to Taikoo station and one of the exits takes you right into Tower I.

The giants of the shopping world are clustered over the harbor in Tsimshatsui and Tsimshatsui East. From the moment you get off the Star Ferry, in fact, you're drawn into the luxury vortex of shopping plazas, all interlinked **Star House**, **Harbor City** (Ocean Terminal, Ocean Center and Ocean Galleries) and **China Hong Kong City**, containing no fewer than five hotels and hundreds of shops. It's such a mammoth place that an information desk in the Ocean Terminal, staffed by English-speaking guides, will provide you with maps and even a computer print-out of suitable shops to help you find your way through the retail maze.

Some other malls in Tsimshatsui include **Park Lane Shopper's Boulevard** on the Nathan Road side of Kowloon Park and **Park Lane Square**, opposite. The **New World Center** is across Salisbury Road on the southern fringe of the Tsimshatsui reclamation. For the more discerning buyer there are smaller shopping arcades in the Peninsula, Hyatt Regency, Sheraton, Holiday Inn Golden Mile and Regent hotels.

From there, you can wend your way into the heart of Tsimshatsui East and take your pick of a half-dozen shopping plazas around the Royal Garden, Regal Kowloon, and Grand Stanford Harbor View hotels.

JEWELRY

For jewelry lovers Hong Kong offers high-quality diamonds and other gems, at reasonable prices, all of which are exempt from tax and duty charges. Gold and platinum are also competitively priced. As with other shopping, where to go for the best buys is always a problem — before rushing into the first shop you see, it's a good idea to consult HKTA's *Official Shopping Guide*, which tells you what you need to look for in a stone, and lists reputable retailers.

TAILOR-MADE CLOTHING

Gone are the days when you could walk into any tailor shop in Hong Kong and have a man's or woman's suit or dress shirt made in 24 hours at ridiculously cheap prices. A lot of the

24-hour tailors are no longer around, and the conventional ones are now charging prices comparable to designer-label fashion off the hook. Bangkok is a better city for tailor-made clothing. However, one store that is still keeping the tradition alive is the famous and long-established **Sam's Tailor** (2721-8375, Burlington Arcade, 92–94 Nathan Road, Tsimshatsui, whose prices, depending on the material, range from around HK$1,800 to HK$6,000.

THE SPACE-AGE BAZAAR

With its thousands of shops and plazas, Hong Kong is an ideal place to shop for the latest in high-tech consumer products. With the help of the territory's free-port status, as fast as they come off the space-age assembly lines in Japan, South Korea, Taiwan and China they're usually available here — months before they appear in most other countries. And at competitive prices.

But with a combination of spiraling shop rents, increasingly slim profit

Cameras and electrical goods OPPOSITE and tailor-made clothes ABOVE are among the top items on the tourist's shopping list in Hong Kong.

margins, the deteriorating caliber of retail employees and sheer greed, shopping for these goods can be an unpleasant experience. Particular consumer complaints in recent years have been over "bait-and-switch" tactics, where what you get is not what you were shown. Also, components or accessories are often removed from the product boxes and, when the deal is done, the shop assistant claims that these are optional extras — which you must have or the product itself won't work properly, and which he'll sell you at a 50 percent discount because you're such a nice customer. Don't rush into a deal — prices can vary from shop to shop, sometimes considerably.

The Tsimshatsui district is famous for its bargains (and unscrupulous deals) in cameras and consumer electronics, especially in the honeycomb of brightly lit, fixed ghetto blasters that are the cutthroat stores on Nathan Road and back streets either side. Like most of the smaller stores in Hong Kong, these places operate on the principle of high turnover, which means that some of them have profit margins on their most popular lines shaved down to as little as HK$40 to HK$80. Quite honestly, most of them are best avoided. The farther north you go up Nathan Road away from the tourists the cheaper the prices get, and the less pushy the staff become. Go as far as Yau Ma Tei or Mongkok, and shopping for electronic items becomes a lot less high-intensity, though less English is spoken.

On Hong Kong Island, you can try the row of shops running along Queen Victoria and Stanley streets in Central. In Wanchai, try Johnston and Hennessy roads, and in Causeway Bay there's Cannon Street (which leads to the Excelsior Hotel) and Yee Wo Street.

But if you're concerned about getting ripped off, or just don't want to deal with the frequently rude assistants, get a copy of the HKTA's *A Guide to Quality Merchants*, which has a categorized and comprehensive rundown of retail outlets covering all shopping needs.

BARGAINS

Outside the big plazas, there are literally thousands of department stores and smaller shops to choose from, offering just about anything. Their prices are cheaper because their rents are lower, the competition between them is fierce and, as already mentioned, they operate on the basis of a swift turnover. Many of them also cater more to the domestic Chinese buyer, which in some cases means better prices and, in the case of clothing, means some very good deals if you can fit into the generally smaller Chinese sizes.

Starting in the western area of Central District, the **Shun Tak Center** in the Macau Ferry Terminal offers several levels of shops selling the latest in fashion and informal gear. Nearby, the **Wing On** and **Sincere** department stores not only offer high fashion but also reasonable bargains in clothing, luggage, shoes and body-care products, particularly when there's a sale on.

For watches and jewelry, there are dozens of stores running virtually parallel with each other on Des Voeux and Queen's roads. For really good value, the City Chain watch shops — there are around 70 branches scattered throughout Hong Kong — have 30-to 50-percent discounts.

A relatively cheap place for quality men's shirts, suits and casual ensembles is **Crocodile**, which has a number of outlets in Central, Pacific Place, Causeway Bay and Kowloon. Even more popular is the **Giordano** chain of shops (offering casual clothes for both men and women), which initiated the unfamiliar concept in Hong Kong of service with a smile. On-the-spot hem alterations are also done here and goods are exchanged without question. Elsewhere in Central, you'll find haberdashery items on the steps on Pottinger Street and across Queen's Road in "The Lanes." Li Yuen Streets East and West, which run down to Des Voeux Road, have cheap clothing, underwear, shoes, silk wear, make-up, jewelry and Gucci look-alike handbags. **World-Wide Plaza** on Des Voeux Road

has lots of small shops selling much of what's to be found in the lanes.

For mainly Chinese products, try the five floors of the **Chinese Merchandise Emporium** at 92–104 Queen's Road, just past Pottinger Street. The prices are good and styles and quality are steadily improving as the society modernizes. It's also a treasure house of interesting souvenirs — herbal medicines, Chinese teas, mahjong sets, jewelry, carpets and antiques, silk embroidery, fine linen, carved marble and soapstone figures, jade and nephrite jewelry and sculptures, intricate cloisonné and bamboo ware, traditional kites in the form of hawks and ducks, mouth organs, ping-pong sets, calligraphy and painting sets, ornate old-fashioned treadle sewing machines, kung fu swords and tom-toms, dragon masks and even the sturdy Phoenix and Swallow bicycles of China, modeled on the old British workhorse, The Raleigh Roadster.

In Wanchai around the Wanchai Road and Spring Garden Lane area there are stalls and shops selling designer jeans, children's clothes and casual wear for both men and women. Further along in Causeway Bay, the bargain shopping

is more concentrated, largely in the area between Hysan Avenue and the Excelsior Hotel. Again, there's just about everything you'd want on sale in the myriad stores and boutiques that absolutely throng with shoppers. The area is particularly rich in women's clothing and shoes — a popular place is **Jardine's Bazaar**, which is similar to the lanes in Central. Also in the vicinity is another huge Chinese emporium, **China Products**.

No shopping visit to Hong Kong is really complete without a browse through the open market and bargain boutiques at Stanley, which you can reach by taking bus No. 6 or the air-conditioned No. 260 from the Exchange Square terminal in Central. Famous for years for its cut-price clothing and arts and crafts, the market has become a mainstream tourist attraction these days, with tour coaches thundering out there every day. On weekends the place is packed — go there during the week if possible. Stanley isn't as cheap as it used to be and bargaining is no longer common practice. But you won't be disappointed; it's still a good place to shop, and a lot of fun.

In Tsimshatsui, the most interesting place for browsing and buying both day and night is along the "Golden Mile" of Nathan Road, checking out the side streets if you have the time. One area off Nathan Road that shouldn't be missed is Granville Road, which is noted for its cheap clothes, though there are fewer outlets here than there used to be. Most of the shops are outlets selling factory "seconds" and production overruns. If you've got the patience to sort through the endless racks and piles of clothes you'll find some amazing bargains.

For Chinese products, **Chinese Arts & Crafts** in Star House, by Star Ferry, sells happy coats, silk dressing gowns, embroidered linen, inexpensive to very pricey jewelry and jade items, porcelain and antiques, along with rosewood

Delicately painted antique Chinese screens can be found along Central's "Cat Street."

chicken blood
正 鸡 血

furniture and beautiful Chinese carpets. It's good for souvenirs and gifts and, like its competitor in Central, its prices are very reasonable.

For more browsing and buying, **Temple Street** in Yau Ma Tei is Hong Kong's most popular night market; it can be reached by MTR, alighting at Jordan station. From the Jordan Road exit there is block after block of stalls and shops selling fake Rolex, Dunhill and Cartier watches and designer clothes, sunglasses, silk ties, trousers, shirts, sweaters, jackets, suits. You can pick-up electronic key rings that beep, solar calculators the size of credit cards (which also double as FM radios), or FM radios the size of cigarette lighters, or cigarette lighters that double as FM radios. You'll find Nepalese hawkers sitting on the sidewalk selling Nepalese jewelry, masks and colorful bags. You'll see street dentists and Chinese opera, and for HK$50 to $80 you can have some of your fortune told — the full story will cost more.

Tung Choi Street in Mongkok is the "Ladies' Market," selling bright sweaters, scarves, jeans, underwear and makeup.

Back in Yau Ma Tei, another of Hong Kong's traditional open-air bargain centers, the **Jade Market**, under the fly-over near Kansu Street, offers a range of jade, and prices. But be careful, if you know nothing about the stone, don't spend a lot of money unless you have an expert with you.

East of Tsimshatsui East in **Hung Hom**, **Whampoa Gardens** is another place for value for money. When you arrive, if you think you see a large ship in the middle of the shopping area you're not mistaken. The Whampoa hasn't run aground and was, in fact, especially built as a shopping mall — inside there is a Japanese department store, a Chinese restaurant and a coffee shop. Nearby, the **Hong Kong Place** arcade stages a Musical Fountain Show. To get there from Kowloon, take a taxi — if you're coming from Hong Kong Island, Star Ferries will take you directly there.

Out in the New Territories the shopping plazas in the "new towns" at Shatin, Tsuen Wan and Tuen Mun — all conveniently accessible via the MTR/KCR — have added to the bargain market, forced by their locations to undercut the prices in the central tourist districts. If you have the time, they're definitely worth visiting.

ANTIQUES, ARTS AND CRAFTS

For Chinese and Asian antiques, there's really only one place to go, the area in Central starting from the upper end of Wyndham Street, continuing all the way along Hollywood Road until you reach "Cat Street," just by the Man Mo Temple.

Here you'll find a wide range of high-priced boutique-style stores offering everything from Chinese and Thai carved Buddhas to Indonesian masks and batiks, Persian and Indian carpets, rosewood furniture, Thai and Himalayan artwork and a fascinating array of snuff bottles, porcelain, silver jewelry, Korean and Japanese wooden chests and traditional Chinese silk paintings and scrolls.

If the prices frighten you off, there's an irresistible junk shop on the corner of Hollywood Road and Lyndhurst Terrace laden with an incredible assortment of second-hand Western and Chinese collectibles, Mao paraphernalia, watches, cameras, Chinese coins, black and white photos of old Hong Kong and China and books and magazines. For much the same thing, but on a larger scale, hawkers at "Cat Street" display their "antiques" along the pavements of two narrow streets. Take a look at **Cat Street Galleries (** 2541-8908, 38 Lok Ku Road, Sheung Wan, Western District, where a group of shops can be found selling antiques and arts and crafts.

SAFE SHOPPING

Being the frenetic open market that Hong Kong is, the trading rules and practices naturally get a little twisted and bent here and there, and there are certain precautions that should be taken before buying anything of technical or financial value. The first rule is this: don't go shopping until you've obtained a copy of the HKTA's *A Guide to Quality Merchants*. This handy little booklet is packed with information on where to go

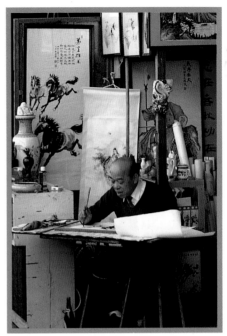

and who to trust on your shopping spree, and it offers the added guarantee of its own membership system — every retail outlet in the book has the HKTA stamp of approval. If you have any complaints or queries about a member, you can contact the HKTA Hotline at **(** 2508-1234.

When you're shopping outside the major retail plazas, take cash and not plastic. Such is the low-profit turnover in most shops, especially the clothing, camera and electronics places, that many retailers put a five percent "handling" charge on the cost to discourage using credit cards.

Always shop around and compare prices before making any decision, and even then make sure that the best bargain price you get includes not only the camera or stereo unit you want to buy but the standard accessories that go with it. For complaints or advice, call the Consumer Council **(** 2929-2222.

Again, outside the major plazas, the question of a warranty on cameras and

Hong Kong's traditional arts. OPPOSITE: Ornately sculptured marble and jade chops in a Man Wa Street store, Western District. ABOVE: An open-air calligrapher's studio offers a hand-painted souvenir.

electrical goods is a constant problem. The best way to tackle it is to shop only where you see the HKTA sign, meaning the establishment has been vetted for good customer service and honesty, and insist that a warranty be provided and stamped with the dealer's chop before you hand over the money.

Don't be timid. Bargain where you feel you can. Go for whatever discount you can get: it's accepted practice in most "freelance" outlets in Hong Kong. But then again, don't lose your cool if you get cold-shouldered. Try at all times to make shopping a fun experience, not a cultural collision — remember that, with the vast variety of stores throughout Hong Kong, and the fierce competition, if one shop won't give you the price you want you'll get it somewhere else.

Don't let touts physically drag you into their shops. It means you're stepping into a tourist trap. When you're buying ivory or jade, shop only at an HKTA-recommended establishment and go there armed with HKTA advice. There are some very clever bone and plastic imitations of ivory around Hong Kong, and plastic and ordinary stone "jade." Remember also that some countries have

banned the import of ivory and that elephants are an endangered species; check with your consulate or trade commission before you bother to look around.

If you're buying Chinese or Asian furniture to ship home, make sure you get all receipts from the retailer, the total price, shipping information and check requirements for disinfestation before or after importation to the destination country. The HKTA advises that on major purchases you take out All Risk Insurance as well to cover the possibility of in-transit damage. Remember also that rattan and certain other Asian woods and materials dry out and become brittle or even crack when they're shipped from constant humidity to centrally heated homes.

Lastly, be careful about the amount of luggage you try to hand-carry onto your plane. For most airlines, United States carriers excluded, there's a size limit to cabin luggage, and there's a team of inspectors inside the departure barrier who are so zealous you'd swear they trained with Delta Force or the SAS. Anything beyond a reasonably sized hold-all will not get through, and you'll leave Hong Kong in anger, when you should have a contented, perhaps over-stimulated and exhausted smile on your face.

Short Breaks

There's no need to spend the entirety of a Hong Kong visit in Hong Kong itself. The outlying islands can make a pleasant break from the hectic pace of downtown, and visits to Macau and Guangdong province are perfectly feasible, even as day trips, though if you want to take a proper look at, say, Guangzhou, you will need to stay overnight.

OUTLYING ISLANDS
Most visitors to Hong Kong base themselves in a city center hotel and explore the territory on day-trips.

Thanks to the efficient transportation system, you can easily see Hong Kong's central highlights in a few days and get out even to the furthest corners of the territory and back again within a day.

But if you'd rather be walking over the hills in Hong Kong's country parks than browsing through the shopping malls of Tsimshatsui, you might like to base yourself in the countryside for a day or so.

The outlying island of **Lantau** is the ideal choice since it offers excellent hiking trails within easy reach of its main village and ferry terminal, Mui Wo (Silvermine Bay). There are several accommodation options in Lantau.

The neighboring island of **Cheung Chau** is another alternative — not so much for hiking, since the island is too small and developed for that, but for easy-going days and nights (there are no cars on Cheung Chau), fascinating strolls through the village or lazy hours on the main Tung Wan beach — it's highly recommended.

Lamma Island is less developed than Cheung Chau, and while on weekends it gets flooded with Hong Kong day-trippers, during the week it is a perfect

place to relax. There are some splendid walks in the hills, and the harborside and beachside restaurants are pleasant places to enjoy lunch or an evening meal.

MACAU
Another enticing option is to extend a visit to Macau beyond a quick day-trip into a relaxing two- or three-day visit. With this length of time, you can not only get to see most of Macau's cultural sights but also catch its Portuguese flavors most enjoyably by lingering over meals in typical Portuguese style — that means several hours spent over a three-course lunch that naturally includes aperitifs (a dry white port, perhaps?), wine and a vintage port with your coffee. Sightseeing after such lunches is invariably a strain: best to follow the Portuguese way and have a quick siesta back at your hotel. Check MACAU, page 203 for more details of its various temptations and for information on how to get there.

OPPOSITE: A Chinese calligraphy set makes a lovely gift or souvenir. ABOVE: The electrified Kowloon-Canton Railway links new towns with urban centers and provides regular services from Hung Hom Railway Station to the border crossing at Lo Wu.

GUANGDONG

A short trip from Hong Kong into Guangdong province is an even more popular extension to a Hong Kong holiday. You can do this on one- to three-day tours organized by tour operators such as China International Travel Service (see TAKING A TOUR, below), or go by yourself.

The quickest, easiest hop is to **Shenzhen**, a Special Economic Zone (SEZ) that lies just across the border from Hong Kong's Special Administrative Region. Shenzhen is a modern, high-rise business city — not so very different from Hong Kong, in fact — but it does have a couple of theme parks which are very popular with Hong Kong visitors and make a suitable destination for a day-trip, especially if you've got kids in tow: Splendid China (China's major monuments and architectural wonders, all in miniature) and the adjacent China Folk Culture Villages (recreations of minority villages, with folk dances and arts and crafts).

From Hong Kong, it's an easy trip to Shenzhen by express bus (call **Citybus** (2873-0818, or **CTS Express Bus** (2764-9803 for details), train (regular services run

from Hung Hom to the border crossing at Lo Wu; call the **Kowloon-Canton Railway** (2602-7799 for timetables) or hoverferry to Shekou, Shenzhen's port west of town (with regular departures from China Hong Kong City on Canton Road or the Macau Ferry Pier). If you'd rather someone else made all the arrangements, there are regular day-trips to Shenzhen's theme parks through tour operators.

Another quick trip to mainland China can be made by hopping across the border from Macau to visit the **Zhuhai Special Economic Zone**. This area, too, is developing at lightening speed, although it's still slower-paced than Shenzhen and in many ways a more attractive place to visit. It has a pleasant stretch of beach and several upmarket holiday resorts and golf courses (playgrounds for rich visitors from Macau, Hong Kong and even the mainland). The birthplace of Dr. Sun Yatsen (China's famous revolutionary and republican) is in Cuiheng village in **Zhongshan** county, just north of the Zhuhai SEZ border (minibuses go there directly from the Macau border crossing), and is the focus of organized day-trips to Zhuhai.

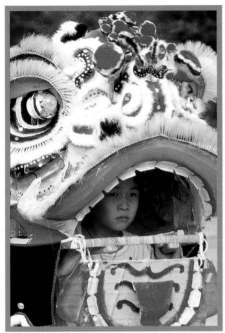

Festive Flings

Hong Kong's spiritual calendar is full of observances, rituals and festivals that govern the Chinese reverence for life, death, good luck, good health, their forebears, their new-born and the various gods that overlook day-to-day life. If you are lucky, your trip may coincide with one of the periodic explosions of feasting, praying, joss-stick burning and gift-giving that marks a major spiritual event.

For exact dates and details of festivals and events, check with the HKTA or their WEB SITE www.hkta.org/festivals/traditional.html.

CHINESE NEW YEAR
The most important observance of the Chinese, their New Year, comes well after the Western event, marked by the first new moon after the sun enters the constellation of Aquarius, and falling somewhere between January 21 and February 19. It is a time of celebration and of reckoning, and it involves a full week of feasting, observances and rituals during which most business in Hong Kong grinds to a crawl or stops altogether. As the magic hour approaches, families, merchants and factory chiefs clean out their homes and offices and settle all outstanding debts. Apartments and homes are decorated with peach blossom trees, kumquat trees, jonquils (Water Fairies) and chrysanthemums. It is at this time that the Kitchen God is believed to visit households to report on the families' conduct during the year, so pictures of the god are worshipped and smeared with sugar or honey so that the reports will be sweet rather than sour.

For the visitor, the atmosphere of Chinese New Year can best be captured by meandering around the enormous

Going to Zhuhai by yourself couldn't be simpler: just walk across the border from Macau. Alternatively, you can take a jetcat directly from Hong Kong's China Hong Kong City ferry terminal. Or consider a tour such as the two-day package from CITS (around HK$2,000), which starts in Hong Kong and includes a quick visit to Guangzhou, Foshan (famous for its pottery and temples), Zhongshan and Macau. You could even leave the tour in Macau and linger there a while before returning to Hong Kong.

If you want to push on farther into Guangdong and visit the capital city itself, **Guangzhou**, catch a minibus from Shenzhen railway station or a bus from Zhuhai. The trip takes about four hours. Directly from Hong Kong, the quickest and most comfortable option is the new high-speed train, which takes just under two hours. Again, there are plenty of tour options to Guangzhou, ranging from one to three days, if you prefer.

If you are visiting just Shenzhen or Zhuhai, it's possible to get visas on arrival, but for trips farther afield into Guangdong you will need to get a visa (see GENERAL INFORMATION, page 218 in GUANGZHOU (CANTON) for details).

OPPOSITE: Door gods and banners are all part of the Chinese New Year festivities, while ABOVE a lion dance adds color to the festive celebrations.

flower markets erected specially for the occasion, in **Victoria Park** in Causeway Bay on Hong Kong Island and **Fa Hui** in Boundary Street, Kowloon. They are a carnival of jostling, jovial couples and families ambling around in search of flowering symbols fit to decorate their homes for the auspicious occasion.

On New Year's Day, the Cantonese dress in their finest new clothes — the children swaddled in brightly colored Chinese padded jackets — and go visiting close relatives and exchanging red envelopes, or *laisee* packets, containing "lucky money." On the second day it's time to visit and exchange *laisee* with close friends. It's also the time to reflect upon any late lunches, long sojourns around the water cooler or office misdemeanors during the previous year. This has traditionally been the day when employers could inform any superfluous or unsatisfactory staff that their services are no longer required — either presenting them with a symbolic piece of chicken or greeting them with the words "Thank you for your assistance in the past year," which in the Cantonese tradition is equivalent to an American vice-president gently telling one of his or her executives, "You've done a great job. What you need now is a rest."

Although mainly a time of rest, reflection and family obligation, Chinese New Year has its pageantry and color too. In China itself, the period features huge Spring Festival parades in most major cities and towns. In Hong Kong, especially in the more "Chinese" villages and centers like Stanley, Aberdeen, Shau Kei Wan and Cheung Chau Island, people celebrate with lion dances to the frenzied thunder and clash of tom-toms and cymbals and, here and there, the crackle and splutter of fireworks — banned for all except official occasions in Hong Kong since the Red Guard troubles of the late 1960s.

But there are numerous other festivals throughout the year that have less of the feasting and formality and far more fun and color.

THE DRAGON BOAT FESTIVAL

Usually held in June, the Dragon Boat Festival is an ancient Chinese commemorative event that Hong Kong has turned into a combined sporting extravaganza and beer fest — with the added underlying attraction of rivalry between Chinese and *gweilo* (Cantonese for "foreign devil" and the name by which Caucasians are often known) teams. The event has traditionally paid homage to the memory of an imperial adviser, Chu Yuan, of the Warring States Period (403–221 BC), who committed suicide by throwing himself into the Mi-Lo River in what is now Hunan province in a desperate act of protest against official intrigue and corruption.

It is said that Chu was so popular and respected that the villagers, hearing of his death, rushed in their boats to the spot where he'd disappeared and beat the water with paddles, banged drums and gongs and threw rice to keep the fish away from his body. It's been a custom since to make offerings of colored packets of rice on the day of the festival, and the symbolic beating of the waters survives in the very nature of the dragon boat races.

Today's dragon boats are anything up to 40 m (131 ft) long, have huge ornately carved and decorated dragon's heads on their prows, and look very much like a hybrid of an ancient Chinese war canoe and a modern racing shell. They're manned by as many as 80 oarsmen, who lash at the water with their paddles to the heavy rhythmic beat of big drums carried in the middle of the vessels. There are many heats, culminating in a grand championship of the three fastest boats, and the races are held over courses that are packed with pleasure junks, launches, ferries and other small craft.

If there's an essential spirit to the competition, it's making as much noise as possible. While hundreds of spectators on the surrounding vessels

A typical New Year welcome at Ocean Park's Middle Kingdom complex.

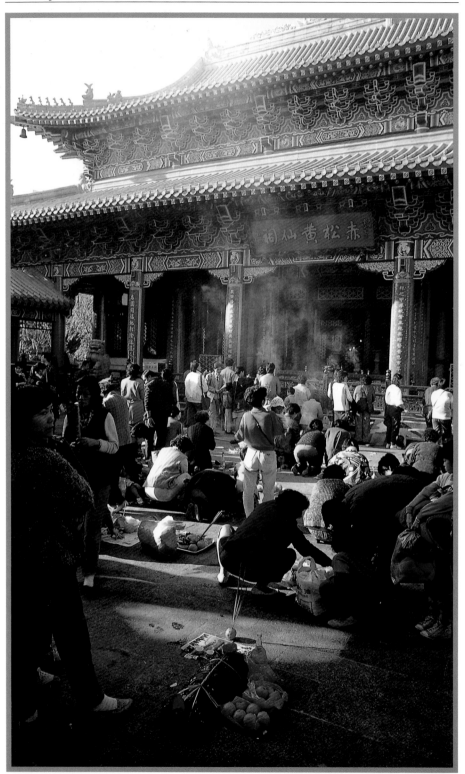

beat gongs to frighten evil spirits away, hundreds of others yell and scream encouragement from the shores as the boats leap and lurch through great explosions and cascades of water thrown up by each massed strike of the paddles, the tom-toms pounding out a kind of primitive blood-curdling tattoo above all the hullabaloo and excitement. Some heats end with boats foundering and sinking with their crews, amid more waves of hysteria. The races are held at a variety of locations in the New Territories, Kowloon and on Hong Kong Island. The HKTA will give advice on the current year's program and venues, and these are also published in the daily and tourist newspapers. A week or so later, it's all done again, with crews from all parts of Southeast Asia and even the West taking part in the strictly competitive International Dragon Boat Races, held on the Tsimshatsui East waterfront.

MOON FESTIVAL

In contrast, there are other traditional events and observances in Hong Kong that are noted more for their reverence and beauty than their decibel level. And none is more beautiful than the Moon Festival, held in mid-autumn on the fifteenth day of the eighth moon (some time around mid-September). Also known as the Mid-Autumn (Chung Chiu) Festival, it combines a Chinese version of the Western harvest celebration with a lantern festival and a fourteenth-century tradition of preparing and eating moon cakes, a sweet confection filled with sesame seeds, duck egg and ground lotus seeds. But it is also a moment of simple nature worship in which thousands of people make their way to beaches and the peaks of Hong Kong's many hills to picnic through the night and gaze upon the full moon.

For the Lantern Festival, there's no better venue than **Victoria Park** in Causeway Bay — the entire grounds festooned with thousands of lighted lanterns ranging from the traditional pot-bellied, candle-lit paper designs to ornate, laser-operated versions that revolve and play music. Another good location is **Stanley Beach**. There, in the full flat glow of the rising moon, the sands are packed with picnickers and moon-gazers; and there are not only lanterns of all shapes and designs to behold — everything from butterflies and fish to tanks and warships — but children also carve castles and ornate patterns in the sands and place hundreds of small candles in them, creating astonishingly sophisticated fairylands of flickering pools and caverns of light.

TIN HAU FESTIVAL

The most revered of all Hong Kong's deities is Tin Hau, the Goddess of the Sea and protector of fisherfolk, and the annual Tin Hau Festival, which falls in April or May, is by far the most colorful and dramatic of all the territory's spiritual events. There are Tin Hau temples all over Hong Kong, but the most popular during the festival is the **Ta Miu** (**Green Temple**) in Joss House Bay. Huge armadas of colorfully decorated junks, launches, cargo lighters, ferries and even harbor tugs flood across the harbor waters to crowd the foreshores below the temple, tom-toms beating, gongs clanging and maybe firecrackers exploding over the decks and bows.

Lions and dragons prance, leap and twist across gangplanks to the shore, and behind them come spectacular, lavishly decorated paper altars loaded with offerings of food, wine, tea, "lucky" money and even toys. And then come the worshippers themselves, carrying giant wrist-thick joss sticks and more offerings of fruit, pastries and even whole roasted piglets. One after another, the cavalcades stream ashore and up through the temple doorways, cramming into the prayer halls and chambers in a murky bedlam of billowing joss smoke, in the thick mists of which hundreds of figures kneel, kowtow and pray to the looming, impassive images.

At the Tin Hau Festival worshippers offer food, joss and prayers at Wong Tai Sin Temple.

Others haul the garish paper altars up the walls to hang on display in the temple rafters. Others shake canisters of bamboo tapers, inscribed with numbers, taking the sticks that slide out of the tight clusters to nearby soothsayers to have their fortunes read for the coming year. And over it all, the drums boom and the gongs clash and whine, and engines grumble and roar as wave after wave of fishing junks and harbor craft pull into the crowded bay.

THE BIRTHDAY OF BUDDHA

The inherent exuberance and excitement of the Cantonese somehow complements, rather than shatters, the more placid, reflective character of Buddhism in Hong Kong. Its major Buddhist monastery and temple, **Po Lin** (Precious Lotus) on Lantau Island, offers retreat, meditation and escape from the urban clamor for most of the year, but during the most important observance, the Birthday of Buddha, held in May, peace and tranquility give way to pandemonium as thousands of worshippers flock across to the island to fill the sanctified air once again with clouds of joss, the blood-stirring thunder of drums and the massed murmur and chorus of prayer. Similar spiritual explosions take place at

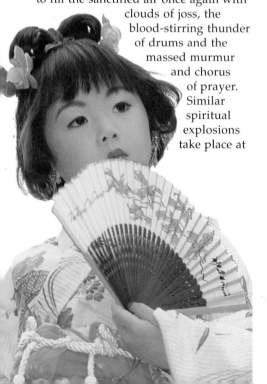

the Buddhist **Castle Peak Monastery**, **Miu Fat Monastery** and the celebrated **Ten Thousand Buddhas Monastery** in the New Territories. Meanwhile, at the **Tam Kung Temple** in Shau Kei Wan, Daoism and Buddhism put on one of their spiritual "double features" in which homage is paid to Tam Kung, the latter-day second patron saint of Hong Kong boat people, and honor is given to the other Great Teaching with a spectacular Washing the Buddha ceremony at the harbor foreshores — with more drums and gongs, more extravagant altars and offerings, and dancing, writhing lions and dragons.

THE FESTIVAL OF HUNGRY GHOSTS

There are ritual occasions in Hong Kong when the full ceremony of ancestor-worship can be seen. The Festival of Hungry Ghosts, for instance, held on the fifteenth day of the seventh moon (August), is the day on which vast symbolic fortunes in gifts and provisions are consigned by ritual fire to the awaiting dead. Hungry ghosts mean underworld spirits who are financially down on their luck, whose homes have leaking roofs, whose television set has blown a fuse, who need a car, bicycle or maybe even a horse and carriage to get around, and hungry or discontented spirits can mean trouble for the living. So on this festive day, all over Hong Kong, the urban pavements, temple forecourts, ancestral halls and grave sites blaze with paper offerings.

CHING MING FESTIVAL

In April an even more astonishing ritual takes place. For the Ching Ming Festival, thousands upon thousands of people flock to the graves of their forebears to pay homage by sweeping, cleaning and repairing the tombs and sites, making offerings of food and,

Children in traditional costumes are a feature of Cheung Chau's Bun Festival. LEFT: A beautifully dressed doll-like young girl. RIGHT: A costumed child "floats" on a pole above the crowds, secured by hidden braces.

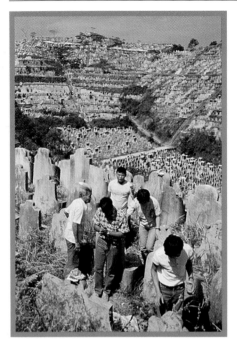

gong bands, ornately decorated floats with tableaux depicting moral themes. Riding majestically above the whole procession, children dressed up in theatrical and historical costumes and painstakingly applied make-up are suspended on the tips of poles with hidden harnesses and metal rods so that they appear to be levitating amidst the banners and flags.

Throughout the week-long celebration, mammoth images of three deities — the Gods of the Earth, Good Luck and Hell — preside over the festivities. But all the feasting and fun is really focused on the central symbol of the festival, three big bamboo towers literally covered with bread buns. These small round loaves are there as offerings to the dead, but at the climax of the festival they are taken down and distributed to the revelers — the idea being to grab as many as possible for good luck in the coming year. Until a few years ago, it was the tradition at each Bun Festival to make a massed scramble up the towers for the buns, but the free-for-all was abandoned when it got out of hand and one of the towers collapsed, injuring several revelers.

in some cases, actually taking out the skulls and bones and polishing them. Bizarre as it sounds, it's actually a rather tender event — it's a family communion and transaction with the dead in which their wishes and needs are anticipated and their blessings sought for the future course of the living. A similar ceremony is held in October during the Chung Yeung Festival.

THE BUN FESTIVAL
There's one other major festival in Hong Kong that began as an observance but has now become more of an extravagant seven-day Mardi Gras. The Bun Festival on the island of **Cheung Chau**, held in April or May on dates that are not announced until about three weeks beforehand, was originally held to placate the spirits, so the story goes, of people murdered by a ruthless pirate who used the island as a base before the colonial British appeared on the scene.

Nowadays it's a huge fiesta that features religious ceremonies, Chinese opera performances and various other cultural displays and, on the third day, a tumultuous parade of lions and dragons, traditional drum, pipe and

Galloping Gourmet

At its most refined, Chinese cuisine is about far more than simply taste or sustenance. It is almost a creed in which diet and certain health-promoting ingredients and tonics are combined with traditional herbal medicine, massage and acupuncture and muscular and breathing exercises, a regimen that goes back several thousand years into Chinese history.

Whether you buy into the Chinese concept of cuisine as tonic, with its *yin* and *yang* notions of "hot" and "cold," the local obsession with food does at least mean that there is no shortage of venues in Hong Kong to sample the best in Chinese cooking. And if the creed of Chinese food is health, its gospel is variety. It is generally acknowledged that Chinese food is a famine cuisine,

its origins going back to the nation's perennial experimentation with all things animal, vegetable and even mineral in the search for enough for its many millions to eat. This gospel, according to the Hong Kong Cantonese, goes like this: "If its back points to heaven, you can eat it," or more colloquially, "If it has four legs and it's not a table, it's edible."

NECESSITY AND INVENTION

The very earliest preparation of food in China was very much like that of the West — first roasted and then boiled or stewed legs and haunches of meat. But the Chinese refined the stewing process — casting heavy three-legged bronze pots and cauldrons called *tings* in which to do it — and arrived at meat that was so tender that it virtually fell away from the bone, requiring only two twigs and nimble fingers to pick it away. Hence the origin of those most unlikely and the most infuriating of eating implements, the chopsticks.

While the nets of the food-gatherers were cast wide for more and more ingredients, the cuisine was gradually refined by experimentation in the kitchens. If it was possible to eat a snail

or a sea slug, it was another thing altogether to actually make it enjoyable, and the cuisine's characteristic refinement of textures, sauces and condiments evolved. The imperial courts and wealthy aristocracy added their important culinary stamp too, encouraging their master chefs to perform great feats of creativity and ingenuity to keep their tastebuds quivering and their senses wallowing in indulgence.

As the cuisine expanded, the harsh limits of the Chinese environment added their say to the way in which it developed. The country's chronic shortage of cooking fuel, for instance, led to the process of speedy stir-frying. It also meant that food had to be cooked in small, fuel-efficient, bite-sized portions, which encouraged the continued use of chopsticks. The generally hot summer climate, and the all-round heat in the south, meant that food could not be kept for long without going bad and perishing, and that meant that the first consideration of the Chinese cook was that the ingredients should be as fresh as the new day. Despite modern-day refrigeration, deep-freezing and chemical preservatives, that principle is still so sacrosanct among the Chinese that fish are kept alive in tanks in the Hong Kong restaurants, right up until it's time for the wok; tortoises, eels, shrimp and prawns also huddle and twitch in baths until the moment of truth. And if you venture into the incredible hullabaloo and pungent aromas of the Chinese Central Market off Queen's Road Central, right across from the Chinese Merchandise Emporium, you'll see the ultimate in fresh-food preservation — live fish laid out on display for the discerning shoppers, skillfully, surgically scaled, skinned and filleted, with their hearts still beating to prove that as far as fresh goes, there's nothing fresher.

OPPOSITE: Filial piety — visiting ancestors' graves at Wo Hop Shek Cemetery during the Ching Ming Festival. ABOVE: Many of Hong Kong's larger international hotels offer exceptional Chinese and Western dining.

FUN FOR ALL OCCASIONS

If food is a religion to the Chinese, restaurants are more than just an occasional place of worship, they are a devotional way of life. The Hong Kong Cantonese spend nearly as much on eating as they do on housing, and this in a relatively confined property market in which the lack of space keeps rents and prices at an astronomical level. More than that, they spend most of their food budget eating out.

Compared with most Western restaurants and the Western etiquette for dining out, all but the most high-priced Chinese eating places are a natural extension of the home. Most Western establishments are for adults only — the average Hong Kong Chinese restaurant is for the whole family. On Sundays, particularly, when most Cantonese businessmen and office workers shrug off their suits and ties and devote their entire attention to family life, their grandparents and their smallest children crowd with them into the casual carefree bedlam of a *dim sum* dining hall or a full-blown multi-story eating palace. While most Western restaurants follow the bistro style of quiet dignity and taste, in keeping with the characteristic Western need for social privacy, the Chinese restaurant is a place in which the ambiance is measured in terms of the number of people who can be packed in at any one time, the noise they make, the gusto with which the food is consumed, the number of children darting and laughing between the tables, the mess that's made and the number of staff who are worn off their feet trying to keep up with the clamor.

Tea is the main beverage, with myriad tastes and blends of its own that have evolved over some 5,000 years — a history as long as that of the food itself. Again, Chinese tea has medicinal origins; its stimulative properties were first regarded as a tonic. It was centuries after its discovery that experimentation began, developing three main categories of the beverage — plain unfermented green tea, semi-fermented and "fruity"

oolongs and stronger, Indian-style black tea. Add to these the various herbal blends — jasmine, chrysanthemum, etc. — and the range is as wide and exotic as that of wine and liquor.

As for hard drink, the Chinese prefer beer, rice wine and cognac with their meals, and they observe a fairly strict control and etiquette in which alcohol complements a meal but very rarely becomes the main course. Although Chinese history celebrates the inebriated poet and writer, and the artist's propensity for strong drink as something quite understandable, extreme drunkenness is frowned upon and you will not often see a Hong Kong Cantonese in his or her cups. You'll know they've had a drink — their faces usually go blood-red on two glasses. But the drinking is done in concert with the food, glasses raised in toast in a dozen different celebrative excuses as each course reaches the table, the food effectively absorbing and neutralizing much of the alcohol intake. Boisterous drinking games are sometimes played, but they rarely go beyond the happy-go-lucky upswing of drinking. When the meal is finished the evening is over. The games cease, the laughter ends and everyone almost abruptly gets up and goes home.

REGIONAL TASTES

The main contributions to Chinese cuisine have come from the imperial courts and the country's principal ethnic groups and regions. The emperors themselves had immense kitchens manned by anywhere up to 4,000 chefs, assistants and service staff to feed and banquet legions of retainers, courtiers, administrators and advisors, extended families and concubines. "Pony express" teams rushed fresh seasonal fruits and delicacies from all parts of the country. Occasionally, the imperial whim added new recipes to the burgeoning compendium of the cuisine: the infamous Empress Dowager, Ci Xi, the last effective imperial ruler of China, is said

A *dai pai dong* (street-side restaurant).

to have dreamed one night of steamed buns filled with pork. They appeared on the imperial menu the next day and have been popular ever since.

As the expanding Moslem empire pushed the Islamic faith down the Silk Road into northwest China, destroying the idolatry face of Buddhism as it went, the Moslem cuisine of lamb and beef kebabs and its flat, unleavened bread, joined the Chinese table. The Mongolians, sweeping down through the Great Wall to wreak the most terrifying destruction and wholesale slaughter that China has ever known, introduced the hot-pot dishes that have also been part of China's regional tastes since the reign of the powerful but short-lived Yuan dynasty.

The culinary customs and creativity of China's various regions, based on distinctive regional foodstuffs and local climates, have contributed much to the vast variety found in its cuisine. Chinese food is categorized into four main regions — the north (Hebei, Shandong and Henan), the east (Jiangsu and Zhejiang, often contracted into *jiangzhe*), the south (usually referring to Cantonese and Chaozhou) and the west (Sichuan and Yunnan).

Northern or **Beijing** style is based largely on wheat-flour breads, noodles and dumplings, the staple of the comparatively austere temperate-frigid climate, and features the foods of the northern and northwestern tribes — the mutton, lamb and beef of the Moslems and Mongolians, served with scallions, leeks, pickled cabbage and cucumbers. But against this rather mundane culinary backdrop, the richness and variety of Shandong cooking adds a regional flair. The Shandong chefs were the maestros of the imperial courts in Beijing, famous for their delicate sauces and ingredients stir-fried with vegetables, crab, shrimp, chicken or meatballs. Of all the dishes, none ranks in stature or popularity with that abiding star of the northern cuisine, the Beijing duck, with its golden brown, crispy-thin basted slices of skin and flesh wrapped in unleavened pancakes with salty plum sauce and fresh scallions.

Eastern or **Shanghai** cuisine is noted for its chicken and seafood dishes, especially fish, shrimp and crab, its rich tastes and its extravagant use of garlic and sesame oil. In fact, it's the richest and oiliest of the regional culinary styles, so oily that steamed bread is often served instead of rice to soak up the juices, and so rich that at one stage in its history its leading chefs were accused of preparing "unnecessarily elaborate dishes and overly opulent banquets." Although Shanghai itself was only a small, nondescript fishing port until the British forced it open as a trading concession, Hangzhou had a far more illustrious history — as the capital of the hard-pressed but culturally glorious Southern Song dynasty — and its contribution to eastern Chinese cuisine has been aristocratic and quite considerable. Nanjing (Nanking), west along the Yangtze River, added its famous smoked meats. As for Shanghai, it contributed an annual culinary fever, triggered in the autumn months, when gourmets and common diners go wild over seasonal Shanghai hairy crab.

The **western** cuisine, originating from the mountainous, misty **Sichuan** province, is the spiciest of all the regional types, reflecting both the character of the people and the need for "heating" foods in the damp and comparatively chilly climate. The citizens of Chongqing and Chengdu like to describe themselves as the fiery "Latins" of China. The cuisine is certainly hot — as one noted expert on Chinese food described it, "the poor sister of the lot, but one with a slightly vicious tongue." Green and red chilies, garlic, ginger and peppers are liberally used to spice up the food. A lot of oil is used too. The effect with most dishes, Sichuan prawns and pork and wind-dried beef recipes for example, is a reasonably mellow jolt to the senses. But anyone who's had the courage to try the province's common *piece de résistance*,

Many Chinese restaurants in Hong Kong not only offer good food but fun too — here a foursome plays a game of *mahjong*. OVERLEAF: The ornate floating seafood restaurants at Aberdeen.

Sichuan Hotpot, will tell you that for much of the meal you can only nod your appreciation (or shock) — you're too speechless and tear-stricken to do anything else.

It is **southern** or **Cantonese** food that is the most widely known, most popular and, by many accounts, the supreme regional cuisine of China. It is born of the crowded, richly fertile subtropical lands and waterways of the southeastern provinces, and it offers an absolute wealth of foodstuffs and ingredients — chickens, ducks, pork, geese, pigeons, prawns, crabs, lobsters, along with a similar variety of vegetables, tropical fruits and melons. It is recognized as the lightest of the regional cuisines, with particularly wide use of the stir-fry technique; and it's also noted for its combinations of meat and fish and other seafood, and meat dishes pepped up with oyster or lobster sauces. Another specialty is red roast pork, a delicious and deservedly popular dish.

But the southern cuisine's most renowned specialty, a sub-cuisine of its own, is its *dim sum*, or "little heart" delicacies, mainly light bite-sized steamed or fried pork, prawn, beef or squid recipes usually cooked in pasta jackets or bean-curd skin and taken with tea from breakfast time, through lunch and into the early afternoon. *Dim sum* tea-houses are among the biggest, most ornate, most popular and most packed of all the restaurants in Hong Kong. To lunch at one of them you have to get there very early — not long after 11 AM — otherwise you'll join crowds of hopefuls standing around in the raucous dining rooms pressing against the crowded tables and waiting for the lucky ones to finish their meals and leave. When you finally manage to grab a table, the various delicacies are brought around on trolleys, many of them in bamboo steaming baskets. You choose whatever catches your fancy and when the meal is over the check is calculated from the number of empty baskets. In some more modern *dim sum* palaces the dishes are ticked off a card.

Special Interests

COOKERY CLASSES

Gourmets love Hong Kong because of its huge choice of cuisines and restaurants, particularly its excellent Chinese cuisine. During the HKTA-organized Hong Kong Food Festival, held every March, there's a chance to learn a few secrets from master chefs and well-known cooking personalities such as William Mark, Chan Tung and Doreen Leung through the "Hong Kong at Home" program of cooking classes, jointly organized by the HKTA and the YMCA Domestic Center. Eight classes are offered during the festival, costing HK$380 each. As there's a maximum of only 12 people per class it's advisable to book at least a week in advance.

Another Food Festival program, Cooking with Great Chefs, features executive chefs from some of Hong Kong's finest restaurants and hotels, who demonstrate two or three recipes and then help course participants to recreate the dishes. While the "Hong Kong at Home" course concentrates on mainly Cantonese family dishes, this program features everything from Mexican to Mediterranean fare, Japanese to East-meets-West. Again, each class costs HK$380 and there's a maximum of only 15 people per course. Contact the HKTA well in advance if you would like to participate.

Outside of Food Festival times, **Chopsticks Cooking Center** (2336-8433, G/F 108 Boundary Street, Kowloon, is one of Hong Kong's best known cooking schools, with courses ranging from half day through to several months. The Peninsula Hotel also has occasional cooking courses.

The **Towngas Cooking Center** (2576-1535, Basement, Leighton Center, 77 Leighton Road, Causeway Bay, has cooking classes every Wednesday morning. Attendance can be arranged through the HKTA or through directly ringing the center.

HISTORICAL TOURS

The HKTA organizes several excellent tours that aim to provide a deeper insight into Hong Kong's social, cultural and religious life. **The Heritage Tour** of the New Territories takes visitors to some of the finest classical Chinese sites in Hong Kong, including the beautifully restored eighteenth-century walled village of Sam Tung Uk, the eighteenth-century Man Shek Tong ancestral hall (a tribute to ancestral worship) and the opulent stately home of Tai Fu Tai, a nineteenth-century scholar of the gentry class. The tour leaves four times a week and costs HK$305 per person.

The HKTA also runs other Heritage Tours in Hong Kong and Kowloon, all of which are recommended.

TAI CHI

Get up early in the morning in Hong Kong, and you will see practitioners of tai chi going through their routines in parks and public places. A recent innovation is free public lessons in English for visitors to Hong Kong. The venue is the Tsimshatsui Waterfront Promenade, behind the Cultural Center, directly to the right of the Clock Tower

as you are facing north from the Star Ferry Terminal. Lessons begin at 8 AM on Tuesdays and Wednesdays, and last for an hour. These lessons are subject to changes in time, however, so it is a good idea to ring the HKTA (2508-1234 beforehand.

For more information about tai chi in Hong Kong, contact the **Hong Kong Tai Chi Association** (2395-4884 WEB SITE www.hkstar.com/~yancheng/taichi/main.html, 11th Floor, 60 Argyle Street, Lee On Building, Kowloon. Most of its classes are available on a monthly basis, but it is also possible to negotiate for something shorter.

LANGUAGE

While it's possible to study Cantonese in Hong Kong, it's a better idea to study Mandarin, which is easier and can be used throughout the Chinese world. Obviously the best places to do this are in Taipei or in Beijing. But it's also possible to study in Hong Kong. The **Yale in China Language Program** at the Chinese University of Hong Kong (2609-6727 FAX 2603-5004, Shatin, New Territories, is recommended for serious students.

Taking a Tour

Tour operators today can get travelers to Hong Kong either overland or by air with stopovers en-route for those that want them, but usually in combination with a visit to highlights of China. Hong Kong itself is a dream to get around in, and only the least intrepid traveler need consider a tour if Hong Kong is their only destination. For those looking to combine Hong Kong with a taste of the "real China" however, a tour is a good idea.

Most of the big established operators provide escorts with a sound experience of China and Chinese culture, who take care of everything from visas to meals.

Chinese noodle-making skills are exhibited at some of the Food Festival programs organized by HKTA.

Their competitive prices generally include international travel to and from Hong Kong and China, all internal travel, full accommodation and meals, cultural excursions, Chinese interpreters and guides and airport taxes.

UNITED STATES
Abercrombie & Kent International
((630) 954-2944 TOLL-FREE (1 800) 323-7308 FAX (630) 954-3324 E-MAIL info@abercrombie kent.com, 1520 Kensington Road, Oak Brook, Illinois 60523, is one of the big names of package tourism, and offers not only tours to Hong Kong and China but to all corners of the world. Tours, such as its Highlights of China, an eight-day jaunt around some of the best of China, are extremely popular.

For a company that specializes in Hong Kong and China, **China Voyages** ((1 510) 559-3388 TOLL FREE (1 800) 914-9133 FAX (1 510) 559-8863, 1650 Solano Avenue, Suite A, Berkeley, California 94707, is recommended. Apart from tour packages, they also offer customized tours. A wide variety of tours is on offer at any given time from the United States, Hong Kong and Beijing. China Voyages also offers a number of "flexible city packages" that get travelers to a Chinese destination and provide accommodation, leaving you free to explore under you own steam.

CANADA
Pacific Rim Travel Corporation ((250) 380-4888 TOLL FREE (1 800) 663-1559 FAX (250) 380-7917 E-MAIL pacrimtc@pinc .com, 419–1207, 8-1501, Glentana Road, Victoria, British Columbia V9A 7B2, is a tour operator with special interests in Hong Kong and China. Along with general tours of China, they also offer specialist tours and tours led by China experts.

BRITAIN
Voyages Jules Verne is probably Europe's biggest and most experienced Hong Kong and China tour operator, with

Repulse Bay and its sought-after condominiums overlooking Hong Kong's most popular beach.

offices in Hong Kong and Beijing to help smooth out accommodation and itinerary problems. The company also has a wide range of tours to China and Tibet, and can also take in North Korea, the Republic of Mongolia and Russia. The Trans-Siberian/China rail route is another possibility. For brochures and detailed information, contact their London office: **Travel Promotions Ltd**. ((020) 7616-1000 FAX (020) 7723-8629 E-MAIL sales@vjv.co.uk, 21 Dorset Square, London NW1 6QJ.

Regent Holidays ((0117) 921-1711, 15 John Street, Bristol, is another tour operator that offers Trans-Siberian packages, but the difference is they're aimed at individual travelers. For those who want the comfort of knowing everything is organized but don't want the group-tour experience, this tour company is recommended.

For the standard package experience with a reliable and well established operator, **Hayes and Jarvis (Travel) Ltd**. ((020) 8748-5055 FAX (020) 8741-0299, Hayes House, 152 King Street, London W6 0QU, is a good choice. Not only do they do some very reasonably priced combination tours that include Hong Kong and China, but their basic one-destination packages inclusive of accommodation are among the most reasonably priced around.

Swiss-based **Kuoni Travel** has tours of all kinds. They have many offices around Europe, including one in the United Kingdom: **Kuoni** ((01306) 740500 FAX (01306) 744222, Kuoni House, Dorking, Surrey, RH5 4AZ, England.

AUSTRALIA

Adventure World ((02) 9956-7766, 76 Walker Street, North Sydney, has the most comprehensive package tours to Hong Kong and China of any Australian operator, and also offers specialized tours.

Australia's most well established tour operator is **Flight Centers International — Sydney** ((02) 9267-2999, Bathurst Street (corner of George Street), North Sydney 2090; **Melbourne** ((03) 9600-0799 TOLL-FREE 1800-679943, Level 7, 343 Little

Collins Street, Melbourne 3000; **Brisbane** ((07) 3229 5917 TOLL-FREE 1800-500204, Level 13, 157 Ann Street, Brisbane 4000.

HONG KONG

It's possible to fly to Hong Kong and pick up a tour on arrival, either to see just the sights of Hong Kong and Macau or for trips farther afield into China.

Given its small size, Hong Kong has perhaps more tours crossing its length and breadth than anywhere else in the world. A good place to get an overview of what exactly is on offer is the HKTA WEB SITE tour page at www.discoverhong kong.com/eng/touring/tours. At last count, it had more than 60 tours covering Hong Kong, the New Territories, Kowloon, and the Outlying Islands, and a small number of tours to nearby destinations over the border in Guangdong province.

With such a large number of tours and the diversity of interests they cater to, it would be foolish to make specific recommendations. Essentially they divide into **City by Action**, which covers such things as golfing, scuba diving and trail walking; **City by Cruise**, which offers night cruises with a buffet, junk charter and evening pre-dinner cruises; **City by Cultural Diversions**, which takes you behind the scenes at a Cantonese opera and on a guided tour through a local market among other things; and a number of other categories that take in the city by day and by night, in its rural splendor and in the rush of the transport system.

Several private operators offer tours: **MP Tours Limited** (2118-6235 or 2845-2324 organizes one-hour **open-top tram tours**, which trundle from Central to Causeway Bay and back five times a day every day (including a Night Tour starting at 7:45 PM daily, except Friday and Saturday).

Gray Line Limited (2368-7111 FAX 2721-9651 has a variety of land tours and harbor cruises, most of which cover very much the same ground as the HKTA tours. Gray Line's **dinner cruises** offer some unadulterated romance, however: For HK$630 per person you can cruise the harbor on a modernized Chinese pleasure junk and then enjoy dinner at the Revolving 66 Restaurant, on the 62nd floor of Wanchai's Hopewell Center. Gray Line also organizes trips farther afield, to Macau, Zhongshan and Shenzhen's two theme parks.

Splendid Tours & Travel Limited (2316-2151 FAX 2721-7014 has similar tours on offer as well as a Splendid Aberdeen Night Cruise for HK$680, which includes a Chinese seafood dinner on the famous floating restaurant in Aberdeen.

Watertours of Hong Kong Limited (2739-3302 FAX 2735-1035 offers some of the most popular tours in Hong Kong — a trip on a Chinese-style motorized junk to the outlying islands of Lamma, Lantau or Cheung Chau or the seafood haven of Lei Yue Mun. Their Cheung Chau and Islands Hopping Tour, for example, runs daily except Sunday and costs HK$240 adult (HK$160 child).

Do-it-yourself **walking tours** are increasingly popular in Hong Kong. The HKTA publishes five excellent little booklets (complete with basic maps) to help you find your way around Central and Western District, Yau Ma Tei, Cheung Chau, Lantau or Sai Kung. They're on sale at the Information and Gift Centers for HK$30 each.

For trips into the Chinese mainland, China International Travel Service (CITS) and China Travel Service (CTS) offer everything from a one-day hop over the border to two- to three-week grand tours. The head office of **CITS** (2732-5888 FAX 2721-7154 is in Kowloon, at 13/F, Tower A, New Mandarin Plaza, 14 Science Museum Road, Tsimshatsui East; there's also a branch office (2810-4282 at Room 1807, Wing On House, 71 Des Voeux Road, Central. The **CTS Head Office** (2522-0450 FAX 2851-0642 is at CTS House, 78-83 Connaught Road, Central, Hong Kong; with a branch office (2521-7163 FAX 877-2033 in the China Travel Building, 77 Queen's Road, Central; the Kowloon Branch Office (2721-1331 is in Tsimshatsui, First Floor, Alpha House, 27–33 Nathan Road, Hong Kong.

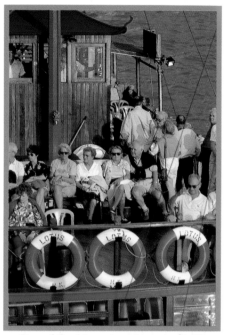

One of the biggest and most reliable agencies for either tickets to or tours into China from Hong Kong is **Abercrombie & Kent** (865-7818 FAX 2866-0556 E-MAIL akhkg@attmail.com, 19th Floor, Gitic Center, 28 Queen's Road East, Wanchai.

Thomas Cook Travel Services (HK) Ltd. (2853-9933 FAX 2545-7477 E-MAIL infobox@thomascook.com.hk, Unit 2210-218, Level 22, Tower 1, Millennium City, 388 Kwun Tong Road, Kwun Tong, Kowloon, is another long-established operator with standard and customized tours to China. They are able to handle most bookings in China, including flights, internal train travel and hotels.

Harbor boat tours are one of the most relaxing ways to see Hong Kong.

Welcome
to
Hong Kong

ON JULY 1, 1997, one of the most extraordinary events in modern history took place, as 156 years of colonial rule in Hong Kong came to an end. Following the Sino-British Joint Declaration on the future of Hong Kong, signed in 1984 and lodged with the United Nations, the sovereignty of Hong Kong — one of the most successful capitalist countries in the world — reverted to communist China. Under a unique arrangement referred to as "One Country, Two Systems," Hong Kong became a Special Administrative Region (HKSAR) of China, with promises of a high degree of autonomy and the freedom to continue its capitalist lifestyle for 50 years after 1997.

Whether such promises were to be trusted seemed to be the furthest thought from the assembled crowds' minds at midnight, June 30, as the Union Jack and Hong Kong flags were lowered and the new SAR Bauhinia-flower flag was raised. For good or for bad, the feeling seemed to be, Hong Kong was being reunited with the Motherland. And, given that the new China was less about Maoist sloganeering than making a quick buck, chances were it would be for the good.

It was a far cry from 1841, when the island, annexed by the British as part of their imperial booty from the first Opium War with China, was dismissed as a "barren rock." It had soon astounded everyone by burgeoning into a major trading center and "Emporium of the East." From the start the island was flooded with Chinese from Canton (Guangzhou/China) and the southern provinces fleeing famine and the harsh rule of the Manchu Qing dynasty, most of them with nothing to lose and thus, with thrift and hard toil, everything to gain. With this grab-happy cheap labor force harnessed by the colony's second major attribute, its nineteenth-century British and European adventure capitalists — dour ledger-worshipping successors to the "merchant princes" whose cannon-bristling East India-men had first forced China to open up to trade — Hong Kong couldn't help but make money.

Its magnificent sheltered harbor and its position as an offshore haven, distanced from the collapse, chaos and civil conflict into which China was sliding, gave it some advantage over the mainland treaty ports, where there was always the threat, and often the fact, of "native" unrest. As British maritime power grew, as steam replaced sail, and as the first transoceanic flying boats began linking the capitals of the Far Eastern and Pacific empire, Hong Kong's strategic position made it one of the busiest crossroads of the world.

And thus it has remained through the vicissitudes of the twentieth century. When World War II ravaged Shanghai and the communists virtually shut the city down in its wake, Hong Kong welcomed its former rival's merchant class. And when China began to tentatively open its doors to the outside world, Hong Kong was there again, a window on the forbidden Middle Kingdom and a conduit for China's burgeoning trade with the outside world. Even the handover of 1997 failed to take the winds out of Hong Kong's sails. It is as prosperous, busy and noisy as ever.

For many travelers today, Hong Kong is a night or two of luxury at the end of a grueling China trip, or perhaps a shopping stopover en-route to another Asian destination. This is a pity. Hong Kong may be Asia's most international, cosmopolitan city, but it is nevertheless a Chinese city. Some 98 percent of its population is Chinese, and it is they who give the city its character, its energy. And for anyone who wants to see a Chinese city at its push-and-shove best, nowhere can beat Hong Kong. It has the best of everything: the best food, the best shopping, and the best nightlife. To be sure, there's the colonial overlay that itself makes for some fascinating exploring, but it is little more than an overlay. Behind the British colonial legacy and the air-conditioned malls are bustling seafood restaurants, parks where daybreak sees crowds of tai chi exponents, temples where the air is thick with wafting incense. Nearby China may offer grander vistas, but tiny Hong Kong packs a lot of punch. It is one of the miracles of the modern world, a "barren rock" that has emerged as the richest, most energized place in the Chinese world.

As tycoons and architects tried to outdo each other by building ever bigger and grander commercial monuments, Causeway Bays' skyline became a study in early Manhattan neo-classicism.

The City
and Its
People

EVERY DAY ON THE STROKE OF NOON, a cannon is fired on the waterfront of Causeway Bay on Hong Kong Island, marking the passing of another 24 hours of high-paced business and pleasure in this, the world's most incredible and exotic center of capitalism.

The Noon-Day Gun doesn't just mark the time, it announces achievement and change — for at the frenetic pace that business goes on in the tropical heat and urban clamor of Hong Kong, a 24-hour period may have seen a new multistory hotel or restaurant open its doors in a celebration of gongs and tom-toms and prancing dragons and lions, a new consortium formed to drive a new tunnel under the harbor, break the ground on a new multimillion dollar high-rise commercial and residential development, or build a new futuristic banking headquarters. And while the cannon signals the end of that day's business race, it's also the starter's gun that triggers the Hong Kong business world out of its blocks for the next mad 24-hour dash for profits.

The origin of this noon-day ritual says as much about the philosophy of Hong Kong's approach to business as it does about the business itself. It's believed the cannon was first fired a century ago in a ceremonial welcome to one of Jardine & Matheson's cargo clippers, loaded with opium, as it sailed into the harbor. It was this nefarious trade in "foreign mud" with China that gave birth to Hong Kong, that nurtured its founding business and trading houses in its infancy, that set the swashbuckling and quite disreputable tradition and tone of its business world and the sort of people who inhabited it. And, while that world is infinitely more respectable, image-conscious and even virtuous today, it still has a faint ring and clash of cutlass blades, a whiff of musket powder and a slight swagger of the self-made buccaneer in its boardrooms. It is still a place where each noon-day boom on the Causeway Bay harborfront triggers the pursuit of one thing: the fast buck.

The new Hong Kong Special Administrative Region bauhinia-flower flag and the national flag of China replace the Union Jack and Hong Kong colonial flags over the Legislative Building in Central Hong Kong. OVERLEAF: Amid celebrative neon signs proclaiming the return of Hong Kong to China stands the impressive Hong Kong Convention and Exhibition Centre — built especially for Hong Kong's 1997 handover ceremony.

FIRECRACKER ISLAND

There have been so many booms in Hong Kong's 150-year flicker of history that to study its development is like watching a fizzing firecracker, waiting for the next bang. Every five years or so this tiny island and small wedge of mainland territory, an ant-hill of less than seven million people, bursts its seams with ambitious, even impossible, business dreams, and five years later it has not only achieved every one of them but is about to do it again.

It became an offshore refuge and new business base for Shanghai textile barons and their money, fleeing the communist revolutionaries. With the many millions of dollars and even manufacturing equipment that they brought with them, the colony retooled, fattened and diversified — no longer just a huge island emporium and port of free trade, but an emerging manufacturing center too, churning out textiles and toys. By the 1960s it had not only gone through a new development boom but was in a near-permanent state of change. Once again,

From the turn of this century until World War II, only one treaty port outshone it, and that was Shanghai with its vastly bigger, even cheaper labor market, its huge textile industry and its direct access via the Yangtze River to the resources and trade goods of central China. But even then, Hong Kong was virtually "twinned" through business links and joint investment with the "wickedest city on earth" — through the Hongkong and Shanghai Banking Corporation and the wealthy, powerful Kadoorie and Sassoon hotel families, for example. And when Shanghai collapsed, first in the horrific Japanese bombing and wartime occupation, then in the communist revolution of 1949, Hong Kong was there to pick up the pieces.

Southeast Asia was in the grip of a violent convulsion, and again Hong Kong was in the right place and ready at the right time to take advantage of it.

That convulsion was the Vietnam war, a conflict to which the United States committed more than half a million military personnel and an immense amount of arms and supplies. By 1966, Hong Kong was not only the main Southeast Asian transshipment point for Vietnam war materials — its harbor packed with freighters — but it was also one of the most popular R&R (Rest and Recreation) venues for the American troops, and for the next decade played host to something like 3,000 free-spending GIs a month.

WINDOW ON THE WORLD

But by then the colony had also been taking advantage of a far greater and even more lucrative conflict, and one that underscored not only its innate, imperishable instinct for survival but also its fundamental survival policy — business above all else — and its unique ability to turn even the most unlikely situations to its own favor. While in the 17 years since the Chinese revolution it had become an offshore life-preserver for almost

"legitimate" exports to other countries. On top of that, Hong Kong provided a base, or enclave, for Beijing's trade and diplomatic negotiations and capitalistic endeavors that lay conveniently outside the walls of the revolutionary socialist society.

If the prospect of a communist society practicing capitalism in Hong Kong was surprising enough, Hong Kong's own wheeling and dealing was simply amazing — it was playing international high stakes' poker with almost every card in the pack marked. It was a sovereign British colony

two million mainland refugees, it had also quite incredibly become the communist government's main international trading base, communications center and source of something like US$5 billion a year in desperately needed foreign exchange.

The American embargo on "Red Chinese" exports had fallen like a ripe plum into Hong Kong's lap. It became a "laundry" for Chinese products, vast amounts of which went in one end of its port and emerged the other end as Hong Kong products with new certification to prove it. With China's own transport and trading infrastructure still struggling to repair itself after the many years of civil war, Hong Kong was also the key transshipment point for

on the surface, but quite prepared to accept instruction from Beijing on key issues behind the scenes. It was anti-communist and a haven for many anti-revolutionary Chinese, yet it was acting as banker, business agent and sales representative for the communist government. It was supporting the American Vietnam war effort on the one hand, as a funnel for war supplies, while on the other hand it was helping circumvent the United States' embargo on mainland Chinese products. And it was making a fortune out of it all.

Hong Kong then and now. OPPOSITE: Pedder Street is dominated by its old clock tower in the late 1860s. ABOVE: A modern-day eventide view of the Manhattan-style skyline of Central District.

CARNABY STREET EAST

In 1966 Hong Kong was at the height of its first resounding boom, and the face of the society reflected it. It was a time of wealth, youth and a burst of hedonism after the post-war and post-revolutionary austerity. Its late-1950s' image of the "World of Suzy Wong" had slipped into a micro-skirt, false eyelashes and Mary Quant eye-shadow, put a Beatles record on the turntable and headed for what was then called the *discotheque*. With its unique blend of Chinese character and red London buses, Hong Kong was "Carnaby Street East."

The island's Wanchai bar district fronted directly on to lapping harbor waters, sampans and American warships, and at night it was teeming and jumping with hordes of United States servicemen and their military police, tourists, local expatriates and young Chinese office workers. Its bars and discotheques were packed with bar-girls, hostesses and seething masses of dancers. The most popular, crowded, exciting "in" place, and the one with the loudest pop music, was the Cave. Its main rival was The Den at the former Hong Kong Hilton, where partiers gyrated to the beat of the Stones or the Beach Boys or swayed gently in the late hours to Paul McCartney's "Michelle" or Frank Sinatra's "Strangers in the Night."

The Hilton was the most popular business and recreation hotel for tourists, American military officers and executives and Vietnam correspondents, and one of three hotels which at that time dominated the Hong Kong scene. On the island's Central District waterfront, massively impressive in that era of comparative low-rise development, the Mandarin (today it's called the Mandarin Oriental) was for British businessmen and visiting Foreign Office bureaucrats who liked a bit of brass and leather with their roast beef and gin. And on the Tsimshatsui waterfront on the other side of the harbor, almost monumental in size, architecture and reputation, famed throughout the whole world for its guardian lions, its fountain, its unending streams of Rolls-Royces and its cavernous gathering place of the interna-

tional jet-set — its lobby coffee lounge — stood the Peninsula Hotel.

Amid tall columns, crisp linen tablecloths, potted plants and bustling teams of waiters and uniformed bellhops, guests sat in the lobby of the Peninsula, on the southern tip of "forbidden" China and the main overland routes of the entire Eurasian landmass, and watched the "in" people of Hong Kong and the rest of the world go by — the great stars of Hollywood, Shaw Bros movie starlets, wealthy ex-Shanghai industrialists, United States congressmen, Commonwealth

prime ministers, United Nations officials, British aristocracy, Indian princes, Asian and Western tycoons and the new giants of the British business world, the pop idols. Marlon Brando was there, so was Danny Kaye, and so too were Steve McQueen, Doug McClure and Richard Crenna, filming *The Sand Pebbles*. And seen through the same soaring lobby windows was an absolute fairyland scene — from the twinkling lights of the harbor and its ships to the island and its rising Mid-Levels and Peak and the eastern reaches of Wanchai, Happy Valley and Causeway Bay, all of it ablaze with lights as though it were a huge diamond, encrusted with millions of precious gems. Many of those gems, at the eastern end of the island, were the lights of thousands of squatter huts, shanty dwellings of tin, scrap timber and even cardboard, built on the hillsides by the thousands of refugees who had poured across the border from China.

In that year of 1966, Prince Charles paid a visit and the colony's British community went wild, filling the So Kon Po Government Stadium and the streets with thousands of Chinese schoolchildren waving Union Jacks. A "Buy British" trade drive was launched and the Union Jacks came out again, along with British food, industrial and consumer displays, British fashion

a man traced the outline of your stockinged feet on a sheet of paper — and come back two days later with a pair of brand new, handmade, high fashion, and cheap, shoes; when the same nineteenth-century, free-wheeling, laissez-faire principles that had guided the colony's business and prosperity since the first shot of the Noon Day Gun were still manifestly successful.

And it was also the year of reckoning, when the special laissez-faire license and "borrowed time" that had built the colony's fortunes suddenly ran out.

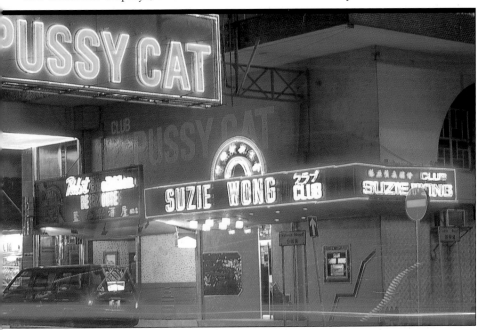

shows, British beer, British pop stars and a lot of British pomp. The Australians left their mark on the colony that year too — a whole team of Aussie journalists working on one of the daily newspapers abruptly picked up and departed Hong Kong en masse, taking thousands of dollars' worth of tailored suits and other clothing with them, along with radios, cassette recorders, television sets, watches, jewelry — even a brand new car — and leaving a lot of Hong Kong merchants stuck with nothing more than some hire purchase deposits.

It was that kind of year, the swinging era when fortunes were being made and flamboyantly shown off in public, when you could sit and work at your office desk while

RED GUARDS AND REALITY

Two calamities hit Hong Kong in 1966 — one was a natural disaster (or perhaps, in the context of that time, an act of God) and the other a momentous political act — which together suddenly brought home to Hong Kong-ites the implication of all those "fairyland" shanty lights in the squalid squatter areas that spilled down many of the colony's hillsides.

In June, one of the heaviest unbroken monsoonal storms in Hong Kong's history dumped so much rain that parts of the

Hong Kong's famous red-light district has calmed down somewhat since the heady days when strings of nightclubs awaited the United States fleet.

slope of the Peak and Mid-Levels, and the hillside above Causeway Bay, collapsed. The mud-slides caused incredible damage, and even loss of life, at one point smashing into the foundation pillars of a high-rise block of flats and tearing the building to the ground. Disaster of that scope wasn't particularly new to Hong Kong — landslides were a regular occurrence in monsoonal storms, and so too were violent and destructive typhoons, which boil up out of the Pacific to smash against the South China Coast from July to October every year. But what the 1966 tragedy showed was that Hong Kong could no longer go on simply making money and ignoring its own infrastructure, safety and welfare. The immediate lesson of 1966 was that a huge and costly public works program was needed to shore up and strengthen all hillside places where land slips were likely to occur.

The second calamity was the launching by Chairman Mao Zedong (Mao Tse-tung) of his Great Proletarian Cultural Revolution, and the unleashing of the Red Guards, some of whom immediately began denouncing the imperialist regimes of Hong Kong and Macau. The Cultural Revolution ignited just as public outcry and unrest were coming to a head in Hong Kong over a proposal to hike up fares on the Star Ferry. Both fire and tinder came together in violent riots in the teeming, tenement-packed streets in the urban hinterland of Kowloon.

For two weeks, in the interminable rain, the tourist Mecca of Tsimshatsui and the deeper districts of Mongkok and Sham Shui Po looked like an urban battleground. Police and army Land Rovers veered through the almost deserted streets with riot-clad crews and anti-missile metal grids over their windscreens and doors. The stately colonial stone and glass façade of the Peninsula Hotel was boarded up, and riot shutters guarded the hotels, stores, banks and money-change kiosks along Salisbury and Nathan Roads.

In the back streets, fires blazed in the night, casting a hellish glare over huge mobs of screaming, chanting, rock-throwing rioters and, confronting them, deep,

heavily-armored and shielded ranks of police and Gurkhas — the British Army's long-standing strike force of Nepalese mercenaries — advancing under big banners emblazoned with Chinese characters warning the crowds to disperse or be gassed, or possibly shot.

Again, Hong Kong was no stranger to civil unrest — there had been labor strikes in the 1920s and riots in 1952. But, like the rains and mud-slides, the 1966 outbreak exposed the bare bones of social neglect, exploitation and discontent that lay under Hong Kong's swinging image. When, in the following year, there was another natural calamity — this time a crippling drought — and even more violent and prolonged riots, including an incident in which a mob

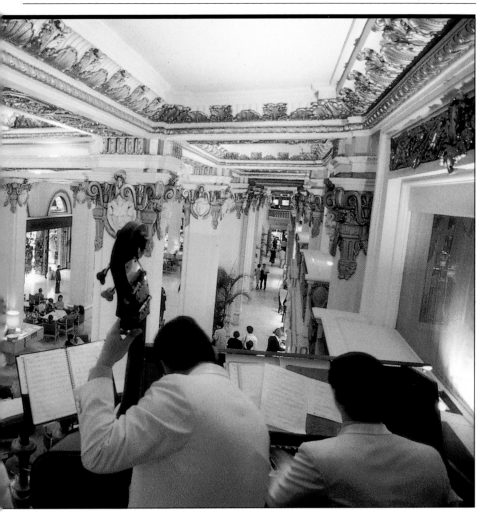

besieged Government House chanting slogans from Mao Zedong's *Little Red Book*, it was obvious that radical and fundamental reforms had to be made to the way in which Hong Kong conducted its business and its community.

Thousands of its people were stranded without homes, and many of those who were crammed into the packed tenements of back-street Kowloon were without adequate sanitation, healthcare, education, social welfare and many other facilities and amenities. The police force and civil service already had a growing reputation for corruption, and Chinese salaries were ridiculously low compared with those of the British and other foreign expatriates — less than one-tenth of the *gweilo* (foreign devil)

incomes even at middle management levels (if, indeed, Chinese employees could ever break into middle management positions anyway).

Momentous and inevitable decisions were made at that time. Laissez-faire had to end, or at least be moderated and reformed to produce a caring, rather than exploitative, society. Hong Kong had to shed its buccaneering attitude and begin to regard itself as a serious and possibly permanent society, not a temporary dwelling and business house living on borrowed time. And in typical Hong Kong style, it threw itself headlong into major reform — and another huge development boom began.

Old World grace and charm at afternoon tea in the renowned lobby of the Peninsula Hotel.

GOING FOR BROKE

By the mid-1970s, Hong Kong was well into a massive building boom that was completely changing its physical character and social attitude. Suzy Wong had thrown away her stiletto heels and slinky *cheong-sam*, settled down, got an office job and joined the PTA. If the transformation aroused a twinge of indignation and regret among the hedonists, it offered a new sense of hope and inspiration to thousands of immigrant Chinese families who, only a few years before, had crept across dark, guarded borders, run the coastal waters in packed sampans and junks, or swum across Deep Bay or the inlet south of Shataukok, and now demanded and deserved a society with

some permanence and sense of concern in which they could build decent lives. Also, it had not escaped the calculations of the government and business world that Hong Kong could not succeed in its next stage of development — from trade, textiles and toys to trade, international banking and finance and electronics — without a vastly improved housing and public transportation infrastructure that would keep its working population reasonably happy.

So, by 1974, the first Cross-Harbor Tunnel had been built, providing speedy, direct access between the island and the mainland districts. The Lion Rock Tunnel had been blasted through the tall hills just north of the Kowloon urban sprawl to free the traffic bottleneck that had existed on this key

to today's modern international airport on Lantau, was being expanded, its harbor runway — streaking out into the harbor waters on reclaimed land — already one of the world's most thrilling examples of space-saving engineering, providing a spectacular touchdown right in the heart of a high-rise beehive in Kowloon. Work had started on the huge Kwai Chung container terminal, destined to become the main export conduit for Chinese trade.

THE NEW CITIES

But all this paled against the central showpiece of the development boom — a multi-billion dollar resettlement scheme to develop three rustic, sleepy rural centers in the New Territories — Shatin, Tsuen Wan and Tuen Mun — into huge "new towns," or satellite cities, providing public housing and full social amenities for one million people. When the first blueprints were made public, it looked like another urban nightmare — the plans calling for a population of 90,000 in one gigantic skyscraping housing estate alone.

There was an echo of Hong Kong's old laissez-faire attitude in the arguments that were put up to defend this construction of one of the most massive, tightly crammed high-rise public housing projects on earth. The Chinese were accustomed to living this way, one argument went — they even preferred it. The development's promoters were on much more realistic ground however when they pointed to the space-saving factor — Hong Kong's largely hilly terrain, making it difficult to create sprawling low-rise tract housing. But even then it was apparent that one million working people were going to be poured into huge industrial dormitories, thrown up relatively cheaply on reclaimed land, while the hillsides were to be kept free for high-profit luxury private condominiums.

Of all the development schemes under way in 1974–1975, the "new towns" had the biggest question mark over them. There were costly development projects under way on the social and recreational fronts

route to Shatin and the New Territories. On Hong Kong Island, initial work had already begun on the Aberdeen Tunnel, carving through the island's central mountain to Aberdeen, Repulse Bay and Stanley on the southern side. And an even bigger, far more ambitious tunnel system was also under way, the US$2.2-billion Mass Transit Railway (MTR), a high-speed subway that would switch the bulk of Hong Kong's public transportation underground and solve the enormous "people pressure" in its urban streets.

Two other gigantic projects, the Plover Cove and High Island reservoirs, were under way in the New Territories to solve Hong Kong's chronic high-summer shortage of fresh water. Kai Tak airport, the forerunner

Hong Kong's commuter ferries provide an inexpensive and enjoyable way to see the sights.

too. New sports stadiums were to be built in Wanchai and on the roof of the new Kowloon–Canton Railway terminus at Hung Hom; a new ultra-modern Space Museum and Planetarium on the waterfront at Tsimshatsui; and a huge US$25-million marine playground, Ocean Park, featuring aquariums, marine zoology, wave tanks, whale and porpoise shows, a cable car system, fairground rides and cultural gardens, on the Brick Hill headland between Aberdeen and Deep Water Bay on the southern shore of Hong Kong Island.

poured off the Jumbo 747s at Kai Tak Airport, and 70,000 Vietnamese boat people struggled ashore from leaking ramshackle sampans and junks — and cargo freighters that had rescued them at sea — to be herded into makeshift refugee camps and, as their numbers swelled, locked up in concentration centers. Not surprisingly, the general health of the community suffered — a report in 1979 claimed that between 20 and 50 percent of the population was suffering from some degree of stress-related mental illness.

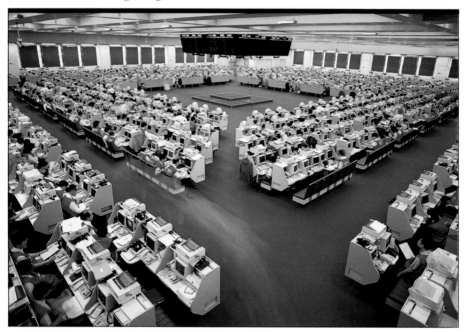

On the island and in the tourist and commercial centers of Kowloon, the face of Hong Kong in the latter half of the 1970s was one of continual noise, overcrowding, stress and chaos. Whole streets were being excavated and districts ripped apart in the work on the MTR and other projects; pneumatic pile drivers shrieked and thumped on dozens of building sites right through the day and sometimes into the night; cherished landmarks of the colonial era, notably the old Kowloon–Canton Railway Station, Tsimshatsui, disappeared in the frenzy of redevelopment, adding to the trauma of some of the more traditional sections of the British community. And amidst it all, some two million tourists a year

But already, the signs of a new, far more just and realistic community were beginning to appear.

With the combined pressure of Beijing and local outrage, along with a couple of notorious court cases, the Royal Hong Kong Police was brought to heel — with the setting up of the watchdog Independent Commission Against Corruption (ICAC). The Hong Kong Festival, launched in earlier years to counteract the adverse publicity of the Red Guard confrontations and riots, had now been turned into the annual Hong Kong Arts Festival, combining public relations with a bid to lift the community out of what had been a profit-oriented cultural wasteland.

What had been a colony was now a "trading territory" — it distinctly said so in all Hong Kong Government Information Service releases. The government's Information Officers were also under distinct notice that anything questionable they wrote about Hong Kong would be discussed over tea in Guangzhou or Beijing that same day. There was a coincidental and gradual breaking of the political and commercial umbilical with the "Home Government" in Whitehall. First, a decision by Hong Kong to break away from sterling and link its currency to the

divine authority in the rich property and development fields.

Another momentous change was about to take place in Hong Kong, and one that explained everything — the sudden massive social development, the slow but steady erosion of its ties with the British Crown. It was a change that would, once and for all, test Hong Kong's unique ability to turn every challenge to its own advantage. It was more than just a change, it was a crisis. Hong Kong was to be returned to the sovereignty of China.

United States dollar, then a certain distancing of this burgeoning enclave — now one of the top 20 trading and industrial centers of the world, and potentially its third richest financial capital — from the staggering, crisis-ridden, and comparatively impoverished economy of Britain.

The "territory's" own economic structure began to change significantly, with high-tech production rising to dominate the manufacturing sector. Its financial structure saw an even more significant change — mainland Chinese investment moving in, and "communist" corporations suddenly challenging the long-established Old Boy network of British and Western corporate powers that had enjoyed almost

CHINA'S FRONT DOOR

In 1841, the Union Jack flew only over Hong Kong Island. In 1860, after the second Opium War, China's Qing dynasty government had been forced to cede the waterfront district of Kowloon, up to what is now Boundary Street. Thirty-eight years later, the British took a 99-year lease on the hinterland, what is now the New Territories, and 233 more islands.

After the 1949 revolution the communist government in Beijing disowned all colonial agreements, quite rightly pointing out

OPPOSITE: Hong Kong's Stock Exchange is one of the world's busiest. ABOVE: High-rise housing in Shatin — Hong Kong's first designated "new town."

that they had been obtained under military duress. But Hong Kong was allowed to continue existing and serving Beijing's interests under British administration. The internal rule and day-to-day running of the "colony" were left to the British, but most key decisions on defense and diplomatic affairs required Beijing's approval — and, just in case the British were tempted to exert full colonial autonomy, Beijing occasionally demonstrated the sort of overwhelming *fait accompli* Hong Kong faced by flooding the territory with thousands of "illegal immigrants."

It became apparent from the moment Mao Zedong died, when the ultra-revolutionary Gang of Four were crushed and imprisoned and when the head of the Chinese "revisionist" moderates, Deng Xiaoping, rose to power, that the status of Hong Kong was in question. China's sudden swerve to the semi-capitalist path was accompanied by a new open, but more aggressive, foreign policy. Deng himself made it clear where the future lay by donning a Texan ten-gallon hat at a rodeo while on a visit to the United States. The Chinese military turned its jets, tanks and guns on neighboring Soviet-backed Vietnam to put it in its place. And it was made clear that the futures of Hong Kong, Macau and even nationalist Taiwan were now to be settled.

In Hong Kong, word rippled down through the expatriate business community that it was time to begin a strategic retreat. Outside the highest levels of government, the feeling was that Hong Kong's value to China, and thus its reason for existence, had run its course — a capitalist China flinging its door wide open to the rest of the world would hardly need a special offshore trading base and diplomatic window any more. That feeling rose to panic when, in 1982, British Prime Minister Margaret Thatcher visited Hong Kong on her way to the first talks on its transfer back to Chinese control in the year in which the lease would run out on the New Territories, 1997.

The Hong Kong stock market slumped, and the hugely inflated property market took a nose-dive with it. Some of the biggest Hong Kong corporations, headed by Jardine & Matheson, let it be known that they were transferring their financial bases elsewhere. Two major property companies collapsed and had to be bailed out, and there was a temporary run on a leading bank. Capital flew out of the territory with the speed of migrating swallows. Amongst the Hong Kong Chinese there was a sudden rush for immigration to the United States, Britain, Australia and just about any other non-communist country that would take them, and up to 40,000 people a year began leaving Hong Kong, in what became a serious drain of middle-management expertise. In Britain, the "Hong Kong lobby" of parliamentarians and business chiefs, bolstered by the Falklands victory, fiercely rattled their sabers against this cowardly sell-out in the face of over one billion mainland Chinese.

But in fine traditional style, Hong Kong recovered quickly from its initial panic, took a good hard businesslike look at the situation and did what it had done in the midst of all crises of the past — looked for the opportunity for profit. A new restaurant opened in Central District, for example. Its name? "Nineteen 97."

The old-fashioned method of transporting goods. ABOVE: A wide-beamed junk-style "lighter" hauls cargo from a mid-harbor freighter. OPPOSITE: The Yau Ma Tei typhoon shelter harbors a colorful array of lighters.

MONEY AND POLITICS

As any visitor to Hong Kong will immediately confirm today, the much-feared Anglo-Chinese agreement didn't sink the territory at all, nor did it even make a dent in its phenomenal economic growth. Hong Kong has continued to boom after Beijing takeover, and is showing every sign of continuing to boom now that the takeover is history. Indeed it has taken vigorous advantage of the economic expansion that its absorption with the mainland economy promised.

Indeed, 1997 in retrospect is memorable less for the "historic" handover than for the great crash of the Asian economic "miracle." Less than a month after Hong Kong had been reborn as the SAR, Thailand was fighting off speculative attacks on its currency, a battle that was to drain its foreign reserves and lead to a massive devaluation of the baht. Before long, the "Asian flu" had spread to Malaysia and Indonesia. Similar attacks were fended off in Hong Kong, and within two years high-tech excitement was fueling another boom on the bourses.

Chinese corporations have continued to invest heavily in Hong Kong, particularly in the property market. The huge Bank of China building, a monolithic architectural hybrid of steel, glass and Chinese imperial arrogance, has planted Beijing's standard right in the heart of the territory's business community. Despite increasingly exorbitant office rents and real estate costs, foreign corporations have continued to pour into the territory, and the SAR continues to be the favored regional operations center for foreign businesses.

Fear of the Chinese takeover now seems somewhat dated. But for those who remember the Tiananmen massacre, Beijing politics remain a specter, even if they have so far had little impact on the day-to-day running of Hong Kong. On the night of June 2, 1989 the Beijing authorities sent tanks and troops into Tiananmen Square to crush the student pro-democracy movement. Up until that night, when mass killings took place, Hong Kong's business community and a growing number of its

people took the view that despite the prospect of coming under Chinese Communist Party rule, the "Open Door" policy and rapid economic changes in China would lead to political and social liberalization as well. The Tiananmen Square massacre proved that despite all the other fundamental changes taking place in China, the Communist Party did not intend to relax its grip on the country.

Hong Kong's reaction was equally dramatic. Mass demonstrations of more than a million people at a time, Chinese and expatriates together, poured through the streets in protest against the Tiananmen crackdown. An underground escape system went into operation to help Chinese democracy activists on the run from the authorities to get out

to the West. There was another emigration panic, with Hong Kong Chinese — mostly skilled middle management — seeking citizenship in Canada, Australia, Britain and any other country that would admit them. Beijing's view of Hong Kong perceptively shifted: while it was still a much-coveted political and economic asset, come 1997, it was now also a potential hotbed of resistance and possible insurrection against authoritarian rule.

Since Tiananmen Square, Hong Kong's relationship with its new masters has followed two distinct tracks. On the economic track, even the horror of Tiananmen and a subsequent hardening of Communist Party rule have been largely ignored in the clamor to take advantage of business opportunities

in China. On the political track, the collapse of world communism, leaving China and North Korea as the last bastions of Marxist authoritarianism, produced a British-led administration in Hong Kong, with wide domestic and international support, which, far from being the caretaker government that one might have envisioned diligently putting the books in order for Beijing's triumph in 1997 — actually began redefining and reforming Hong Kong's political institutions to strengthen its hand in the inevitable power-play with Beijing after the takeover.

Hong Kong's container port at Kwai Chung in western Kowloon is the busiest in the world — it started off as the "laundry" port during the United States' embargo on "Red Chinese" products.

The City and Its People

The appointment of Chris Patten, a tough British Tory Party strategist and former MP, as Governor of Hong Kong in 1992 brought to an end a tradition of British Foreign Service mandarins who tended to bow to China's demands as though it was still the fashion to bear tribute to imperial Beijing. In a sense, they were right: first Mao Zedong, then Deng Xiaoping, both elevated to cult status at the tip of the Communist Party pyramid, simply copied the imperial structure of authority and administration that had existed for many centuries before the 1949 revolution.

But under Patten's governorship, the scholarly myths of 5,000 years of Chinese history and culture were swept away. Far from being the Middle Kingdom, endowed with the innovation, wisdom and exoticism that have fascinated China scholars for years, China was seen as a politically and socially backward, over-populated, under-educated Third World monolith with a brutal, self-protective ruling structure that lacked the worldliness, experience and insight required to safeguard Hong Kong's basic freedoms after 1997.

In the end, the prospect of enormous wealth in the economic partnership with China has far outweighed real and nagging fears of post-1997 rule. The thousands who fled the territory in search of foreign citizenship after the Tiananmen massacre have been drifting back — many missed the energy and opportunities of Hong Kong. After all, it cannot be denied that much of this tiny, ultramodern, ever-burgeoning territory's special allure is its belief that nothing short of catastrophe should stand in the way of business.

THE FUTURISTIC CITY-STATE

Hong Kong today is a thriving, highly efficient city-state. Where the great social programs of the 1970s and 1980s provided it with an ultramodern infrastructure — public transportation, telecommunications, parks and playgrounds, social services and business facilities — the 1990s mostly transformed the territory's commercial skyline.

"Ego architecture" is what it was called — a multibillion-dollar scramble by the territory's new tycoons to outdo each other in the scale, design and sheer audacity of new skyscrapers and commercial malls. No sooner had the 70-story Bank of China thrust skyward over Central District than an even bigger, architecturally grander monolith, Central Plaza, streaked upward out of the new harborfront business district of Wanchai, this one setting a new trend for Hong Kong in early Manhattan neo-classicism. It's a design trend that you'll see right along the Central–Wanchai–Causeway Bay commercial corridor in new high-rise creations like Number Nine Queen's Road (The Galleria) and the Entertainment Building in Central District, the giant Times Square in Causeway Bay and a host of other smaller commercial and office complexes that have sprouted up on both sides of the harbor.

While Hong Kong has been roundly accused of ripping up its history, it is creating a new architectural heritage that is evident in the landmarks of the past three decades — buildings like Jardine House near the Star Ferry and the cylindrical 66-story Hopewell Center in southern Wanchai representing the first great burst of growth in the 1970s, supplanted in the 1980s by the enormous steel and glass citadel of Exchange Square and the novel futuristic architecture of the Lippo (formerly Bond) Center and the main headquarters of the Hongkong Bank, and then all of them giving way to the granite towers and turrets of the neo-classic 1990s. Where shopping malls like The Landmark,

ABOVE: "One country, two systems" — China has agreed to continue Hong Kong's capitalist lifestyle until 2047. OPPOSITE: Like an apparition from the movie *Ghostbusters*, the 78-story monolithic Central Plaza streaks upward out of the harborfront business district of Wanchai.

with its vast atrium, in Pedder Street Central was the last word in luxury, multifunctional shopping environments in the 1980s, now the huge Pacific Place complex, with two lofty atriums and three sprawling levels of shops and department stores, restaurants, office towers and three hotels — the Marriott, Conrad and Island Shangri-La — and the equally dramatic Times Square have become the new showplaces.

In infrastructure, too, the second Cross-Harbor Tunnel linking Kowloon Bay with Quarry Bay has been joined by a third from

Meanwhile, the world's longest covered outdoor escalator system has been built up to the Mid-Levels from Central District — a distance of 800 m (2,620 ft) — to make getting up and down the steep streets easier for walking commuters and to reduce Mid-Levels traffic congestion.

THE COLONIAL GEOGRAPHY

The never-ending outward and upward expansion of Hong Kong is mostly a result of its geography. The early colonialists took

western Kowloon to Kennedy Town on the western harborfront of Hong Kong Island. This third tunnel's construction was part of one of the world's largest civil engineering projects: the building of Chek Lap Kok Airport off Lantau Island. The project was the most ambitious new development in Hong Kong's history, and included a new highway, a new MTR line and the world's heaviest and longest road-and-rail suspension bridge — the 2.2-km (1.4-mile) Tsing Ma Bridge, Lantau Island's first "fixed crossing" to the mainland. After some initial hiccups, Chek Lap Kok Airport, despite dire predictions, has been an enormous success — and for anyone who remembers crowded former Kowloon Airport, a welcome relief.

an island that covered only 68 sq km (26 sq miles) of land space, with most of that space unsuitable for large-scale development, its 552-m-high (1,811-ft) backbone rising virtually from the water's edge. It had absolutely no natural resources beyond its 44 sq km (17 sq miles) harbor — but the harbor was immediately its most prized and potentially powerful asset.

Early *gweilo* development took place along the waterfront of Victoria, or what is now more commonly known as Central District, on the only immediately available skirt of reasonably flat land. Their Chinese camp followers erected their raucous, sprawling, densely packed shanty town further to the west, in what was for many years marked on the maps as Chinatown but is now known as Western District.

As development gathered pace it pushed in two directions, up the steep slopes, or Mid-Levels, of the tallest hill overlooking the harbor, the Peak, and east along the harborfront through Wanchai and another indent of reasonably flat land at Happy Valley — where another fever epidemic struck its first settlers, driving the British back toward Victoria and instilling all sorts of fears and superstitions in the Chinese. Above Happy Valley, a natural pass through the

steep hills provided a vital road through what was named Wongneichong Gap to the island's southern beaches at Repulse Bay and Aberdeen.

As the first road cut through the ocher-colored soil of the hillside, the Chinese protested that the British had severed the spine of a dragon that reposed in the hills, destroying the island's *fengshui*, or natural harmony of spirits and elements, and laying the settlement open to great misfortune. They didn't have to look too far for the evidence of the dragon's wrath — successive epidemics continued to cut like scythes through the merchant and military ranks, and lawlessness reigned throughout the infant colony, with constant violence, burglary, robbery

and piracy. Hong Kong's second major geographical development came in 1860 when, as part of the final settlement of the first Opium War of 1841, the Qing government ceded Kowloon Point, the mainland wedge of what is now Tsimshatsui, and the strategic Stonecutter's Island. This not only gave the colony a bit more elbow room and a mainland foothold but also more effective control of the harbor.

In 1898, having fought the second Opium War to force China to open her doors to trade, the British dictated another deal, this one a 99-year lease in which the present-day geography of Hong Kong was established — the island, the mainland Kowloon district, the hinterland New Territories stretching up to and slightly beyond the Shumchun River, now called the Shenzhen River, and 233 more islands. It gave the colonial government a total 850 sq km (328 sq miles) of territory.

THE HUMAN GEOGRAPHY

Nowadays, it is this aspect of Hong Kong that is the least known to outsiders and a surprise to them when they get here. Often it's not until they arrive there that they realize how big Hong Kong really is. Aside from the main island and the large rump of territory across the harbor, two of the myriad other islands, Lamma and Cheung Chau, are big enough to support large mixed Chinese and foreign expatriate communities, while Lantau Island is twice the size of Hong Kong Island itself.

The tenacity with which the early British traders and settlers clung to this "barren" place can be understood when you consider the territory's position within the geography of southern China. It lies at the eastern side of the mouth of the Pearl River, the major access to the sea for the key river of the south, the Xi Jiang, and part of a vast network of waterways that reaches right up into the heart of China. Guangzhou, the southern gateway to China, lies just over

Two photographs taken in around 1890 show a far more tranquil Hong Kong. OPPOSITE: Before the emporium — a view of the modest skyline of Wanchai and almost barren Mid-Levels. ABOVE: A Chinese artist in a Wellington Street studio specializing in "photographic" portraits.

The City and Its People

100 km (66 miles) to the northwest — and this doorstep proximity is now of considerable value to both cities, giving Hong Kong a close, reasonably efficient trading and investment partner, and a source of food, and Guangzhou a ready supply of capital and much-needed consumer technology.

But it is the human settlement of Hong Kong that has really established its present-day geography. Just as the prospect of one billion people confined in 15 percent of the land-space can be regarded as the most fascinating topographical feature of China, Hong Kong's 6.8 million population crammed into 10 percent of a relatively infinitesimal 1,070 sq km (328 sq miles) pimple of land has never ceased to amaze the outside world. A decade ago, the urban beehives of the island waterfront and Kowloon were so overcrowded that three square meters (32 sq ft) per person was considered to be an acceptable living space, and the district of Sham Shui Po had a population density of 165,000 people per square kilometer (427,000 per square mile) — the highest the world has known.

It is this struggle to fit all its people in that has given Hong Kong its dramatic human topography, the massive high-rise development of its two main urban centers and the satellite towns of the New Territories. And, just as dramatically, the geography has been changed and re-sculpted over the past century in another continuing thrust for more living space — large-scale reclamation of harbor side and seafront land.

ENGULF AND DEVOUR

When the first traders, merchants and soldiers began building the colonial settlement, Queen's Road was their first main thoroughfare on Hong Kong Island, and it ran right along the harbor foreshores. Before the island had even been officially declared a colony, trading depots, warehouses and wharves were being built on reclaimed land on the northern side of the road, and from that point on the waterfront was steadily devoured — and the harbor gradually narrowed — by successive waves of development.

As early as 1851, when a fire virtually destroyed the "Chinatown" settlement to the west of Victoria, new land was claimed from the harbor, around what is now Bonham Strand, to build a new community. Four years later the first reclamation work began along the eastern harbor front, extending the Happy Valley district into the sea. Over the next few years another reclamation project created a *praya* along the Victoria harborfront that pushed Queen's Road back from the water — but by 1890 this new land-space had become so overcrowded and unsanitary that it was overtaken by another big reclamation scheme, and the old *praya* is now Des Voeux Road, deep in the heart of Central District. Successive reclamation schemes extended Kennedy Town and

Wanchai into the harbor waters, and "pestilent swamps" on the foreshores of Causeway Bay and the mainland Yau Ma Tei were filled in and quickly turned over to commercial development. Right into the 1920s, the scramble for new land continued — the Wanchai waterfront was pushed further into the harbor, creating the teeming urban tenement area between Hennessy and Gloucester Roads; Kai Tak was extended into the harbor on the mainland side to create room for the colony's early land-based airstrip; and other reclamation work created new harborfront space at Sham Shui Po and Laichikok. In the most dramatic reclamation project of all, the runway of Hong Kong International Airport, Kai Tak, was later built entirely on reclaimed land, creating what is

virtually a fixed flight-deck in the harbor and, for travelers, one of the world's most awesome arrival and take-off experiences.

By the late 1950s, so much of the harbor front of Hong Kong Island was earmarked for reclamation that engineers began to worry about the effect it would all have on the harbor currents. It took a major research project to settle the fears — a 23-m (75-ft) scale model of the harbor, with electronically operated weirs creating "tides," was constructed at a hydraulic research plant in England. Tests showed where the land could be extended without damaging the colony's most valuable asset.

You can still enjoy fresh air and open spaces on Hong Kong's outlying islands — this one is Lamma — before such peaceful spots catch the eye of developers.

Since then, the harborfront around Central District has marched on beyond Connaught Road, creating land-space for the General Post Office, City Hall, the former British Forces headquarters, the Mandarin and Furama Hotels and the soaring Jardine House and Exchange Square. In Wanchai, another massive reclamation scheme has doubled its area, creating the harborfront area on which the Academy for the Performing Arts, China Resources Building and Wanchai Stadium now stand. To the east, the Island Eastern Corridor streaks across reclaimed land that has doubled the land-space of North Point, Quarry Bay and Shau Kei Wan.

On the Kowloon side, the Kowloon–Canton Railway Terminus, Kwai Chung container port and the huge Tsimshatsui East development all stand on land that was once harbor waters. Out in the New Territories, reclamation has provided much of the land-space for the huge "new towns" of Shatin, Tsuen Wan and Tuen Mun. In all, more than 220 sq km (85 sq miles) of extra land has been squeezed from the sea bed over the past century and a half.

As Lantau Island is developed, easing pressure on the rest of the territory, more land will be reclaimed around its hilly coastline for more high-rise residential and commercial centers. And the geography of Hong Kong continues to change, as with the Macau Ferry Terminal, which radically altered the harbor front face of Western District.

BETWEEN THE MONSOONS

If the struggle for living space has molded much of the topography and character of Hong Kong, the struggle with its distinctive climate has been just as dramatic. The island lies just south of the Tropic of Cancer, which makes it possibly tropical. But it also lies virtually at the point where the southern and northern, or summer and winter, monsoons collide over Southeast Asia — and that has made it a place where only mad dogs and Englishmen could probably have envisaged settling, survived, and developed the huge urban society that it is today. It was Hong Kong's position between the monsoons that

brought the British and European traders in the first place. In the days of sail, the huge canvas-laden merchant ships rode the summer monsoons north to the Chinese coast, stopping over in the "Fragrant Harbor" to take on fresh water and repair any damage before continuing up the Pearl River to Guangzhou. The winter monsoon, its winds originating in the frigid reaches of the Siberian steppes and blowing south right down through China and into the northern Pacific, carried the fleets on their first stage home to the West.

Around March every year, as these mighty wind systems change, the warm southern monsoon meets the cooler, waning winter monsoon over the South China Coast, and the result is muggy moisture-laden air that blankets Hong Kong, settling in thick clouds over the Peak and the Mid-levels of the mountains and drenching everything it touches. The summer months — May through September — see regular and sometimes torrential rains and, during the hottest months, in July and August, temperatures soaring to between 27°C and 34°C (81°F and 93°F), along with humidity in the 90s.

Not surprisingly, Hong Kong is the answer to every air-conditioning salesman's dream, and its newer urban development, particularly in busy Central District and Tsimshatsui, seems to reflect the enervating climatic conditions — enclosed walkways and pedestrian flyovers connect many of the big shopping plazas and hotel arcades so that you can scurry from one frosty, blissful air-conditioned haven to another with only an occasional exposure to the sauna outside.

From October through December the northern monsoon takes over, its icy winds abating and softening by the time they reach

the east of Hong Kong, lashing the territory with their stormy outer bands. Mercifully, it's only on occasions that they hit Hong Kong head-on.

Two typhoons scored direct hits within months of Commodore Bremer's historic landing in 1841. Tuesday, September 22, 1874, a particular violent one almost devastated the colony, the *Hong Kong Times* recording this vivid description of the disaster: "The rain descended in torrents: the wind blew with the violence of a tempest, the rage of a whirlwind. Vessels staunch

this far south, moderating the climate to pleasant sunny days with 21°C to 25°C (70°F to 77°F) temperatures and a relatively parched 70 percent humidity. From there, January through March is cool, about 14°C to 21°C (57°F and 70°F, and April in the mid-20°C (mid-70°F) range.

But the most fearsome climatic feature that the territory has had to face, and still faces each year, is the typhoon season. These powerful cyclones rear up out of the Pacific south of the Philippines each summer and surge northwards to hurl themselves one after the other at the Chinese mainland. They carry tremendous volumes of rain and winds of up to 200 km (125 miles) an hour and they usually cross the China coast to

and strong were driven about the harbor or onto the shore like children's toy craft. Roofs were torn off as by the hand of a mighty giant; trees were uprooted by the hundreds; rows of buildings were blown down in a moment, many of the inhabitants being buried in their ruins. The harbor water overflowed across the Praya — dashing aside and carrying away coping stones that weighed in the tons. The work of destruction went on without intermission for hours; and it may be said that there is not a single house in the Colony but what has suffered."

OPPOSITE: Tea-making is a 5,000-year-old tradition. ABOVE: Indulging in opium was the core of the Anglo-Chinese trouble in the nineteenth century.

Altogether, 35 huge merchant ships were either sunk, driven ashore or badly damaged, along with hundreds of junks and sampans. More than 2,000 lives were lost in Hong Kong and Macau. In the hinterland of Guangdong province, the death toll reached an horrific 100,000.

In September 1906 an even more destructive typhoon hit — this one killing 10,000 people in just one and a half hours, sinking or crippling 141 British and European ships and destroying more than 2,000 Chinese craft.

it's going to cross the coast close to or perhaps right over Hong Kong — and by then the entire population has gone home to sit it out. Windows are taped or fitted with storm shutters. Shop fronts and hotel façades are boarded up. Work sites are battened down to prevent what is now the main danger of these annual visitations: flying building material and debris in the streets. The radio and television network issues constant bulletins on the strength and direction of the storm. For tourists, snug and safe in their hotels, the only danger or

The most recent destructive *tai-feng* (big wind) was Typhoon Rose in 1971, which hit the territory head-on with 150-knot winds that actually broke the anemometer and dumped 288 mm (11.23 in) of rain in just a single day.

The territory now has a very advanced and effective early warning system that gives the community plenty of time to batten down for a "big blow." As a typhoon or "tropical storm" is spawned and begins its northward rampage, it is tracked by weather satellites and reconnaissance planes, and if it looks like it is coming close to Hong Kong a series of typhoon signals go up. Signal No. 1 means there's a typhoon building in the region. Signal No. 10 means

inconvenience that a typhoon presents nowadays is the possibility of a delayed departure from the airport or the train and ferry terminals.

Somehow, against all these political and physical odds, Hong Kong has more than justified the faith and the colonial dream — however antiquated and piratical it may seem to be from these more honorable times — that fluttered with the Union Jack on the flag staff on Possession Point on January 26, 1841. Even more remarkably, that dream has been realized in the face of an even greater challenge — a partnership of what must certainly be the two most distinct and incompatible cultures on earth: the British and the Chinese.

THE CULTURAL CONTRAST

Right up until the development boom and sudden political shift of the 1980s, an integral feature of Hong Kong's vivid cultural character went on show each Saturday afternoon on a neatly trimmed oval of green turf right in the heart of Central District. There, in the grounds of what is now a public park, Chater Garden, British cream-and-white cottons flapped in the damp breeze while the sharp thwack of leather on wooden bats gave a faint, waning echo of British imperial tradition and power amid the general downtown clamor of traffic, trams and construction site pile drivers.

This Saturday cricket match, as religious to the British community as Sunday services in St. John's Cathedral and the firing of the Noon Day Gun, took place right under the towering, austere façade and red-lettered Chinese sign of what was then Maoist Beijing's main commercial and political base in Hong Kong, the Bank of China. This striking contrast of cricket and communism was for many years a much-photographed symbol of Hong Kong and the tenuous circumstances in which it existed — a borrowed place living on borrowed time.

But it also represented a much wider contrast, that of two largely alien cultures, British and Chinese, which had somehow managed to settle together and function side by side in Hong Kong, to harness their various qualities and skills to a common goal — prosperity — and to still retain their own cultural traditions and characteristics. While the British enjoyed their sedate pursuit of maiden overs and silly mid-ons right below the bastion of Chinese communism, an antique Chinese sailing junk might have been tacking its way ponderously down the harbor, a traditional Chinese funeral might have been wending its way through the packed streets in a cacophony of clashing cymbals, thundering tom-toms and wailing pipes, or thousands of Cantonese might have been flocking to pay their annual homage to Tin Hau, the Goddess of the Sea, pouring across the harbor in decorated sampans and fishing junks to Po Toi Island or Joss House Bay, on the southern shore of Clear Water Bay.

If there was any real measure of cultural exchange, it still placed each culture on the fringe of the other. The British and other foreign expatriate groups enjoyed the Tin Hau Festival and other Chinese cultural events just as the Cantonese enjoyed Christmas — but only as spectators, swiveling their camera lenses from the edge of the melee, never really to share the spiritual impulse of the occasion. If there was a point at which both cultures could actually find common ground and speak each other's language, it was in the business office or the

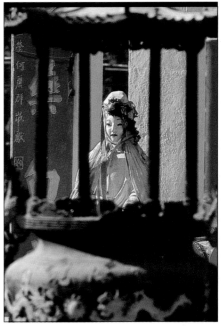

boardroom, or in the one major "cultural" pursuit in which distinctions are blurred because it is another proving ground of the mutual lust for the fast buck — Hong Kong's paramount and incredibly wealthy gambling institution, horseracing.

Since the redevelopment of Central District and, significantly, since the gradual changing of the guard from Western to Chinese political and commercial power, the Cricket Club has moved to a more roomy but far less dominant site above Happy Valley on Wongneichong Gap Road. But the cultural contrast remains, and thankfully so, for it

OPPOSITE: The compelling character make-up of a Chinese opera singer. ABOVE: Incense burner and Buddhist deity.

provides perhaps the most colorful and exciting of all Hong Kong's tourist attractions. And it also bears testimony to the extent to which the Lion and the Dragon have been able to lie down together, and each occasionally get a wink of sleep.

WIND AND WATER

In many respects, Hong Kong's colorful and often dramatic cultural character exists because of the tenacity with which the vastly predominant Cantonese population maintains

its Chinese beliefs and traditions. In other respects, it prevails because of a constant and tenacious Cantonese struggle to drive a coach and horses through the slightest loophole or loose clause in the territory's laws.

In the midst of such high-tech high-rise development, many Chinese cling, for example, to the traditional *fengshui* ("wind and water"), a mixture of belief, superstition, divination and geomancy which is aimed primarily at placing man in his most harmonious relationship with the physical and spiritual world about him. When a new apartment is being furnished and equipped, a *fengshui* geomancer may be called in to position the furniture so that it conforms with the *qi* or spiritual breath of the universe.

Mirrors are often strategically placed in Cantonese homes to block or deflect the path of evil spirits and influences.

This 4,000-year-old science created havoc and apoplexy with Western attempts to modernize China in the early treaty port days. When the first railway line in China was built between Shanghai and Wusong it was bought up by Chinese investors and then destroyed for fear that the speed of the trains would disrupt the *fengshui* of thousands of people living along the route. When the first telegraph line was strung between Guangzhou and Hong Kong it aroused Chinese outrage and opposition because in their eyes it would weaken the southern capital by linking it directly with the inauspicious Nine Dragons said to be residing within the earthen bowels of Kowloon.

But even today, homes and offices in Hong Kong are sometimes evacuated and then exorcised by *fengshui* experts to get rid of "ghosts" and malevolent influences, as happened a little over a decade ago with an entire floor of the Inland Revenue Department. The movie tycoon Run Shaw is said to have consulted *fengshui* geomancers about the site of his huge production center at Clear Water Bay. When the Hong Kong Hilton rented its ballroom for a particularly important land auction, the development company conducting the sale brought in a *fengshui* man to check the ballroom's harmony before bidding began. He decided that the sale would be a big success if the ballroom doors remained open throughout the proceedings, several windows were blacked out to block evil spirits and the cocktail bar, of all things, was rearranged in an L-shape.

Fengshui enjoyed an upsurge of popularity during the initial "new towns" resettlement and development in the New Territories. Any new home that didn't conform to the most propitious *fengshui* siting brought an immediate complaint — and a demand for compensation — from its occupants. It was a constant headache for the hard-pressed planners of the government's Public Works Department, and it may have been motivated less by spiritual concern than the opportunity for base coin, but it also tended to be an effective grassroots defense against a wholesale process of uprooting and re-housing in which human comfort and needs may not, on occasions, have been given a high priority. It was taken seriously, nonetheless, and especially when it became known that one of the PWD's Chinese departmental heads responsible for settling *fengshui* issues had himself brought in a geomancer to check the location and surrounding influences of an apartment that he was interested in buying.

It's difficult to say just how deep-rooted these beliefs remain in the present-day mini-Manhattan of Hong Kong, but it's estimated that there are still around 100 geomancers at large and still a fair proportion of the population that will not sign a business contract, take a trip, buy or build a home, select a grave site, bury their dead, or choose a wedding date without consulting the vital signs first.

THE BAMBOO RULE

But whatever its present-day strength, *fengshui* is an interesting cultural phenomenon for the role that it has symbolically played in the division of power in Hong Kong. Just as the British administration often found it prudent and expedient to back down and pay lip service to its beliefs, so it has had to give ground on more major cultural and political issues over the years to accommodate its vastly overwhelming 98 percent Cantonese population and to keep the essential profit-making machinery of Hong Kong running smoothly.

In fact, for an undemocratic colonial government, ruling largely through the personal power of its governor and a non-elected Executive Council (with a partially elected Legislative Council responsible for passing policy into law), the British were reasonably even-handed and non-interventionist in their dealings with the Cantonese, preferring to guide rather than govern and to bend like bamboo rather than stiffen like oak in the face of Chinese pressure. Their most obvious stamp on the society was the civil law and order that allowed the territory to develop to its present extent. They also took a hard and uncompromising line against spitting in the streets and other public places, much to the relief of visitors and young Chinese alike. They discouraged littering, at least in the most popular urban tourist districts. Quite

naturally, considering their obsession with "man's best friend," they strictly banned the eating of dogs — or at least drove it underground. They even managed to encourage the Cantonese to form British-style queues for buses, ferries and other public services and facilities — an accomplishment that can only really be appreciated when you experience the mob frenzy and struggle for any essential service throughout China itself.

But for the most part the British allowed, and even encouraged, the Hong Kong Cantonese to be themselves, to freely observe

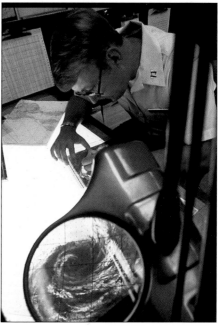

their own traditions, rituals, beliefs and lifestyles. And it is this cultural freedom that has given Hong Kong its unique color and excitement on the one hand — and, on the other, preserved much of the most fascinating aspects of Chinese culture that were dealt a destructive body-blow in the Red Guard rampage of China's Cultural Revolution. The result has been a society that appears to be constructed almost entirely of steel, concrete and glass at first glance, but underneath is a constant and whirling pageant of Chinese social and spiritual life.

OPPOSITE: Sampans hustle between moored fishing trawlers and junks in picturesque Aberdeen.
ABOVE: A meteorologist interprets radar and satellite pictures of weather disturbances to give advance warning of typhoons.

WORLD OF THE LIVING DEAD

Alongside the fear of spirits and worship of gods, there lies the most vital of all the spiritual impulses and disciplines of the Chinese — ancestor worship. Its importance in Chinese culture cannot be overstated — it is the bond, or thread of continuity, that ties their remarkable 5,000-year-old civilization together and has enabled them to keep it virtually intact, and its main traditions, customs, beliefs and rites unchanged, to the present day. It is also the discipline that has maintained the ancient social codes of Confucius, keeping them firmly established as both the base and most powerful creed of the Three Teachings, setting the rules by which the society is structured and leaving individual matters like faith, hope and fortune to the two religions.

The essence of Confucianism, like many other basic Chinese traditions and beliefs, is the pursuit of social harmony. Its abiding principle is this: if people know their allotted place within a society, and are taught to accept it, they'll achieve a measure of contentment; and contentment means peace. The broad picture of Confucianism is a vast pyramid — peasant or laboring masses at the base and the emperor or ruling elite at the topmost tip — with each teeming class or level in between submitting and kowtowing to the one above.

And there are levels within levels. Not only are wealth, birth and social role and status honored, but age is respected and even revered, filial piety elevates parents close to godliness and, most fascinating of all, ancestors are not only diligently recorded, honored and worshipped — they are placed in the realm of the living dead, an underworld which is the mirror-image of the living society and in which their comforts and needs must be taken care of as if they were themselves alive.

This reverence for the dead adds its own color and somewhat bizarre ritual to the spiritual pageantry of Hong Kong. At any time in the city streets, people may be seen setting fire to paper replicas of jewelry, furniture, washing machines and, in the years to come, probably micro-computers too — the flames consigning these comforts and luxuries to needy ancestral spirits in the underworld.

ABOVE: The imposing Government House in Upper Albert Road, built in 1855. OPPOSITE: Hakka women dressed in their traditional headdress are still a frequent sight throughout the New Territories countryside.

Hong Kong
Island

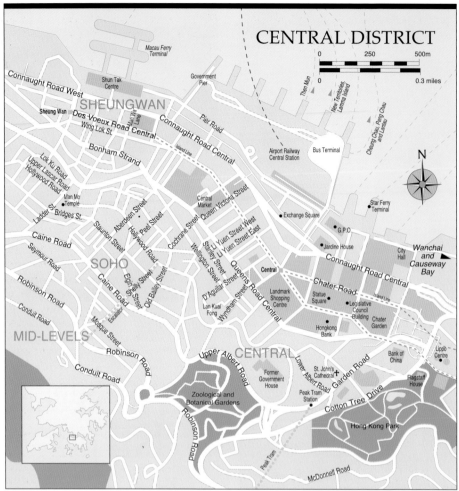

CENTRAL DISTRICT

0   250   500m

0   0.3 miles

Macau Ferry Terminal

Shun Tak Centre

Government Pier

SHEUNGWAN

Sheung Wan   Des Voeux Road Central

Connaught Road West

Wing Lok St.   Pier Road

Lan Wa Lane

Connaught Road Central

Bonham Strand

Island Line

Airport Railway Central Station   Bus Terminal

Then Mun

New Territories, Lamma Island

Cheung Chau, Peng Chau and Lantau

N

Lok Ku Road

Upper Lascar Road

Hollywood Road

Man Mo Temple

Central Market   Queen Victoria Street

Star Ferry Terminal

Ladder St.   Bridges St.

Staunton Street

Aberdeen Street

Hollywood Road

Peel Street

Cochrane Street

Li Yuen Street West   Li Yuen Street East

Exchange Square

G.P.O.

Caine Road

Seymour Road

SOHO

Caine Road

Elgin St.

Old Bailey Street

Graham Street

Wellington Street

Stanley Street

D'Aguilar Street

Wyndham Street

Queens Road Central

Central

Chater Road

Jardine House

City Hall

Wanchai and Causeway Bay

Connaught Road Central

Robinson Road

Conduit Road

Mosque Street

Escalator

Landmark Shopping Centre

Lan Kuai Fong

Statue Square

Legislative Council Building

Island Line

Chater Garden

Hongkong Bank

MID-LEVELS

Robinson Road

Conduit Road

Upper Albert Road

CENTRAL

Lower Albert Road

Garden Road

Bank of China

Lippo Centre

Former Government House

St. John's Cathedral

Peak Tram Station

Flagstaff House

Zoological and Botanical Gardens

Cotton Tree Drive

Robinson Road

Hong Kong Park

Peak Tram

McDonnell Road

WHEN PEOPLE SAY HONG KONG, they are usually referring to the Hong Kong Special Administrative Region, or SAR, which includes Kowloon, the New Territories and the outlying islands. But to be specific, Hong Kong is the island of the same name. It's a tiny place of just 77 sq km (30 sq miles), but for those who live there it is the center of the world, and many of them rarely leave — at least not to the benighted regions over the other side of the harbor in Kowloon.

Hong Kong may not exactly be rich in sights, but it is like nowhere else on earth to wander around and ogle at. Central is the obvious first destination, and if you are not staying there already it is likely to be the first stop as a matter of course if you take the Star ferry from Tsimshatsui. Central

is the jumping off point for what is probably Hong Kong's most famed tourist attraction: the funicular ride to Victoria Peak, with its ultra-exclusive residential properties and stunning views of the harbor. Wanchai has long shed itself of its shady Suzie Wong connotations and is mostly another commercial hub, but it still has more than its fair share of nightlife and dining. Causeway Bay is more shopping and office space, but with a younger, more Japanese character than establishment Central. Stanley draws in visitors for its Stanley Market, but is otherwise another exclusive residential area. Shek O, on the southeast of the island, is one of Hong Kong's few getaways, with a beach and some picturesque village homes (along with prestigious mansion-style homes for the rich).

While it's possible to race around and see the main sights of Hong Kong Island in a day, it's far better to give yourself several days or more. It might be a small place, but it's amazingly compact.

CENTRAL DISTRICT AND THE PEAK

All roads in Hong Kong lead to Central District, the financial and bureaucratic hub of the territory. All the important action takes place there, where the major boardrooms of the business world cluster around this humming powerhouse of key banks, the combined stock exchanges, the huge office blocks and the most established of the big business hotels.

Central District begins on the waterfront, at the foot of its high-rise office skyline, at the **Star Ferry Terminal**, from where the packed harbor ferries have labored faithfully for more than 100 years to and from the "other side." Since the Cross-Harbor Tunnel and MTR went into operation, the harbor ferries have become more of a sedate and scenic short harbor cruise than a vital transportation link, but they're still packed at peak hours (though it's unlikely you will be wanting for a seat), and they give visitors and residents alike a chance to relax and catch their breath in the constant urban clamor. A first-class trip costs only HK$2.20, the cheapest scenic cruise in the world.

Alongside the ferry terminal stands the General Post Office, a huge edifice that is nonetheless dwarfed by the towering **Jardine House**, Hong Kong's pioneer skyscraper which, when it was first built, sank slightly on its reclaimed harbor foundations, with startling results — the minute shift made thousands of small tiles decorating the building's façade pop off and endanger pedestrians below. Protective nets had to be strung around the tower to avoid people being brained. It has since been safely re-clad.

Adjacent to Jardine House, **Exchange Square** is home of the nerve center of Hong Kong's business world, where the Hong Kong Stock Exchange soars up in a spectacular cliff-face of curved glass — and here you can start your tour of Central District, which is compact enough to be explored on foot.

The covered pedestrian overpass alongside Exchange Square will take you in two directions — one going straight ahead across the roaring stream of traffic on Connaught Road into **World-Wide Plaza** and **Swire House** and into the temperature-controlled shopping atrium of **The Landmark**, and the other west along the harborfront side of Connaught Road passing Hong Kong Central MTR station (linking Hong Kong Island to Chek Lap Kok Airport), and ending at the twin silver towers of the **Shun Tak Center**, home of the **Macau Ferry Terminal**, and the beginning of Western District.

Before the Macau Ferry Terminal, another walkway crosses Connaught Road into the **Hang Seng Bank Building** and continues over Des Voeux Road to the top floor of Central Market. At the end of that walkway you'll find the **Mid-Levels Escalator**, the world's longest covered outdoor escalator (800-m/875-yd) running above street level up Cochrane Street, across Hollywood Road, up Shelley Street to Robinson Road in the Mid-Levels, then making its final ascent to Conduit Road. The escalator is only one-way, though, going down in the mornings from 6 AM until 10 AM, and then up until 11:30 PM. Travel time is around 20 minutes.

CHINATOWN

Veteran residents of Hong Kong still chuckle now and then over an American visitor who once hit town for the first time and immediately asked: "Where's the Chinatown?" But there is, in fact, a "Chinese" neighborhood: Western District, beyond the Shun Tak Center, known as that not for its particularly traditional Chinese character but because few foreigners have moved into it over the years.

Hong Kong's earliest land surveys and maps named it "Chinatown" because it was where the first wave of immigrant Cantonese, flooding across from the mainland, set up their mat shed homes and shops. Although the burgeoning office development in Central is now pushing into it, with more and more companies attracted by the lower rents, it is still a district in which much of the old Chinese character has survived.

Its stores are strictly Chinese, many of them selling Chinese provisions, rice, tea, herbal medicines, clothing and textiles and practical arts and crafts that are definitely not on sale just for tourist mantelpieces. And they've retained a great deal of their traditional style and decor — old swishing ceiling fans and inner gloom while the modernized boutiques of Central glitter with decorative chrome and plate glass.

Of all the retail and residential districts of Hong Kong Island it is the most inscrutable, and well worth exploring. The open, heaped wooden barrels of Western's rice stores and strange and odorous dried animal organs and vegetation of its herbal medicine shops squat below packed tenements from which pet finches twitter and sing from rattan cages hung outside the windows. In the provisions stores, amid a planned chaos of dried foodstuffs and mounds of fresh fruit, you can still see fresh eggs being checked against naked light bulbs to ensure they're not fertilized, and "thousand-year eggs" being unearthed from their chemical burial mounds where they've been cured in alkaline ash for not a thousand years but maybe a few hundred days, turning their whites brown and yolks green, and their taste slightly metallic and very tart.

The residents of Western District reflect the character of the area itself — conservative, traditional in pursuit and taste, clinging with great dignity to that which the heady and progressive pace of change in Hong Kong has allowed them to salvage from their 5,000-year-old culture. But it won't remain that way forever. Already, the district's skyline is sprouting commercial offices, and along its harborfront one of the newest major reclamation schemes is about to mushroom with new development, matching the growth of the remarkable **Macau Ferry Terminal**, with its shopping mall and huge jetfoil pens — looking for all the world like a space-age German U-boat depot. Opposite here, on the corner of Connaught Road and Morrison Street you'll find **Western Market**, a reconstructed 1858 Edwardian building, selling mainly souvenirs and fabrics, along with a Chinese restaurant on the top floor. Nearby

in **Man Wa Lane** there are rows of stalls selling traditional soapstone chops, or seals. If you want them to, the artisans will translate your name into Chinese characters and engrave it on the seal — an interesting, inexpensive souvenir. From there wind your way through the streets and alleys of shops selling anything from batteries, electrical products and cheap clothing to funeral offerings, snakes, herbal medicines and teas and one-man printer stalls — where a business card or the like can be set up quickly in movable type and printed on a hand-operated platen press — until you reach "Cat Street" flea-market and antique shops and Man Mo Temple at the end of Hollywood Road.

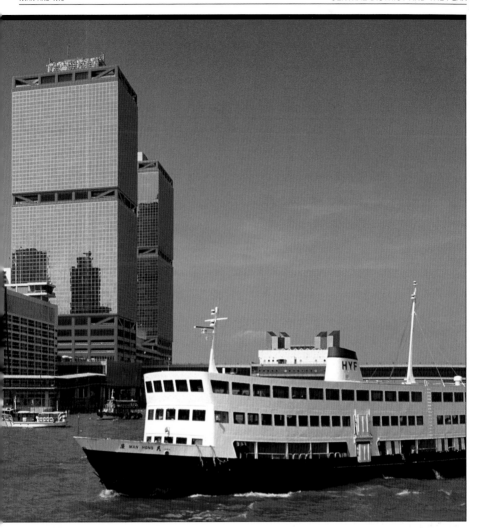

MAN AND MO

The 1840s **Man Mo Temple**, with its ornate green tiled roof, bell tower, smoke tower and main hall of prayer, is dedicated to the God of Civil Servants, Man Cheong, and a famous second-century warrior, Kwan Kung, or Mo, since deified as the God of War, and guardian deity of pawnshops and curio dealers for good measure.

In typical Chinese fashion, the temple celebrates war, peace and commerce, and is a sacred place for Buddhists and Daoists alike — a prime example of the cultural exchange, or mutual "borrowing" of each other's gods, that made it possible for both religions to exist in harmony rather than confront each other in China. Being on the edge of Western District, Man Mo is a "working" place of worship, not a tourist attraction, and this has to be kept in mind when you're visiting.

In the main hall, huge incense coils hang from the ceiling; each one donated by a worshiper and, as they smolder and smoke for anything up to two weeks, symbolically broadcast prayers and pleas to the gods. As for the deities themselves, garish, richly costumed and blackened images of Man and Mo sit together on the main altar, and in front of them their tools of trade — a pen for Man, the scholarly deity, and an executioner's

A cross-harbor ferry passes the high-tech façades of the Victoria Hotel and Shun Tak Centre.

sword for Kwan Kung, symbolic of his own execution in the fierce intrigues of his time. "Years ago, the sword of every public executioner used to be kept in the local Kwan Kung temple," says Joyce Savidge in *Temples* (Hong Kong Government Publications), one of the most informative and brightly illustrated guides to the territory's temple trail. "After an execution the presiding magistrate would always call at the temple to worship — and to make sure that the ghost of the criminal didn't follow him home."

From Man Mo Temple, you can pop into one of Hong Kong's newest museums: the **Museum of Medical Sciences** (2549-5123 (9 AM to 5:30 PM, closed Mondays). This is one of the first museums in the world to compare traditional Chinese and Western approaches to medicine. It's housed in the former Old Pathological Institute, an historic red brick building at 2 Caine Lane, Mid-Levels, just up Ladder Street from Man Mo Temple. Alternatively, continue up **Hollywood Road** or more antiques and curios. Here you can either break your journey and go back down to the shops in Queen's Road Central or hop on the escalator for a Mid-Levels tour.

If you decide on the latter, as you go up the stretch from Caine Road to Mosque Street you'll see on your left the old **Jamia Mosque** with its striking green-and-white minaret. Reaching Robinson Road, a short walk west takes you to **Ohel Leah Synagogue**, now integrated into a massive high-rise residential development. Built in 1902, it's the only surviving synagogue in Hong Kong, and China. Services are held daily; for more information call (2801-5442. Back on the escalator, take the last stretch to Conduit Road.

At this point you have two choices — walk directly back down the steps running alongside the escalator to Central, or walk east to the start of Conduit Road to a path that will take you straight into the **Zoological and Botanical Gardens** (6 AM to 7 PM daily), with its elegant pink flamingos, Mandarin ducks, peacocks and other exotic birds, along with orangutans, gibbons and other animals. In the early mornings the gardens are a popular meeting place for people practicing tai chi, the ancient, disciplined ballet-

like series of martial and breathing exercises that tone up the mental and physical constitution. From the gardens you'll get a good view of the former Government House directly below. Once the official residence of the British Governor, the building was erected in 1855 and features an interesting tile-roofed tower added for observation by the Japanese occupation forces when they seized Hong Kong in World War II.

Exiting out of the gardens, walk down Garden Road to **St. John's Cathedral**, a beautiful old church built in the late 1840s and constructed in the shape of a cross from bricks brought from Canton (Guangzhou/China). It combines early English, Gothic and Norman architecture. Services are held daily. For information call ((8852) 2523-4157. Through the church grounds, Battery Path leads you back down to Queen's Road Central where you're within easy striking distance of shops, hotels, Lan Kwai Fong, the trams and the MTR, and Statue Square. Around this roughly ornamental pedestrian mall stand the two most striking contrasts of tradition and twenty-first century Hong Kong — the Hongkong Bank and the Legislative Council Building.

<hr>

STATUE SQUARE AND AROUND

On one side of Statue Square, the arched colonial stone architecture of the **Legislative Council Building** (formerly the Supreme Court), often referred to as the Legco Building, recalls the days of drum tattoos and musketry, cabin trunks and tuxedos, the reign of the great ocean liners and flying boats, gin slings and fox-trots and all the other trappings and trimmings of Empire. And right across the street, parked like a visitor from outer space between the headquarters of Standard Chartered Bank and the old Bank of China, stands the futuristic **Hongkong Bank Building** (more popularly known as the Hongkong and Shanghai Banking Corporation, its traditional name).

There's nothing quite like this astonishing edifice of high-tech industrial architecture anywhere in Asia, and probably anywhere else in the world, and nothing else has aroused the sort of passions that still reverberate through the Hong Kong business

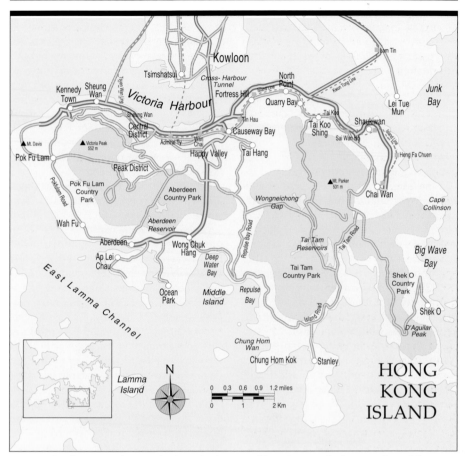

community. Some people consider it aestheti-
cally imprudent and even downright ugly,
and certainly not the sort of image that a
banking institution as traditional as the
Hongkong and Shanghai should project.
Such opinions, mired in a bygone era, should
be left to stew in their own juices. For anyone who finds the idea of ambitious breaks
with tradition uplifting — which, after all,
is the intention — the courageous design
is every bit as brilliant as that other most
controversial post-war architectural project,
the Sydney Opera House in Australia. Designed by Sir Norman Foster and built in
1985, the Hongkong Bank Building is as
striking today as it was more than 15 years
ago when it first flung open its doors. Highlights include the soaring lifts in the massive glass atrium, not to mention the fact
that you can actually walk underneath the
building (it is mounted on props) and gaze
up into it.

Next door, at the intersection of Queensway and Garden Road, is China's riposte
to the Hongkong Bank headquarters — the
Bank of China Tower, a gigantic 70-story,
315-m-high (1,033-ft) landmark with a soaring cubist-style design. Designed by local
architect I.M. Pei, it replaced the nearby Bank
of China building, a post-World War II structure that in its day was Central's most imposing. When the Hongkong Bank went for
bust with its sci-fi skyscraper, the Bank of
China took up the gauntlet and outdid them
with this tower, several meters (20 ft) taller
than the Hongkong Bank headquarters. It
was completed in 1990.

There is more soaring modern architecture in nearby Admiralty. The colonnaded
façade of the **Lippo Center** and the sheer
gargantuan size of **Pacific Place** both remind
that Hong Kong is still a thriving international financial hub, despite 1997's change
of ownership. Pacific Place is the more

interesting of the two to explore. While little more than an upmarket mall, it is a particularly impressive example of one, and its downstairs food hall is an excellent place to grab lunch.

TEA AND BRONZWARE

In Hong Kong Park on Cotton Tree Drive you'll find **Flagstaff House**, a renovated 1940s colonial building with a distinct Greek neoclassic style to it. Formerly home of the Commander of the British Forces, the building now houses the **Flagstaff House Museum of Teaware** (2869-0690 (10 AM to 5 PM, closed Wednesdays), featuring exhibitions of Chinese tea, porcelain and pots and much of the tea-making equipage from the latter centuries of this 5,000-year-old culture.

For more Chinese relics, the Hong Kong **University Museum & Art Gallery** (2975-5600 (9:30 AM to 6 PM, 1:30 to 5:30 PM Sundays, closed public holidays) on Bonham Road, has an interesting exhibition of Yuan dynasty bronzeware, artifacts from the Warring States period and Indian Buddhist sculptures. To get there take bus No. 3 from Edinburgh Place, or No. 23 from Causeway Bay.

TO THE PEAK

A short stroll up Garden Road to Lower Albert Road — just past St. John's Cathedral — will take you to St. **John's Building**. At its base is the lower terminal of the "funicular railway," or the cable-operated **Peak Tram** (a free, topless double-decker bus also runs to the tram from the Central Star Ferry terminal). Climbing smoothly up a sheer series of hillsides, so steep in some places that it would be necessary to stand at a 45-degree angle to move from your seat, it ferries passengers 397 m (1,300 ft) up the 552-m (1,811-ft) **Victoria Peak** which dominates Hong Kong Island — and to one of the most breathtaking views anywhere in the world (see BRACE YOURSELF FOR THE PEAK, page 11 in TOP SPOTS).

In days gone by, the Peak was strictly for the colonial officials — and those who accrued the riches that came to Hong Kong — who lived on the hill. A measure of one's business or bureaucratic success was how close you could reside to the top — a physical manifestation of class status. The Peak is still Hong Kong's paramount status symbol, but it is nowadays open season for anyone who cares to make their way up there. Sprawling mansions nestle in the folds of the upper slopes and right along its highest ridges. Before you are too quick to envy them, think of the unpleasant spring and early summer weather, when humidity often blankets the Peak in an impenetrable cloud.

In 1995, the old Peak Tower was torn down — replaced the following year by a somewhat controversial, HK$400-million seven-story complex in the shape of an upturned bowl, designed by British architect, Terry Farrell. This new **Peak Tower** contains not only the tram terminus but also a major entertainment center, including restaurants and shops, a Dragon Train computer-operated ride through Hong Kong's history, a motion-simulated Peak Explorer ride and a branch of the popular Ripley's Believe It or Not! Museum (see FAMILY FUN, page 47 in YOUR CHOICE for more details).

Adjacent is the ultramodern **Peak Galleria**, housing the chic **Café Deco Bar & Grill**, upmarket shops, an indoor fountain and an underground car park. Miraculously, the **Peak Café**, which was originally built as a sedan chair shelter in 1901, still stands, but only because there was such a public protest against the developers' plans to replace it.

From the terminus a pathway (Lugard and Harlech Roads) circles the peak like a collar, and a one-hour stroll provides panoramic views of the entire harbor and its twin urban beehives, along with the islands of Lantau, Cheung Chau and Lamma. Another path (Mount Austin Road) leads right up to the summit for an even more dramatic 360-degree view: on a clear day the islands in the south and the mountains in the New Territories can be glimpsed.

WANCHAI AND CAUSEWAY BAY

The crowded, high-rise tourist corridor of Wanchai and Causeway Bay begins on the

The Peak Tram affords a panoramic view of Hong Kong Island and Kowloon.

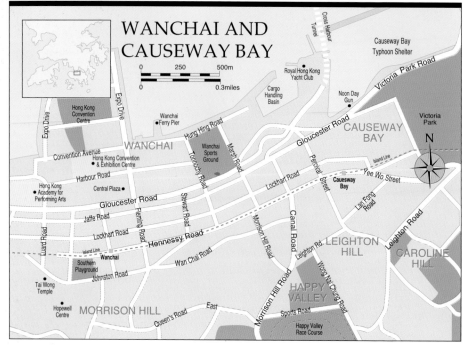

eastern side of the Admiralty and Pacific Place complexes, where the glassed edges of the business citadel soften into the glowing crimson and gold of Wanchai's neon-packed entertainment district.

As with all other urban areas of Hong Kong, getting there is easy — you can take the MTR from Central or Admiralty, and take a look at the world's biggest and most crowded connecting underground concourse at the same time, or you can take a Star Ferry from Tsimshatsui direct to Wanchai, or you can allow yourself another of Hong Kong's traditional and slightly more sedate experiences and travel there by tram from Central. For a flat fee of HK$1.20 these grinding, rumbling double-decker antiques shuttle back and forth all day and late into the night right along the northern corridor of Hong Kong Island, linking its western and eastern extremities from Kennedy Town in the west, through Central, Wanchai, Causeway Bay and Taikoo Shing and Shau Kei Wan in the east. While they labor and clang their way through the dense urban traffic above ground, the MTR streaks along virtually the same route below. Not so long ago the century-old system was earmarked for the

chop, but they're such faithful work horses, still carrying many thousands of passengers a day, and such an abiding symbol of Hong Kong, that the planners backed down in the face of the fierce public protest that was bound to follow.

On the Wanchai waterfront, at the beginning of Harbor Road, is the **Hong Kong Academy for Performing Arts** and the **Hong Kong Arts Center**. Most cultural events are held in the evenings, but during the day, **Pao Galleries** (10 AM to 8 PM daily) on the fourth and fifth floors of the Arts Center has regular art exhibitions. Opposite, an entire block houses the integrated **Hong Kong Convention and Exhibition Center**, the **Grand Hyatt Hotel** and the **New World Hotel**. The Hong Kong Convention and Exhibition Center's dramatic extension out into the harbor is one of the most eye-catching features of Hong Kong's harborfront and skyline, with a distinctive sculptural curved roof inspired by the image of a seabird soaring into the sky. Finished just in time to host the Change of Sovereignty Ceremony on June 30, 1997, the

The Hong Kong Academy for Performing Arts and the Hong Kong Arts Center in Wanchai with Central Plaza in the background.

155,000-sq-m (1.67-million-sq-ft) extension is purpose-built for meetings, conventions and special events and has a Grand Foyer whose 30-m-high (98-ft) glass wall drop gives spectacular 180-degree views of the harbor.

Across the street from there you can't miss the massive 78-story **Central Plaza**, Hong Kong's tallest building, which also claims for itself the dubious distinction of being the "tallest poured concrete structure in the world." There is a free viewing podium on the 46th floor.

is the 66-story **Hopewell Center** with its breathtaking scenic elevator ride and eye-in-the sky revolving restaurant.

On the way to Causeway Bay, consider taking a tram around Happy Valley to view the district's prime attraction, the **Happy Valley Racecourse** which, like its bigger and more modern sister track over in Shatin, swells with massive crowds on race days.

The main reason to go to Causeway Bay is, of course, to shop, whether day or night, in the boutiques and giant Japanese department stores. Indeed, it's easy to forget that

From here several overpasses cross to Gloucester Road and into Wanchai — to its nightclubs, bars, Chinese stores and restaurants, open markets and crowded alfresco food stalls and shops. At the beginning of Queen's Road East, just past Pacific Place, are rows of shops specializing in rosewood and mahogany furniture, along with carved camphor chests. Farther along, and of historical interest, the **Hung Shing (Tai Wong) Temple** has been around for some 130 years, and is a popular spot to have fortunes told. The quaint **Wanchai Post Office** was built in 1912, and now serves as an Environmental Resources Center (2893-2856 (10 AM to 5 PM, closed Wednesdays). Towering behind these two small images of Hong Kong's past life

Causeway Bay has any other attractions, but there are several worth seeing. One of the best of them happens on the waterfront in a small garden opposite the Excelsior Hotel and World Trade Center, where it's possible to watch the firing of the famous **Noon Day Gun**, whose origin to this day is still disputed, but is widely believed to have originated in the 1840s under the auspices of Jardine & Matheson. Nearby, the **Causeway Bay Typhoon Shelter** houses junks and sampans alongside the luxury craft of the Hong Kong Yacht Club. It is a pale shadow of its former self, with not many sampans or junks left these days, but still worth a look.

To the east of the Excelsior Hotel, the recently revamped **Victoria Park** is host to legions of early morning tai chi devotees and, in the late afternoons and evenings, to older residents taking their prized caged birds for walks. During the Chinese New Year and Mid-Autumn festivals the park is packed with celebrating crowds. It has a jogging track, swimming pools and tennis courts. To the east of the park, at the beginning of Tin Hau Temple Road, the seventeenth-century **Tin Hau Temple** is, like other similarly named temples around Hong Kong, dedicated to the Goddess of the Sea and well worth a visit, as is the restored octagonal **Lin Fa Temple** on Lin Fa Street.

From here, go up to Tai Hang Road to where you'll see a large white pagoda standing in the shadow of monolithic housing estates. This is the **Aw Boon Haw Gardens** (also known as Tiger Balm Gardens) (open 9:30 AM to 4 PM, daily), founded in 1935 with the profits from that famous balm that cures everything from a headache to a rattlesnake bite. The "garden" is grotesque but fascinating, full of grottoes, pagodas and colorful statues of mythical Chinese figures and animals. One particular tableau depicts Judgment and Hell, where saints and miscreants alike are judged on their earthly behavior. For the unlucky ones, the punishments are awful — tongues torn out, bodies sawn in half and a host of other gruesome consequences.

Heading east from Causeway Bay, the MTR or trams continue to **Taikoo Shing**, a housing development in Quarry Bay, where the four Cityplaza towers offer bargain and upmarket shopping in air-conditioned comfort and convenience, and even an ice-skating rink.

Farther down the line is **Shau Kei Wan**, once a pirate lair, now the home of one of Hong Kong's biggest fishing fleets. Here, at the end of Shau Kei Wan Main Street by the waterfront, is a cluster of temples and monasteries. Notable among them is **Tam Kung Temple**, whose deity is a locally inspired God of Weather and Good Health, and which plays an extravagantly colorful central role in the annual Tam Kung, Tin Hau and Buddha's Birthday festivals. What distinguishes Tam Kung from other gods is his age — he's said to have been only 12 years old when people began worshipping him.

Also worth visiting in Shau Kei Wan is the **Hong Kong Museum of Coastal Defense** (2569-1500, 175 Tung Hei Road (10 AM to 5 PM, closed Thursdays). Housed in a former fort, the museum documents the history of defense along southern China's coast from the Ming period onwards; it also has a walk where restored armaments are on display.

Continuing on the MTR, two stops past Shau Kei Wan, is Chai Wan, the end of the line and home to the **Law Uk Folk Museum** (2896-7006, 14 Kut Shing Street (10 AM to 1 PM, 2 PM to 6 PM, 1 PM to 6 PM Sundays, closed Mondays). A Hakka home with more than 200 years of history, it has been preserved and also features an interesting history of Hakka settlement in Hong Kong and the migration route through southern China taken by the family who once lived here. Take the B exit of Chai Wan station and look for the signposting to the museum.

THE ISLAND TRAIL

From Central District, the main tourist route leads over or through the island's central mountain spine to Aberdeen, Repulse Bay and Stanley. They're easy to get to: if you're not on an organized hotel tour you can take the No. 6 bus from the Central Terminal at Exchange Square to Repulse Bay and Stanley, crossing the mountain through Wongneichong Gap and passing the garden swathe of the Hong Kong Cricket Club along the way. Or you can take a more scenic route on the air-conditioned express bus, also from Exchange Square, via the Aberdeen Tunnel and Deep Water Bay. For Aberdeen itself, take No. 7 or No. 70.

Aberdeen is still the most fascinating fishing and boat-people haven in Hong Kong, with thousands of fisherfolk still living on a small clutter of surviving junks and their successors, new-style bullet-nosed trawlers. Along the waterfront you'll be approached by very aggressive old women wanting to give you a personal sampan tour through the junks and to the floating restaurants for

Scenic gondolas glide past an ornamental pagoda at Ocean Park. OVERLEAF: Until quite recently, Stanley was a picturesque fishing village. Today, much of Stanley Bay has been reclaimed, and luxury high-rises have replaced the tin-roofed fishermen's and squatters' shanties.

an outrageous fee. If you say no to their HK$300 offer and walk away they'll quickly chase after you, haggling all the way until they reluctantly agree to around HK$50 per person (for about half an hour's ride).

The town itself has been modernized, with new boutiques and shopping centers replacing much of the old Chinese retail and ship's chandler's sections, but there are still a few places of historical interest such as the 1851 **Tin Hau Temple** on Aberdeen Reservoir Road and the **Hung Hsing Shrine** on the corner of Aberdeen Old Main Street and Aberdeen Main Road.

The island of **Ap Lei Chau**, once a quiet fishing community reached by sampan, is now connected to the mainland by a long soaring bridge and has been developed into another enormous housing estate. But here and there you'll still find fishing families tending their nets, baskets of fresh fish being hauled and slopped ashore and, all the way along the waterfront, boats being built and repaired.

Just south of Aberdeen stands the big boy of Hong Kong's recreational circuit, **Ocean Park and Middle Kingdom** (2873-8888 (10 AM to 6 PM daily). A vast playground and marine entertainment complex built into a sharply rising coastal headland, Ocean Park was financed with funds from the Hong Kong Jockey Club's vast gambling profits and, like Hong Kong itself, it is in a constant state of growth.

An outdoor escalator and cable-car system links its lowland and headland amenities. Several roller-coasters are set dramatically on the edge of the headland, and other attractions include rides, a Film Fantasia-Simulator containing 100 hydraulic seats, an Atoll Reef (the largest in the world), a Wave Cove with simulated waves and a population of seals and other ocean life. Dolphin and killer whale shows can be seen at the Ocean Theater, while an aviary, a Dinosaur Discovery Trail and a children's adventure playground are other options. Adjacent to Ocean Park, and strictly speaking part of the same complex, is Water World. It has its own entrance, and features giant water slides, a wave pool and swimming pools. It's open in summer from June through September.

Middle Kingdom is a slightly tacky trawl through the proverbial 5,000 years of Chinese history, but the arts and crafts demonstrations, theater and Cantonese opera, are worth seeing.

The complex is easily reached from Central by a special Citybus from Admiralty MTR station or, excluding Sunday and Public Holidays, a No. 6 minibus from Star Ferry.

From Ocean Park, the road winds through Deep Water Bay, one of Hong Kong's most attractive small beaches, and along with the Peak one of Hong Kong's most exclusive residential districts. The prestigious nine-hole **Hong Kong Golf Club** can also be found in Deep Water Bay.

A little farther to the east is **Repulse Bay**, another expensive residential district, but with a charming beach area. For the best views of the bay, the restaurant and sweeping lawns of **The Verandah**, the elegant surviving relic of the old Repulse Bay Hotel, is a *de rigueur* stop. Expensive, even by Hong Kong standards, The Verandah is nevertheless the perfect spot for afternoon tea or a candlelit supper — it's also a popular place for young newly weds to have their photos taken on their wedding day.

Meanwhile, the beach in high summer is packed with bathers, especially on weekends. The eastern end features two huge statues, of **Kwun Yum** and **Tin Hau**, a children's playground, fast-food outlets, barbecue facilities and a flea market selling souvenirs and sportswear among other things. Past the Seaview Chinese Restaurant, at the other end of the beach, a seafront walk goes to Deep Water Bay.

Until quite recently, Stanley, the next stop to the east on the "island trail," was a picturesque fishing village. Today, much of Stanley Bay has been reclaimed, and luxury high-rises are replacing the tin-roofed fishermen's and squatters' shanties. It's still worth a visit for its lively market — touristy but fun. For a reminder of what Stanley used to be visit the **Tin Hau Temple**, at the far end of the market, and the old colonial-style Police Station, now a historical monument. Also of interest is the military cemetery opposite St. Stephen's Beach.

Looking out across the marine club and its famous floating restaurants at Aberdeen.

THE HARBOR

The harbor, brimming with hundreds of ships of all sizes and shapes churning the water in every direction, Hong Kong's famous skyline overlooking the scene, is justifiably a trademark Hong Kong postcard view. It's likely to be your most vivid memory of the city.

The simplest way to enjoy the harbor is to take a seven-minute ride on the famous **Star Ferry** between Hong Kong Island and Tsimshatsui on the Kowloon Peninsula. There is also a Star Ferry one-hour cruise around the harbor, operated by **MP Tours** (2118-6235. Similar scheduled harbor cruises on gaily decorated Chinese junks, some taking in dinner cruises around Hong Kong Island, are operated by **Hong Kong Watertours** (2367-1970. Details of these cruises are available at HKTA, most hotel tour desks or from Watertours' boarding piers next to the Star Ferry on both sides of the harbor. See TAKING A TOUR, page 89 in YOUR CHOICE, for more information about these daytime and dinner cruises.

The **Hong Kong Ferry Company** (2542-3081 also operates a wide range of services, and the ones to the outlying islands in particular provide an inexpensive alternative to the organized harbor cruises.

WHERE TO STAY

While Kowloon is not without excellent hotels, including some of Hong Kong's best and the lion's share of budget accommodation, luxury and upper mid-range travelers will find a wide selection of hotels on Hong Kong Island. Staying on the island makes sightseeing a breeze, and also offers the advantage of having the best of Hong Kong's restaurants and nightlife on the doorstep.

LUXURY

Whether it is indeed the best of Hong Kong's hotels is subject to heated debate, but along with the Peninsula in Tsimshatsui the **Mandarin Oriental Hotel** (2522-0111 FAX 2810-6190 E-MAIL reserve-mohkg@mohg.com, 5 Connaught Road Central, is certainly among

the most famous. While the lobby and rooms have a classic, understated ambiance, the hotel has kept up with the times, sporting a state-of-the-art business center and high-speed access dedicated data lines in each of the 487 rooms. Most rooms have balconies, and some have splendid views of the harbor. Making it an even more compelling place to be based, the Oriental also has some of Hong Kong's best restaurants — notably Vong and Man Wah. Other winning features include a swimming pool and — rare in Asian luxury hotels — two tennis courts.

Also in the heart of Central and highly recommended is the **Ritz-Carlton Hotel** (2877-6666 FAX 2877-6778 WEB SITE WWW .ritzcarlton.com, 3 Connaught Road Central. Competition with the Oriental is fierce, and the Ritz-Carlton matches its rival in all but name. Rooms — select from views either of the harbor or of Chater Garden — come with Italianate marble bathrooms, dual-line direct telephones with fast Internet connections, and one of Hong Kong's top Italian restaurants in the northern-style Toscana.

Not far from the Oriental and the Ritz-Carlton is the **Island Shangri-la Hotel** (2877-3838 FAX 2521-8742 E-MAIL isl@shangri-la .com, Pacific Place, Supreme Court Road, Central, which towers 56 floors over the harbor. Given that the hotel has direct access to the massive Pacific Place shopping mall, it's something of a city within a building. The extra large rooms come with a computer "data port" and a full size executive desk, should you need to do any work in Hong Kong. Petrus, the hotel's French restaurant, is one of Hong Kong's best.

The **Grand Hyatt Hong Kong** (2588-1234 FAX 2802-0704 E-MAIL info@grandhyatt.com.hk, 1 Harbor Road, Wanchai, is especially popular with the celebrity set, and it is easy to see why. Tastefully appointed throughout, rooms come with an Internet television, framed photographic prints, down duvets lined with Egyptian cotton, and a host of other thoughtful touches. The hotel restaurants are just as famous, in particular One Harbor Road and Grissini, while JJ's has been one of the most popular nightspots in town for years now.

A junk passes Exchange Square, providing a contrast to Central District's stark architectural wonders.

MID-RANGE

Even the budget hotels are expensive on Hong Kong Island. But there are some moderately priced places to stay—just don't expect the value for money that prevails at most other Asian destinations.

The **Wesley Hotel** (2866-6688 FAX 2866-6613 E-MAIL thewesley@grandhotel.com.hk, 22 Hennessy Road, Wanchai, is surprisingly good value given its location in Wanchai and its overall high standards. Its amenities are

family suite, which comes complete with a kitchenette. A swimming pool and other recreational facilities are available at the adjacent YWCA, while the hotel has a good business center. Standard rooms start at HK$630. Advance bookings are essential as International House is often fully booked long ahead.

For functional but smart accommodation in Causeway Bay, the **New Cathay Hotel** (2577-8211 FAX 2577-8211, 17 Tung Lo Wan Road, Causeway Bay, is a good choice. Close to all the shopping action, it has a good

limited essentially to a business center, but it makes up in the well-appointed and maintained rooms. The basic economy rooms, which come in at just under US$100, are small, but larger rooms, including suites, are available at rates that range up to around US$200. All rooms come with a minibar, satellite television and direct dial telephones.

Not surprisingly, there is very little mid-range accommodation available in Central. A notable exception, however, is the **Garden View International House** (2877-3737 FAX 2845-6263 E-MAIL gar_view@ywca.org.hk, 1 Macdonnell Road, Central. Run by the YWCA, the great advantage of staying here is not only the location, but the fact that for little more than US$100 families can take a

dim sum restaurant (the Cathay Seafood Restaurant), and quiet rooms from around HK$1,100.

INEXPENSIVE

Budget accommodation on Hong Kong Island is so scarce as to be virtually non-existent. An exception is **Noble Hostel** (2576-6148, Flat A3, 17th floor, 27 Paterson Street, Causeway Bay. Rooms here (all with shared bathroom) start at around HK$300. **Ma Wui Hall** (2817-5717, on Hong Kong Island's Mount Davis, is one of Hong Kong's seven youth hostels. Compared to the rest, it is fairly central, situated high above Kennedy Town with great views of the harbor and beyond. If you've got heavy luggage, you'd be best to take a taxi: buses No. 5B or 47 from Central come fairly close but you're still faced with a stiff half-hour walk.

WHERE TO EAT

A lifetime could be spent dining out on Hong Kong Island. Central, Wanchai and Causeway Bay alone have more restaurants than the fraction of the island's full dining potential, and although they are tried and tested favorites, there is always average medium-

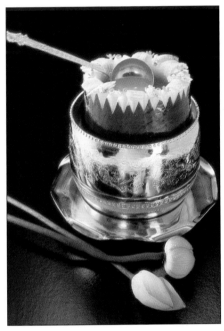

sized city in most parts of the world. The following recommendations represent but a room for some individual exploration. By all means sample the best of the hotel restaurants, but don't forget to head into the streets too.

CENTRAL DISTRICT

The crowded business and banking center of Hong Kong spins like a human treadmill during the day, but is relatively sedate come evenings. The main action is in a wedge of neon signs and strolling crowds bounded by Lan Kwai Fong and Wellington and D'Aguilar Streets. Lan Kwai Fong itself is famous for its nightlife, but is equally worth

exploring for its restaurants, which are legion and generally good. Another good restaurant district, and something of a quieter rival to Lan Kwai Fong, is the so-called SoHo ("South of Hollywood Road") area, off the Mid-Levels Escalator around Staunton and Elgin streets.

Cantonese

One of the best places to experience Cantonese cuisine is the elegant **Man Wah** (2522-0111 at the Mandarin Oriental. Sporting spectacular views of the harbor, this classy

restaurant dispels with the idea that Cantonese should be served under the glare of fluorescent lights in high-decibel environs. The house specialty is the steamed crab claws with ginger and rice wine.

Away from the hotels, the imperial courts of the Chinese cuisine in Central are the **Yung Kee Restaurant** (2522-1624, 32-40 Wellington Street, a multi-story gaudily decorated Cantonese eating place, and the famous **Luk Yu Tea House** (2523-5464, 24-26 Stanley Street,

The many faces of Cantonese culinary extravaganza — the traditional Chinese hotpot OPPOSITE is a typical family dish in the winter months, while melon soup ABOVE LEFT is a popular and light summer soup. RIGHT: An irreplacable staple throughout Asia, different grades and types of rice are displayed in graceful polished casks in this typical Hong Kong rice store.

which is such a popular *dim sum* establishment and restaurant that you virtually need to camp outside overnight to get a table. The Yung Kee is noted for its roast goose, duck and pork, but is strong on a wide selection of Cantonese and Shanghainese specialties. The Luk Yu is, as noted, famous for its *dim sum*, though its roast pigeon is also justly celebrated. The Luk Yee has preserved its art deco, 1933 interior, to great effect, giving it the atmosphere of a bustling tea-house of bygone years.

For affordable Cantonese cuisine in fashionable surroundings, **China Lan Kwai Fong** (2536-0968, 17-22 Lan Kwai Fong, is recommended. Complete with chirping birds in cages, the chief attraction is the 11:30 AM to 3 PM weekend *dim sum* brunch deal, which is a bargain at HK$250 for two. Evening meals feature Shanghai cuisine.

One of a chain that evokes the feel of a traditional *dai pai dong* street-side restaurant, **Dai Pai Dong** (2851-6389, 28 Queen's Road Central, is decorated with nostalgic posters and bric-a-brac. Light snacks, noodle dishes, omelets and sweet soups are featured on the menu, but the real attraction is the various coffees, teas and *yuan yang* (a unique blend of both) prepared and served in a manner that has all but disappeared from the Hong Kong dining scene.

The award-winning **Tai Woo Seafood Restaurant** (2524-5618, 15-19 Wellington Street, has seafood hotpots, steamed garoupa, garlic prawns, sautéed scallops, beef in taro's nest and mango pudding. Tai Woo has other branches on Hong Kong Island, Kowloon and the New Territories, and is a relatively inexpensive choice for traditional Cantonese cuisine. The **Jade Garden** (2524-5098, Basement, Jardine House, 1 Connaught Place, is another less expensive Cantonese restaurant. Specialties include double-boiled duck with parsley and pan-fried stuffed bean curd.

Well worth a visit is **Tsui Hang Village** (2524-2012, New World Tower, 16-18 Queen's Road Central. The restaurant does homage to the home village of Dr. Sun Yatsen, founder of the Republic of China, and is well known for both classic and modern Cantonese dishes such as succulent pigeon and chicken, tasty thick soups and rich fried milk fritters.

Sichuan

The **Sichuan Garden** (2521-4433, 3/F Gloucester Tower (in the Landmark shopping complex) and at Shop 4, The Mall, Pacific Place, specializes in smoked duck with camphor, ducks' tongues, bean curd with minced beef in a pungent sauce and scallops with hot garlic sauce.

Hunan

Another restaurant which will put fire in your belly with lots of chilies and garlic is **Hunan Garden** (2868-2880, 3/F The Forum, Exchange Square, where many dishes are served in the traditional way, in bamboo stems or earthen pots. Levels of hotness are clearly, mercifully, and thankfully indicated on the menu.

Chiu Chow

This cuisine comes from the coastal region around the Chaozhou (Swatow) district of northeastern Guangdong and is similar to Cantonese food, but a little heavier and spicier. It features its own variations of duck, goose and pigeon dishes, along with oysters fried in egg batter and clams in a biting chili and black bean sauce. Chiu Chow restaurants are also noted for their shark's fin and bird's nest soups — the disgorged linings of sea swallow nests, reputed to do wonders for rejuvenation — and a particularly sturdy tea called "Iron Maiden," drunk from tiny thimble-sized cups before and after the meal. One place to try this cuisine is the **Chiu Chow Garden Restaurant** (2525-8246, Basement, Jardine House, 1 Connaught Place. Another popular choice is the **Lippo Chiuchau Restaurant** (2845-4151, which in the winter months is famous for its spicy lamb hot pot, though you will need four people to try it.

Shanghainese and Beijing

The **Shanghai Garden Restaurant** (2524-8181, Hutchison House, 10 Harcourt Road, is a very popular venue for dishes such as "drunken" chicken, fried Shanghai noodles and sweet black sesame dumplings. A more modern venue for Shanghai cuisine is **Ye Shanghai** (2918-9833, Shop 332, One Pacific Place, Admiralty, which even has dancing on Saturday nights.

One of Hong Kong's longest running Beijing-style restaurants is **Peking Garden** (2526-6456, Basement, Alexandra House, 16-20 Chater Road. It has the famous Peking duck, along with beggar's chicken and less famous dishes such as its popular smoked spring rolls. It has branches at the Excelsior Hotel in Causeway Bay, Cityplaza in Taikoo Shing and in the Mall at Pacific Place.

Indian and Sri Lankan

Hong Kong's sizeable Indian community means that it has more Indian restaurants than anywhere else in the region (not including the Subcontinent of course). Most of them are authentic but few offer much in the way of luxury. An exception is **Tandoor** (2845-2299, Third Floor, On Hing Building, 1-9 On Hing Terrace. A northern-style restaurant, everything on the menu is made with freshly imported spices and meals are accompanied by live Indian music.

An establishment that has a well earned reputation for good food and friendliness over the years is **Ashoka** (2524-9623, on 57 Wyndham Street. It's inexpensive and authentic, and very popular with the ex-pat set. In the SoHo district, **India Today** (2801-5959, First Floor, 26-30 Elgin Street, Central, is a little Indian eatery that is a popular place with couples.

For Sri Lankan, the **Club Sri Lanka** (2526-6559, Basement, 17 Hollywood Road, offers very reasonably priced buffet dining.

Japanese

Japanese has taken off in a big way in Hong Kong, and it's rarely far to the nearest sushi shop. One of the most popular is **Tokio Joe** (2525-1889, 16 Lan Kwai Fong, a restaurant that promotes itself successfully as having "user friendly Japanese food." The full gamut of Japanese cuisine (at least its more well known varieties) is available.

Benkay (2521-3344, First Basement, The Landmark, is another popular upmarket Japanese restaurant that offers generic Japanese cuisine.

Thai

For such favorites as spicy *tom yum* soups and red and green curries, king prawns and Thai beer, the newly established **Heartbeat**

Thai by Supatra (2522-5073, 32-38 Ice House Street, is highly recommended. Littered with classic Thai bric-a-brac, the scent of fresh orchids in the air, it's a perfect retreat from crowds of Central. Try the green papaya *som tam* salad — it's a house specialty.

Vegetarian

A casual spot for a vegetarian lunch buffet is the **Fringe Club** (2521-7251, 2 Lower Albert Road, which serves delicious salads, fresh bread and cheeses. You'll need to get here before 1 PM to find a free table. Another

no-frills place is **Vegi-Table** (2877-0901, 1 Tun Wo Lane (next to Petticoat Lane). Its extensive menu includes both Chinese and Western fare, such as congee, Hawaiian bean curd, pumpkin and chickpeas and lots of garden-fresh vegetables, all at bargain prices (and without that bane of Cantonese cooking: MSG — monosodium glutamate).

Though not strictly speaking vegetarian — some meat dishes are also available — **Joyce Café** (2810-1335, 9 Queen's Road Central, caters to well-heeled vegetarians and even to fasters (you will have to figure this one out by taking a look at the menu). Sautéed wild mushrooms, Mexican green

Hong Kong's fresh produce markets are always a hive of activity.

rice and carrot juice combos are popular, as are the take-away vegetarian club sandwiches. It's possible to spend US$100 or more on lunch alone here.

Vietnamese

Since the advent of the "boat people" and their desperate refugee voyages across the South China Sea, Vietnamese cuisine has taken root and flourished in Hong Kong. In ingredients, preparation and style it's probably closest to the Cantonese school of cooking, with the addition of crisp lettuce

are recommended to take a stroll around the Lan Kwai Fong and SoHo areas, where any number of interesting dining experiences can be had. And then, of course, there are the hotel restaurants, many of which represent the best — and most expensive — the SAR has to offer.

For early starters, there are several reputable breakfast spots in Central, headed by The Landmark's mezzanine **La Terrazza** (2526-4200, and the ground-floor **Fountainside Restaurant** (2526-4018. Both feature hearty American and Continental breakfasts.

and fresh mint and an assortment of condiments based on fiery red and green peppers. It features a particularly savory spring roll, eaten in jackets of lettuce and mint, a delicious barbecued prawn with sugarcane, an interesting variety of beef dishes and a range of fragrant meat and noodle-based soups. Probably the best Vietnamese restaurant in town is **Indochine 1929** (2869-7399, 2/F California Tower, 30-32 Lan Kwai Fong, which offers Vietnamese in a setting oozing with French colonial nostalgia.

Western

Central District has so many high quality Western restaurants that making recommendations is no easy task. Adventurous diners

On the hotel dining front, **Vong** (2825-4028, 24th Floor, Mandarin Oriental Hotel, 25 Connaught Road, Central, is only borderline Western, serving French-Asian fusion cuisine. Prices, as to be expected, are high, but Vong is a wonderful place for a splurge, with a roomy setting (a rarity in Hong Kong), splendid views, and light, innovative offerings in a menu that changes frequently. The sampler courses are the best way to appreciate the range of the restaurant's interesting — and usually successful — experiments.

The Island Shangri-La's contribution to luxury dining is the French **Petrus** (2820-8590, 56th Floor, Island Shangri-La Hotel, Pacific Place, Central, where the views, cuisine and service are all of a faultlessly high level. It's one of Hong Kong's best and the perfect place for an intimate dinner or extravagant lunch. Its dress code requires that men wear a jacket.

Back on the streets and worth a recommendation not only for its staying power — it's been around since 1928 — but for the consistently high standard of its food and its convivial atmosphere, **Jimmy's Kitchen** (2526-5293, Ground Floor, South China Building, 1-3 Wyndham Street, is a Hong Kong institution. Essentially it's about generous portions of dishes that will never go out of fashion — a perfect family excursion. The mixed seafood grill is highly recommended, but then anything ordered from the eclectic menu is unlikely to result in disappointment.

Mediterranean cuisine is the specialty at **M at the Fringe** (2877-4000, First Floor, 2 Lower Albert Road, above the Fringe Club. With a classic period design, M has a homey ambiance that belies that inventiveness of the cuisine — the only giveaway perhaps are the eccentric designer chairs. The roast lamb is excellent, as is the suckling pig (a house specialty) and the smoked salmon. It's closed for lunch on weekends.

Landau's (2827 7901, Ground Floor, On Hing Building, 1-9 On Hing Terrace, deserves mention not least because it dominated the more conservative dining scene for so many years from its old Wanchai address. Today it occupies a more spacious venue, and the menu has lightened up a little along with the surroundings. The pig's knuckle, an old favorite, is still on the menu, however, along with many new, more adventurous offerings. Prices are very reasonable, averaging at around HK$300 per head.

It's worth taking a stroll around the Lan Kwai Fong neighborhood at any time of the day or night for a bite to eat. **California** (2521-1345, 30-32 D'Aguilar Street, is a long-runner that is very popular at lunch, serving a satisfying array of hamburgers, open sandwiches and chili dishes. At night, the chrome and sunset and the in-house video monitors wink and flash on supper club diners, and at weekends the dance floor is thrown open to dancers. More highly recommended in the Lan Kwai Fong area is **Va Bene** (2845-5577,

58-62 D'Aguilar Street, a smart Italian restaurant with linen table cloths and a homey atmosphere. The ravioli is recommended, but then there is not a bad note on the menu. The wine list is exclusively Italian.

A recommended venue for sampling the SoHo experience is **Soho Soho** (2147-2618, 9 Old Bailey Street, an intimate diner that serves that most unexpected of things — "modern British" cuisine. And if you associate British with fish and chips, Soho Soho's English standards served with a nouvelle twist will come as a pleasant — in some cases

almost revelatory — surprise. The restaurant is closed on Sundays.

For an ambient Gallic experience, SoHo's **2 Sardines** (2973-6618, 43 Elgin Street, was one of SoHo's pioneers, and is going as strong as ever. The perfect place for an intimate dinner, the restaurant serves far more than just sardines — the stuffed quail is recommended. Also recommended, and the first of the restaurants to open here, in 1994, **Casa Lisboa** (2869-9631, 21 Elgin Street, is

OPPOSITE: Dried seafood on sale in the Western District's Chinatown — shark's fins, scallops, fish maw, squid, shrimp, clams and oysters — the essence of traditional Chinese preserved foods. ABOVE: A live offering from a snake shop in a back-street market. Snakes are used for their bile duct or to prepare "hot" snake soup.

a romantic little haunt serving huge portions of Portuguese dishes.

A treat less for the tastebuds — though they will not be disappointed — and more for the eyes is the **Peak Café** (2849-7868, 121 Peak Road. The cuisine is dubbed "pan-Asian," but by popular consent it is the Indian dishes that come up tops, though Thai and Chinese chefs ensure that their offerings are also authentic. The real reason to head up here, however, is the superlative views — the best in Hong Kong. Be sure to book ahead in order to get an alfresco dining spot.

Causeway Bay come into their own as teeming neon-lit centers of food, shopping and entertainment. In Wanchai, the blazing, beckoning signs of its old Suzy Wong scene, the "girlie" bars and big hostess clubs, now seem tackily outclassed by the area's restaurants and newer nightlife options. In Causeway Bay, the lure of bargain clothing boutiques, even better bargains on the hawker stalls that line the sidewalks, and the huge Japanese department stores — Daimaru, Matsuzakaya and Sogo — that have chosen the district as their own, have turned the area into a

Also on the Peak, the very classy **Café Deco Bar and Grill** (2849-5111, in the Peak Galleria, features a mixture of Asian and Western cuisine and about HK$8-million worth of original art deco items such as a restored 1939 Wurlitzer juke box, a 1930s bronze canopy from a hotel in Miami, toilet basins from the 1920s, an old porcelain and nickel ice box from a New York City church kitchen, a 1920 oyster bar with zinc top, 1925 wall sconces and old brass doors.

WANCHAI AND CAUSEWAY BAY

While Central District breathes a kind of weary sigh of relief in the evening, a financial powerhouse at rest, both Wanchai and

restaurant and nightlife center so packed with people that it's often difficult to find space to stroll on some streets.

Causeway Bay, its main attractions centered on Times Square with its impressive food floor, the Excelsior Hotel and the Japanese emporiums, is mostly about food on the run, but it is not without some fine sit-down restaurants as well.

Cantonese

Fook Lam Moon (2866-0663, 35 Johnston Road, Wanchai, is Wanchai's most famous Cantonese restaurant, where such famous dishes as shark fin and bird's nest soup can be enjoyed in faultlessly classy surroundings. The braised abalone is a signature dish, though most non-Chinese are likely to find the equally famous deep-fried crispy chicken slightly more appealing to their tastebuds. It's a dining experience unlike any other Cantonese, with fine wines on hand and attentive service with a smile. The damage, it goes without saying, will remind you why you don't do this so often.

Forum (2891-2516, 485 Lockhart Road, Causeway Bay, is Causeway Bay's riposte to the Fook Lam. Its chef has made the restaurant famous, and the walls are covered with calligraphy praising his achievements. One dish reigns above all the others — braised abalone. The rubbery ear-shaped mollusk is braised for a full 15 hours in a stock of ham, chicken and beef, and the result (and the price) is truly sensational. It is not unusual for dinner for two to come to US$500, and that is without exploring the wine list.

For less conservative Cantonese cuisine served in spacious surroundings that offer panoramic views of Victoria Harbor, **One Harbor Road** (2588-1234, Eighth Floor, Grand Hyatt Hotel, Wanchai, can easily be recommended as one of Hong Kong's best Chinese dining experiences. Prices are considerably lower than at the two famous dining houses listed above (about half as expensive). The honey roasted pork is a house specialty.

For a *dim sum* experience you won't forget in a while, head to the aptly named **Dim Sum** (2834-8893, 63 Sing Woo Road, Happy Valley. With a setting redolent of old Shanghai, the restaurant offers excellent steamed and fried items from 11 AM to 5 PM and from 6 PM to 11 PM, providing a rare opportunity to have the dim sum experience by night — recommended.

Elsewhere in Causeway Bay, the **Tin Tin Seafood Harbor** (2833-6683 restaurant at 4/F Elizabeth House, 250 Gloucester Road, offers such dishes as sautéed oysters with port wine, shrimps fried with chili and pungent preserved bean curd sauce and Thai-style curry-fried crab. For other home-style dishes, health-enhancing casseroles and "male" and "female" soups, try the renowned **Ah Yee Leng Tong**, which has three outlets in Causeway Bay: at 13 Fleming Road (2573-0402; 503 Lockhart Road (2834-3480;

and Basement, Hang Lung Center, 2-20 Paterson Street (2576-8385, as well as eight outlets in Kowloon, three in the New Territories and three in Wanchai. Lastly, for something completely different, how about some snake soup? **King of Snake 2** (2831-0163, 24 Percival Street (with another branch on Russell Street) is the place to come to sample this popular winter soup, which isn't nearly as disgusting as you may think, but rich, tasty and warming. The restaurant serves other dishes, too, in case you chicken out.

Sichuan

Szechuan Lau (2891-9027, 466 Lockhart Road, is universally lauded as Hong Kong's best and most authentic Sichuan eating house. Unlike so many Chinese restaurants in Hong Kong, it has an appealing understated decor. Favorites include spiced perfumed chicken, kumquat beef and chili and camphor-flavored tea-smoked duck.

Beijing

Established way back in 1948, the **American Peking Restaurant** (2527-1000, 20 Lockhart Road, Wanchai, is Hong Kong's most famous Beijing-style restaurant. The house specialty is, of course, the Peking duck, and this — especially if your trip won't be taking you north to the capital — is the perfect place to sample it. Wash it down with some Tsingtao beer, the nation's most famous brew. Expect to pay around US$50 per head.

Vegetarian

For some traditional Buddhist culinary artistry in which mushroom and bean curd recipes have the shape, texture and even the taste of chicken, pork or beef, try the **Vegi Food Kitchen** (2890-6603, 8 Cleveland Street, Causeway Bay, and **Kung Tak Lam** (2890-3127, 31 Yee Wo Street, Causeway Bay, which specializes in chili-flavored Shanghainese dishes.

Japanese

For a splash out Japanese meal, the Grand Hyatt's **Kaetsu** (2588-1234 extension 7088, is one of the most attractive options in Hong Kong. The minimalist interior is a winner,

An incredible variety of fresh fish and shellfish is available at Hong Kong's markets.

as are the set courses of sushi and sashimi (less expensive than ordering à la carte) and the extensive sake list.

Causeway Bay in particular is a good place to seek out less expensive Japanese dining, largely on account of the numerous Japanese department stores that have made their homes in the area. Outside the department store food halls, a smart restaurant serving generic Japanese cuisine, **Kanetanaka (** 2833-6018, 22/F East Point Center, 545-563 Hennessy Road, is well recommended for its authenticity.

noted for its marvelous harbor views, fountain-decked outdoor terrace and its Saturday night entertainment — come 10:30 PM the tables disappear, a live band or DJ sets up and the trendies pour in to dance and drink the night away.

Indonesian

Shinta (2527-8780, Second Floor, Kar Yau Building, 36-44 Queen's Road East (not far from Pacific Place), offers excellent Indonesian fare such as spicy beef *rending*, *satay* (charcoal-grilled meat with spicy peanut

Korean

For pungent peppery *kim chi*, or assorted vegetables pickled and spiced and then fermented (they're buried in the ground for several months), tabletop barbecues and hotpots, **Arirang (** 2506-3298, 11/F Food Forum, Times Square, is one of Hong Kong's most popular restaurants. The chief draw is the barbecue, and indeed every table comes with its own grill. It may not be a luxury dining experience, but the lively atmosphere and sizzling smells more than compensate.

Indian

Viceroy (2827-7777, Second Floor Sun Hung Kai Center, 30 Harbor Road, Wanchai, has long been a Hong Kong favorite. It's also

sauce), *gado gado* (vegetable salad) and curries, and on Saturday nights a sumptuous buffet. The **Banana Leaf (** 2573-8187, 440 Jaffe Road, Causeway Bay, has Indo-Malay cuisine and has long been a popular place for either lunch or dinner.

Thai

The **Chili Club (** 2527-2872, First Floor, 88 Lockhart Road, Wanchai, was one of the pioneers of Thai cuisine in Hong Kong, and achieved almost immediate popularity, which it has maintained ever since. The food is consistently excellent, and in fact the only thing that can be said against the place is that its popularity makes it difficult to enjoy a leisurely meal here.

In Causeway Bay, the **Golden Elephant** (2506-1333, 11th Floor, Times Square, is another lively and popular restaurant. It pulls in the crowds for its lunchtime buffet, but the evening à la carte meals are recommended too.

Western

It would be remiss not to mention the Grand Hyatt's **Grissini** (2588-1234 extension 7313, in any round-up of Wanchai's Western restaurants. This Milanese restaurant features a superb wine collection — as to be expected at the Grand Hyatt — bakes its own bread, has postcard views of the harbor, winning decor, and serves conventional cuisine with an emphasis on fresh ingredients. Diners should expect to pay US$50 and upwards per head, more if you order wine, but it is money well spent.

Granted it is another example of fusion cuisine, and not strictly speaking Western, but **Tott's** (2837-6786, 34th Floor, Excelsior Hotel, 281 Gloucester Road, Causeway Bay, is difficult to classify — in more ways than one. Open until 2 AM on Fridays and Saturdays, it is as popular a venue for a drink as it is for a meal — bar drinkers get the bird's-eye view of the harbor. The menu is nothing if not adventurous, featuring an interesting range of pizza-style *naan*, among other things. Tandoori salmon is a house specialty and worth trying.

Another interesting Causeway Bay restaurant is **Oscar's** (2861-1511, Podium 3, World Trade Center, 280 Gloucester Road. Offering "modern Australian" cuisine, the barbecue selections are the winners — they come in portions big enough to satiate even the most homesick Aussie.

The Times Square Food Forum in Causeway Bay is packed with excellent restaurants, but **W's Entrecote** (2506-0133, 13th Floor, Times Square, is worth a special recommendation. Ordering is made easy by the fact that if you sit down here you are eating a salad appetizer, a steak entree and a bistro-style dessert. The only decision you get to make is how you want the steak cooked and how big you want it. If this all seems a little processed, the meals are not.

One of Hong Kong's most popular Mexican restaurants is **La Placita** (2506-3308, 13th Floor, Times Square, Causeway Bay. It's Mexican the whole hog, with a bright theme decor and live music in the evenings. The margaritas are celebrated island wide, and the huge La Placita platter is almost a meal in itself.

Harry Ramsden's (2832-9626, 213 Queen's Road East, Wanchai, next to the Hopewell Center, is worth a special mention for bringing authentic fish and chips to Hong Kong. Appropriately, it's open late.

ELSEWHERE AROUND THE ISLAND

Anyone who saw *Love is a Many Splendored Thing* is familiar with the much-publicized gastronomic symbols of Hong Kong: the palatial floating restaurants in Aberdeen. They can be visited directly or by organized tour, or by way of harbor cruises from Central District or Tsimshatsui. The most well known is the **Jumbo** (2553-9111, which is moored beside its sister ships the **Jumbo Floating Palace** (2554-0513 and **Tai Pak** (2552-5953. All are excellent for *dim sum*, seafood (you can select your own from tanks) and the usual Cantonese fare.

Repulse Bay may have lost its graceful time-honored landmark, the Repulse Bay Hotel, but a replica of the romantic **Verandah** (2812-2722, Repulse Bay Arcade, 109 Repulse Bay Road, has been built into the high-rise luxury apartment block that now occupies the site. The perfect place for a candlelit French dinner, everything about this lovely restaurant is faultless. Evening meals cost around US$100 per person, but much cheaper lunch specials are available.

Some Hong Kong residents make the journey out to Stanley not for the cut-price boutiques and stalls of the open market but to dine at **Lucy's** (2813-9055, 64 Stanley Main Street. This intimate Continental restaurant has a changing menu that never ceases to delight, and is particularly loved for its desserts.

Also in Stanley Main Street, the elegant **Stanley's French Restaurant** (2813-8873, 90B Stanley Main Street, was the first Western establishment to open here, and well into

Dai pai dong (street-side restaurants) are a convenient and cheap way to dine out.

its second decade is still one of the best restaurants in the southern island area. Located in an old village house, Stanley's French features two glassed-in verandahs which offer fine views of the bay, and at night you can enjoy rooftop dining. In much the same vein is **Stanley's Oriental** (2813-9988, in the same location, whose menu is a mixture of Asian and Western dishes, served either inside the restaurant or on the verandah. During the day and at weekends both restaurants are quite casual but in the evenings, when the candles come out, more formal attire is expected.

NIGHTLIFE

Hong Kong Island has the cream of the SAR's nightlife, and the best place to start is Central's **Lan Kwai Fong**. Many of the bars are open fronted, which makes taking a quick stroll through the area and identifying which is your kind of place relatively easy. Hot spots come and go, but almost all of Lan Kwai Fong's will be hopping after 10 PM on a Friday and Saturday night, and respectable numbers can even be found mid-week.

Early in the evening the place to be is Wing Wah Lane, where a small convergence of Thai and Vietnamese restaurants share the street with the spill-over from **Club 64** (2523-2801, 12-14 Wing Wah Lane. By 8 PM this area is usually packed with alfresco diners (weather permitting), and Club 64, a downmarket but still convivial haunt, is crowded with happy-hour drinkers.

Around the corner, **California** (2521-1345, 32-34 D'Aguilar Street, is a bar-restaurant that starts off the evening sedately before loosening up for the late night dancing crowd. Close by are the three affiliated venues of **Nineteen 97** (2810-9333, 8-11 Lan Kwai Fong — drinks upstairs at **Post 97**, dinner downstairs in **La Dolce Vita 97**, dancing in **Club 1997**. The three have been popular for a decade, and are still extremely popular places to be seen.

Across the road, the second floor of the California Entertainment Building, the **Jazz Club** (2845-8477 frequently features top international performers, along with their regular, first-rate house band.

Less of a scene is the **Fringe Club** (2521-7251, 2 Lower Albert Road, in the same building as the member's only Foreign Correspondent's Club (a very smart place for a drink if you have a friend with a membership). Drinks are less expensive than in most of the nearby Lan Kwai Fong bars, and it attracts an interesting, diverse crowd, ranging from alternative artists to travelers and the odd journalist.

Another alternative to the Lan Kwai Fong scene is the **Staunton Bar & Café** (2973-6611, 10-12 Staunton Street, at the base of the Mid-Levels Escalator. With wall-length windows, it's the perfect spot to people watch during lulls in the conversation.

Wanchai may once have been notorious as the **Suzy Wong** bar, brothel and nightclub district of Hong Kong, but such days are long gone. It has now become a respectable business and restaurant area. The surviving core of fairly tame topless bars and nightclubs, along with karaoke lounges, discos and bars, is an overpriced and somewhat tired affair compared to the nightlife in other Asian destinations.

For live rock and roll and Suzy Wong and old Hong Kong memorabilia, **The Wanch** (2861-1621, 54 Jaffe Road, is something of a Hong Kong institution and well worth a visit.

It's tempting to leave it unmentioned, but **Joe Banana's** (2529-1811, 23 Luard Street, Wanchai, has been pulling in the late-night party animals for so long that to do so would be considered remiss by many. Not to put too fine a point on it, late night Fridays and Saturdays are a meat market.

On the edge of Wanchai, one of the hottest nightspots in town is **JJ's** (2588-1234, in the Grand Hyatt Hotel, which features live rhythm and blues, disco dancing, videos and excellent bar food.

Twenty-first century Hong Kong — the colonial Legislative Council Building and Statue Square are literally overshadowed by the Hongkong Bank, the new Bank of China Building and the Lippo Centre.

Kowloon

FIRST IMPRESSIONS CAN BE MISLEADING. To those who arrive in Kowloon via the Star Ferry, Tsimshatsui can meet the eye as an extension of Hong Kong Island. In fact, Kowloon is another world. Once you leave the tourist enclave of Nathan Road's "Golden Mile" Kowloon very quickly becomes a Cantonese city: increasingly so the farther north you go.

TSIMSHATSUI

This bustling commercial center right on the tip of the Kowloon Peninsula has long been Hong Kong's main tourist district, the site of most of its tourist hotels and the key shopping area for visitors. During the 1970s and 1980s, the area expanded onto reclaimed land in the harbor. This formed a completely new tourist area, Tsimshatsui East — the area where hotels like the Royal Garden, Regal Meridien, Holiday Inn Crowne Plaza Harbor View and Nikko are now situated.

But for all its reputation and growth, along with its famous Nathan Road "Golden Mile" of shops and department stores, Tsimshatsui has never really matched the high-rise architectural drama of Hong Kong Island's Central District and other harborfront locations. The reason: a long-standing restriction on building heights because of the mainland approach by aircraft landing at Kai Tak International Airport.

All this is changing. With the new airport at Chek Lap Kok and with the vast area of ready-formed flat, open land at Kai Tak already slated for massive redevelopment once the airport here closes down, building restrictions have already been relaxed and Tsimshatsui is starting to mushroom with new skyscrapers.

The new tower wing at the famed Peninsula Hotel, opened in 1994, reflects something of the skyward explosion that's taking place throughout Kowloon. Until the tower was built, this grand dame of hotels was almost lost in the welter of new (if low-rise) business and recreational development that transformed the Tsimshatsui waterfront — including the spherical dome of the Space Museum and Planetarium, the sweeping roof of the Hong Kong Cultural Center and the giant Regent/New World Hotel and commercial complex.

Meanwhile, a wide swathe of reclamation off Yau Ma Tei, west of the peninsula, has extended the waterfront of what used to be a typhoon shelter so deep into the harbor that old Hong Kong hands joke about the days to come when you'll be virtually able to step back and forth from Kowloon to Central.

As Central District does, Tsimshatsui starts at the Star Ferry terminal, with the added convenience of an HKTA bureau on the concourse offering advice, maps and guide booklets on all aspects of tourism in Hong Kong, along with fairly classy souvenirs.

From there, three routes lead into the heart of this people-packed high-rise funland — you can head up the escalator into the mammoth **Harbor City** complex of shops, restaurants and hotels, or you can stroll along the harbor promenade all the way to Tsimshatsui East to more hotels, shopping plazas, nightclubs and restaurants, or walk directly along Salisbury Road and pay your respects to the Grand Duchess of tourism in Hong Kong, the lady who's virtually seen it all, the **Peninsula Hotel**.

Built in 1928, the Peninsula reigned supreme as the center of high society life in Hong Kong through to the late 1970s, and even had the dubious distinction of being the headquarters of the Japanese military administration during the occupation in World War II. It has seen some of the most distinguished and the most flamboyant names of the twentieth century come and go, and even today it's a place where you can play "Place the Face" in its ornate and renowned lobby, trying to recall the name of the features that just passed you by, and what they were doing when you last saw them on television.

The Peninsula's columned architecture has survived with much dignity the latter-day explosion of steel and glass in Tsimshatsui, but only just. In the 1970s, after a proposal to tear the old dowager down was quashed, the rooms and suites were renovated and redesigned to update the establishment without harming the outside frills. But even then, one of her greatest devotees, the ill-fated Harold Holt, Prime Minister of Australia, arrived to stay one day after the face-lift and immediately remarked:

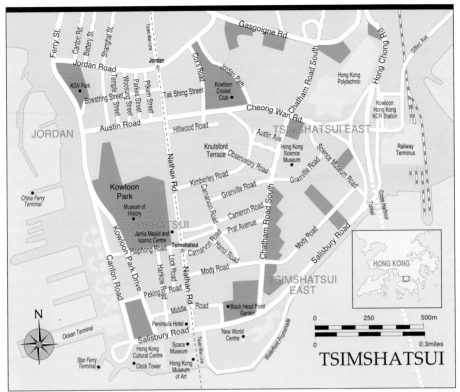

TSIMSHATSUI

"You've changed the pub!" Today, the lobby has been renovated again and a 30-story tower of luxury rooms connected to the hotel has been added.

If you begin your walk at the seafront promenade by Star Ferry, you can study another contrast of tradition and tear-away progress in Hong Kong, the old Kowloon–Canton Railway Station's **Clock Tower**, preserved after much public protest, and beside it the **Hong Kong Cultural Center**. Within the complex is the excellent **Hong Kong Museum of Art** (2734-2167 (10 AM to 6 PM, closed Thursdays). The museum has seven galleries featuring Chinese art from the Han through the Qing dynasties, and two special exhibition galleries — check with the HKTA for the latest exhibitions. Next door, the domed **Space Museum** (2734-2722 (10 AM to 9 PM, closed Tuesdays) has one of the largest and most advanced planetariums in the world, and features a space theater with computerized projection that is so vivid that you actually feel as though you're journeying through outer space. There are performances in

English, but only on certain days and at certain times, so it is best to check with the museum beforehand.

Heading along the waterfront you can take a leisurely stroll to the end of the promenade to **Hung Hom** — the upturned pyramid that can be seen en-route is the **Hong Kong Coliseum**. Next to this is the Kowloon–Canton Railway Terminus (KCR), where the suburban trains serve Kowloon and the New Territories centers up to the border with Guangzhou (Canton), and the expresses go right through to Guangzhou, the jump-off point for almost the entire China trail.

This walk is a must at night, when Hong Kong is lit up, and especially when there is a full, rising moon — it's a dazzling, romantic sight.

Alternatively, take the pedestrian bridge just past the **New World Center** across Salisbury Road to the shopping and hotel district of Tsimshatsui East — here you'll find the major hotels, the **Regal Kowloon**, **Grand Stanford Harbor View**, **Shangri-La**, **Nikko** and **Royal Garden**. Also located here is the **Hong Kong Science Museum** (2732-3232, 2 Science Museum Road, which has around 500 exhibits, more than half of them "hands-on." This high-tech playground is complete with robots, a flight simulator, satellite weather shows, animated skeletons of everything from the human DNA structure to dinosaurs, virtual reality demonstrations, various scientific exhibits and, hanging above it all, Cathay Pacific's first aircraft, a DC-3 called *Betsy*. The Science Museum is open Tuesday to Friday from 1 PM to 9 PM and weekends 10 AM to 9 PM.

Close by is the newly relocated **Museum of History** (2724-9042, 100 Chatham Road South. It's no major attraction, but the collection of memorabilia from the old colonial days has a certain charm that makes the museum worth a visit, particularly for British travelers.

From Tsimshatsui East you can head west back to Tsimshatsui via Granville Road, perhaps stopping at **Kowloon Park** on Nathan Road for a much deserved break. The park has extensive sports and recreation facilities — restaurants, an indoor heated Olympic swimming pool, a games hall, a playground, an aviary, a Chinese Garden, a bird lake and other ponds and gardens. The park is also another ideal place to watch tai chi (or *taiji*) exercises in the morning. Bird-fanciers, who bring their caged birds here to air them, show them off, compare them with other birds and listen to their song — and even sometimes walk them about on delicate leashes — can be seen here too. Some of the finches, thrushes and more exotic lovebirds and parakeets change hands at up to HK$1,000 each, and the passion with which they're regarded by the Chinese — in Hong Kong and indeed throughout China — can be seen in the elegant wicker and bamboo cages, some of which cost HK$10,000 alone, and their delicate little ceramic water and seed pots.

If you're visiting the park on a Sunday, local amateur musicians put on a variety show, free of charge, from 2 PM to 5 PM.

Almost next door is the **Jamia Masjid and Islamic Center** (2724-0095, which was built in 1984 for the Muslims in Hong Kong. Guided tours can be arranged, but by appointment only.

AROUND KOWLOON

Kowloon is not rich in attractions, but it's interesting to explore all the same. Transportation is for the most part very simple, with the MTR reaching almost every point of interest in the area.

YAU MA TEI

Temple Street is actually closer to Jordan MTR station (one stop north of Tsimshatsui) than to Yau Ma Tei, but it's a good introduction to Kowloon all the same. It may be a regular tourist haunt, but it has a lot more character — with its street theater of Chinese opera, fortune tellers and street dentists — than does nearby Nathan Road. The market area bustles even by day, but it really comes into its own at night.

Close by, on the corner of Nathan Road and Public Square Street is **Tin Hau Temple**. Best visited during the day, this is a complex of four temples, originally built in the late 1870s, but refurbished in 1972 after a fire destroyed the temples' wooden roofs and rafters. It's a popular spot to have one's fortune told.

Two blocks west, at the junction of Kansu Street and Battery Street, the **Jade Market** sprawls its precious wares right across the sidewalks every day from 10 AM until around 3:30 PM. As harmless — and orderly nowadays, unlike times past — as it all looks, this is not a place for novices to shop for jade, unless you don't mind paying through the nose for something is perhaps not what it is claimed to be.

MONGKOK

In **Yuen Po Street**, near the Mongkok Stadium (Prince Edward MTR station is closest), you'll find a whole lane devoted to bird shops, and you may even witness a "bird-fight," in which two prized warblers, put together in a cage, will try to bully each other into submission — without actually touching each other. The market is open daily from 7 AM to 8 PM.

A capsule elevator takes shoppers to the upper levels of a Tsimshatsui East shopping plaza.

SHAM SHUI PO

Farther down the MTR line at **Cheung Sha Wan**, a five-minute walk from the station will take you to an area of street markets which cluster around one of Hong Kong's proudest but often neglected cultural sites, **Lei Cheng Uk** (2386-2863 (10 AM to 1 PM, 2 PM to 6 PM, closed Thursdays) on Tonkin Street in Lei Cheng Uk resettlement estate. This museum marks the site of a Han dynasty tomb dating from the years 206 BC to AD 220.

selling joss sticks, colorful paper offerings and souvenir paper windmills — which the Chinese believe will blow away bad luck — and a nearby arcade full of soothsayers and palmists. It's here, along with the Man Mo Temple in Central District, that you can have your own fortune told in the traditional way by shaking the *chim*, a bamboo canister full of tapers, each of which has a number in Chinese on it. You shake and shake until one detaches itself, and its number is written on a scrap of paper. You take this to one of the soothsayers nearby.

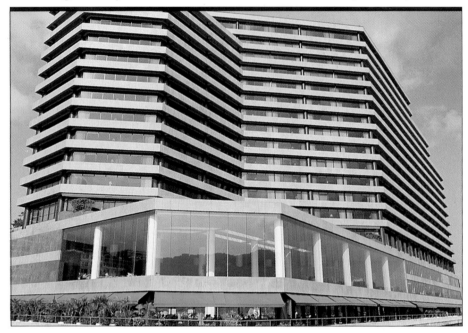

When the vault was discovered in 1955 some pottery and bronzeware were found inside.

WONG TAI SIN

The **Wong Tai Sin Temple** on Lung Cheung Road near the MTR station of the same name, is dedicated to the deity who's become the patron saint of horserace punters. Glittering in the midst of high-rises, it was built in 1973 on the site of an original place of worship, its most treasured relic being a portrait of Wong Tai Sin brought to Hong Kong from China's southern Guangdong province 70 years ago.

What makes the temple particularly fascinating is a surrounding cluster of stalls

You can put the powers of Wong Tai Sin to the test by shaking out two numbers, the race and the runner, and taking them along to the nearest off-course betting shop. You never know.

CHI LIN NUNNERY

Close to the Diamond Hill MTR station, Kowloon's latest attraction is also perhaps its most impressive. The **Chi Lin Nunnery** (9 AM to 4 PM, closed Wednesdays) may not be a historical attraction (it was opened in early 2000), but the wooden buildings were constructed in faithful Tang dynasty style, using wooden pegs instead of nails. Take the C2 exit from Diamond Hill MTR station.

The expansive gardens are also a pleasant place for a stroll, and are open from 7 AM to 7 PM daily.

WHERE TO STAY

Accommodation in Kowloon almost invariably means accommodation in Tsimshatsui, which has not only the SAR's best budget deals and some very good value (by Hong Kong standards) mid-range hotels, but also some of the world's most outstanding luxury digs as well. And given that it's only seven minutes to Central on one of the world's most spectacular ferry rides, little is lost by staying off the island, and indeed, for those Hong Kong bound, a very pleasant start to the day is gained.

LUXURY

The **Peninsula** (2920-2888 FAX 2722-4170 WEB SITE www.peninsula.com/hotels/hk/hk.html, Salisbury Road, Tsimshatsui, is Hong Kong's most venerable hotel. The doors swung open in 1928 and the rich and famous have been arriving ever since. High standards are affirmed in countless tiny details, the classic look of the rooms, complete with marble bathrooms, fax machines and CD players. The hotel's restaurants are among the best in Hong Kong, notably Gaddi's and Felix, designed by avant-garde French designer Philippe Starck.

The **Regent** (2721-1211 FAX 2739-4546 WEB SITE www.regenthotels.com, 18 Salisbury Road, Tsimshatsui, is strongly oriented to the needs of the business traveler, but this does not mean it scrimps on luxury. Indeed it has been voted the Pacific Rim's top hotel by readers of *Condé Nast*. With unrivalled harbor views and facilities comparable to the rest of Hong Kong's best hotels, it is another contender for the world's top hotels list. Amenities include a heated outdoor pool, a gymnasium, solarium and facilities for the disabled.

Not quite in the same league as the Peninsula and the Regent, the 780-room **Sheraton Hong Kong Hotel and Towers** (2369-1111 FAX 2739-8707 E-MAIL res_hongkong@sheraton .com, 20 Nathan Road, has a superb location overlooking the harbor, and is a reliable luxury choice. Less expensive and right in the heart of things — expect furtive sellers of Rolexes to accost you as enter and leave — is the **Holiday Inn Golden mile** (2369-3111 FAX 2369-8016 E-MAIL reserv@goldenmile.com, 50 Nathan Road, Tsimshatsui. It's the perfect place to stay if you are on a shopping holiday, and is also very popular with business travelers.

MID-RANGE

The **Kowloon Hotel** (2929-2888 FAX 2739-9811 E-MAIL khh@peninsula.com, 19-21 Nathan

Road, Tsimshatsui, is one of Hong Kong's best upper mid-range deals. Located behind the Peninsula Hotel, for approximately a third of the price of staying at the latter, you can stay here and use the Peninsula's swimming pool and other facilities. All rooms have fax machines and complimentary e-mail service, and the "telecenter" system allows Internet access through the television. Room rates are around US$200 for a double.

The huge **Salisbury YMCA** (2268-7000 FAX 2739-9315 E-MAIL room@ymcahk.org.hk,

Huge hotels like the Regent OPPOSITE have sprung up in Tsimshatsui East, a tourist city built on land reclaimed from Victoria Harbor on the eastern shores of the Kowloon Peninsula. Corinthian columns RIGHT decorate this Kowloon shopping mall.

41 Salisbury Road, Tsimshatsui, has long been a favorite of repeat visitors to Hong Kong. The health club is widely celebrated (with squash courts, two swimming pools and even a climbing wall), the rooms are spacious and service standards are very high. The newly renovated rooms even have modem lines nowadays. It's arguably Hong Kong's best economy choice in terms of accommodation, and as a result it's wise to book well in advance. Room rates start at less than US$100, and weekly packages are available.

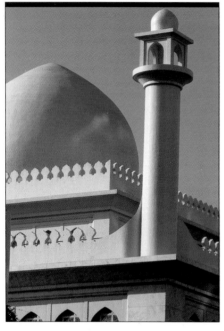

Popular with business travelers, the **Guangdong Hotel** (2739-3311 FAX 2721-1137 WEB SITE http://gdhk.gdhotels.net/en/home/, 18 Prat Avenue, Tsimshatsui, has an excellent location in the heart of bustling Tsimshatsui. It has Cantonese and Continental restaurants, along with a business center.

There is cheaper accommodation in the Kowloon area. The Salvation Army-run **Booth Lodge** (2771-9266 FAX 2385-1140, 11 Wing Sing Lane, Yau Ma Tei, has standard rooms from HK$620 but you need to book well in advance. Another inexpensive choice is the **Caritas Bianchi Lodge** (2388-1111 FAX 2770-6669, 4 Cliff Road, Yau Ma Tei, where singles are around HK$750, doubles HK$850.

INEXPENSIVE

The epicenter of Hong Kong's budget accommodation is the notorious Chungking Mansions. For more than three decades the 17-story, four-block tower that houses nearly 1,000 guesthouses, shops, sweatshops and restaurants, has been a refuge for travelers passing through Hong Kong on a budget. It's probably something of a miracle the place has never burned down, and in the late 1990s moves were finally made to improve the fire safety of the building, a change that closed down many of the fly-by-night guesthouses and pushed up prices in many others.

The majority of Chungking's offerings are not for the faint-hearted. One exception is **Chungking House** (2366-5362 FAX 2721-3570, Block A, Fourth Floor. A superior guesthouse, Chungking House has a coffee shop, laundry service, a dining area, tour desk and a total of 75 rooms. Those who can bring themselves to join the A block elevator queue will find themselves pleasantly surprised once they reach the Chungking House foyer.

The **Carlton Guesthouse** (2721-0720, Flat 7, 15th Floor, B Block, is also recommended. It has well-maintained rooms from HK$200.

For dormitory accommodation, the long-running **Travelers' Hostel** (2368-7710, Block A, 16th floor, is one of the most popular places, and also has a budget travel center for onward bookings into China and elsewhere. It's difficult to recommend this place, but if it's true budget accommodation you're after it has perhaps the cheapest around: dormitory beds from HK$40.

If you can't bear the closet-size rooms of Chungking Mansions, the interminable queues for the lifts or the 24-hour bazaar bustle in its ground floor shopping arcade, there are plenty of reasonable, if slightly pricier alternatives nearby. Recommended is the **Victoria Hostel** (2376-0621 FAX 2376-2609, Middle Floor, 33 Hankow Road, which has both inexpensive dorm beds (from HK$35) and rooms from HK$200.

Up in Yau Ma Tei, the **King's Hotel** (2780-1281 FAX 2782-1833, 473-473A Nathan Road, Yau Ma Tei, is as the name suggests less a guesthouse than a hotel, and probably Hong Kong's cheapest, with rooms starting at HK$300. It's not exactly the lap of luxury, but it's perfectly tolerable for a night or two if you are just passing through.

WHERE TO EAT

Kowloon doesn't offer quite the diversity of dining that Hong Kong Island does, but there is still an enormous choice of fine dining in this part of town. Budget travelers will generally find it easier to keep costs down in this part of town, while those looking for luxury dining will find no shortage of places to indulge.

CHINESE CUISINE

Cantonese

For superb Cantonese cuisine in sumptuous surroundings, the **Spring Moon (** 2315-3160, First Floor, Peninsula Hotel, has few peers. It's worth a visit for the ambiance alone, which is pure 1920s Shanghai. Prices, as to be expected, are far from inexpensive, but given the quality of the service and the food are extremely reasonable. The restaurant's *dim sum* menu concentrates more on quality than on variety, and the result is *dim sum* that are among the best in town.

Less expensive and less impressive on the decor front is **Dynasty (** 2734-6600, Fourth Floor, New World Renaissance Hotel, 22 Salisbury Road, Tsimshatsui. The food, however, is on a par with Hong Kong's best. The deep-fried pigeon is a favorite, and highly recommended, particularly if you have never tried this Cantonese treat before.

Less expensive again but highly rated is the **T'ang Court (** 2375-1133 ext 2250, First Floor, Great Eagle Hotel, 8 Peking Road, Tsimshatsui. The restaurant has a strong wine list, a seasonal menu, and offers a delicious baked chicken in salt as one of its house specialties. Reckon on around US$50 per head, more if you order wine.

Shanghainese and Beijing

The art deco **Wu Kong (** 2366-7244, Basement, Alpha House, 27-33 Nathan Road, is one of Kowloon's most famous Shanghai restaurants. It's a relatively inexpensive place

to dine, and while it can be a little rowdy at times in the Chinese style it's a great place to sample Shanghai cuisine.

The main branch of **Peking Garden (** 2735-8211, Third Floor, Star House, 3 Salisbury Road, is in Central, but this one is a perfectly good place to tuck into some Peking duck. Prices are reasonable.

Vegetarian

Bodhi (2366-8283, First Floor, 32-34 Lock Road, is a good place to try Chinese vegetarian cuisine, which is about replicating

the tastes and textures of meat rather than celebrating vegetables. To the Western palate the results are not always happy, but it is nevertheless a cuisine worth sampling. Bodhi has a wonderful selection of beancurd, fungi and bamboo shoot dishes.

Seafood

For adventurous seafood lovers, the village of Lei Yue Mun, on the eastern, Kowloon tip of the harbor, shouldn't be missed. Select the seafood from rows and rows of tanks that line the alleyways and then take the "catch" to one of the nearby restaurants that

OPPOSITE: The minaret of the Kowloon Mosque in Nathan Road. ABOVE: The birds easily outnumber the customers in this Kowloon restaurant.

do a brisk trade in cooking up customers' shopping trawls. The view of the harbor from here provides a unique perspective. Take the MTR to Kwun Tong, and from there either a Kowloon Motor Bus (KMB) No. 14C or minibus to the Sam Ka Tsuen terminus.

INTERNATIONAL

Indian

Curry lovers are well taken care of at the famed **Gaylord Indian Restaurant** (2376-1001, First Floor, Ashley Center, 23-25 Ashley Road, where tandooris are a specialty and where you can watch breads and kebabs being prepared for clay-oven baking. It's one of Hong Kong's longest running Indian restaurants, and dishes culled from the gamut of Indian cuisines — everything from northern-style tandoori to southern Goan fish curries. Authentic Indian live music accompanies the meals, and prices are reasonable at around HK$250 per head.

Japanese

Hong Kong Island is the place for Japanese dining. One novel establishment to try in Tsimshatsui is **Ah-So** (2730-3392, 159 Craigie Court, World Finance Center, South Tower, Harbor City, Canton Road, which calls itself "Hong Kong's Only Floating Sushi Bar" — the food being served from floating "boats."

Western

Au Trou Normand (2366-8754, First Floor, 63 Carnarvon Road, has been a fixture on the Kowloon dining circuit since 1964. It has relocated now to new premises, but retains its character all the same. Serving classic French cuisine (nothing too adventurous here), it has been outclassed in recent years by the arrival of a new breed of international restaurant, but it still represents good value for reliable cuisine. The escargots in butter are a house specialty. Dinner for two costs a little over US$100.

Providing you don't mind doubling the expense (approximately), **Gaddi's** (2315-3171, The Peninsula, Salisbury Road, Tsimshatsui, is one of Hong Kong's top French restaurants, offering impeccable service, decor and cuisine. Everything about this place oozes class and style. The set meals are re-

markably good value, starting at HK$500 per person.

For top-of-the-range Italian, **Sabatini** (2733-2000, Third Floor, Royal Garden, 69 Mody Road, Tsimshatsui East, is a worldwide chain of the highest order. The emphasis is on a fresh ingredients, and this passion for simple things is reflected in the unostentatious decor. The linguini alla Sabatini is a house specialty, as are the antipasti — on display — and the terrific desserts. Dinner for two with wine can run to US$200.

Mistral (2751-2870, B2, Grand Stanford Intercontinental Hotel, 70 Mody Road, Tsimshatsui, is a less pricey place to sample excellent Italian cuisine. Meals are served in an atmospheric and yet roomy environment, and staff are knowledgeable about the menu. The roast lamb is a house specialty.

Last of the hotel restaurant recommendations, but definitely not least, is **Felix** (2315-3188, 28th Floor, The Peninsula, Salisbury Road, Tsimshatsui. If ever dining out was a total experience it is in this Philippe Starck-designed interior. In fact, for travelers in the know, it is as much a tourist attraction as a place to dine (or take a less expensive drink at the bar). The cuisine is called "Pacific Rim," which essentially allows the chef a lot of latitude to experiment with influences ranging from Thai to Japanese to Californian.

The Tsimshatsui branch of **Jimmy's Kitchen** (2376-0327, 29 Ashley Road, is as popular as its brother in Central. It's basically about filling up with excellent home-style food — whether that be steak, an Indian curry or a Thai soup — in high-class pub-like surroundings.

For those who are simply looking to fill up, there's an endless number of American restaurants in Tsimshatsui. **Dan Ryan's Chicago Grill** (2735-6111, Shop 200, Ocean Terminal, Harbor City, Canton Road, is a good example of the bar-with-hearty-steaks-and-burgers theme, and as its kind is rather good. **Planet Hollywood** (2377-7888, 3 Canton Road, is best avoided unless you have children with you; the **Hard Rock Café Kowloon** (2377-8118, 100 Canton Road, does a better job on the food front.

Hostesses in a replica of a vintage Rolls Royce await customers at Club Bboss.

NIGHTLIFE

Tsimshatsui is the nerve center for most of Kowloon's nightlife. Some of Tsimshatsui's pubs have a tired air, but the scene continues to reinvent itself, as with the arrival of pubs like **Delaney's** (2301-3980, Basement, 71-77 Peking Road. Delaney's was imported piece by piece from Ireland, giving it an authenticity missing from most others in the area. It has a good selection of draft beers and hearty pub lunches and dinners.

also mentioned in WHERE TO EAT above, is another restaurant that also doubles as a bar.

Jazz fans should head to the **Blue Note Jazzzz Bar** (2721-2111, Kowloon Shangri-La Hotel, 64 Mody Road, which has a quiet ambient atmosphere and features classic jazz.

For those interested in Tsimshatsui's opulent hostess clubs, **Club Bboss** (2369-2883, LG/F New Mandarin Plaza, 14 Science Museum Road, is the big name and has been for years. It's a vast 6,510-sq-m (70,000-sq-ft) luxuriously appointed dance-lounge, in which guests are driven to their plush,

For the old style of Tsimshatsui pub, **Ned Kelly's Last Stand** (2376-0562, 11A Ashley Road, has been around as long as almost anyone can remember, and has a decor that celebrates the folk hero of the bush-ranging era. The roof of the place is blasted off in the evenings by a traditional Dixieland jazz band.

Rick's Café (2367-2939, 4 Hart Avenue, is another long-runner, and more a bar than a pub. The *Casablanca*-theme decor was cool in its day, but is now just another fixture on the Tsimshatsui scene.

For a drink in sophisticated surroundings, pop into **Felix** (see WHERE TO EAT, above), where exorbitant prices are offset by the futuristic interior and the fabulous views from the bar area of the harbor. **Dan Ryan's,**

discreetly positioned personal "relaxation zone" in a full-sized battery-powered replica of an antique Rolls-Royce. Bboss boasts no fewer than 1,000 hostesses on its books, up to 400 of whom will be on duty any night of the week. Dressed in glitzy evening dresses or elegant thigh-split traditional silk *cheong-sams*, they're supervised by a legion of *mama-sans* who carry walkie-talkie radios to keep in touch with customer requests. Silly amounts of money, it goes without saying, can be spent here, and the place exists as a testament to the power of the dollar in Hong Kong.

ABOVE: A local trio belt out a disco beat in Rick's Café in Kowloon. OPPOSITE: The Star Ferry boat approaching Kowloon Pier.

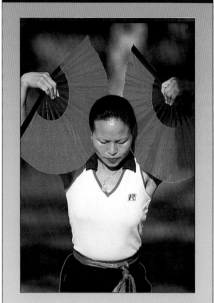

The
New
Territories

NOT SO LONG AGO, the New Territories were little more than farmland dotted with the odd village or two. Over the last few decades, however, massive development has created the "new towns" that rival downtown Kowloon. Fortunately, the countryside is still far from being obliterated altogether, and the New Territories remains a good place to escape from the bustle.

SHATIN

The crowds surge into Shatin in the autumn and winter months, when the horses are running at the huge Shatin Racecourse, the first major stop on the trail through the New Territories. It's an exciting place to see a race (see SPORTING SPREE, page 35 in YOUR CHOICE). Shatin is also the home of the huge **New Town Plaza**, a good spot for luxury bargain shopping, featuring the Yohan Department Store with its vast basement food hall, an indoor computer-controlled musical fountain, an outdoor ampitheater for cultural shows and orchestral concerts, a mini-golf course, a children's playground and tennis courts.

An even more spectacular local facility is the **Hong Kong Sports Institute** (2681-6888 near the racecourse, a giant Olympic-standard complex that includes a 250-m (820-ft) velodrome, an athletics field, an "energy room" full of weightlifting equipment, a hall for table tennis and fencing, a training pool, 12 squash courts, a judo hall, an indoor sports hall with room for two tennis courts or eight badminton courts, a huge gymnasium, 15 outdoor tennis courts, and restaurants and snack bars. It's the pride of Hong Kong's sporting world, described by the President of the International Olympic Committee as the best he'd seen in 130 countries, and it's open every day for visitors from 8 AM to 10 PM. The trouble is, you can't use it. Most of its facilities are booked out by major multi-nationals and corporations in Hong Kong.

Shatin's only bona fide tourist attraction is the remarkable **Ten Thousand Buddhas Monastery** (9 AM to 5 PM daily) behind the Shatin Railway Station. It takes at least half an hour to get to it, climbing 431 steps, but it's worth the effort. In the main hall are not 10,000 but 12,800 Buddha images lining the walls, while an effigy of the temple's founding abbot, Yuet Kai, preserved and covered with gold leaf, can be seen in a glass showcase. Along with the large gilded Buddhas that preside over the main altar are tall decorated images of the 18 *luohans*, the disciples of Sakyamuni Buddha. You'll also find a fierce mounted image of Mo, or Kwan Kung, the God of War, standing guard in one of the halls, along with the God of Wisdom, riding a huge blue lion, and the Goddess of Mercy, Guanyin.

In **Tai Wai**, just west of **Shatin**, there's an interesting walled village called **Tsang Tai Uk**, which was built as a stronghold by the Tsang clan in 1859, and a few minutes' walk away, near Tai Wai KCR station, the Daoist **Che Kung Temple** (7 AM to 6 PM daily), dedicated to a deified general credited with saving the area from a plague.

Shatin is also home to the **Chinese University of Hong Kong**, which has a superb collection of more than a thousand Chinese paintings and calligraphic works, 300 Han and pre-Han bronze seals and 400 jade flower carvings in its **Art Gallery** (2609-7416 (10 AM to 4:45 PM, 12:30 PM to 5:30 PM Sundays, closed public holidays).

TSUEN WAN

From Shatin, the New Territories trail leads to the **Chuk Lam Shim Yuen Monastery** (7 AM to 4 PM daily) at Tsuen Wan, whose name translates as "Bamboo Forest Zen Monastery" due to the fact it was first established in a bamboo mat shed in 1927. Now an ornate, sprawling temple with a sweeping, curved and tiled roof, it houses three of the largest "precious Buddha" images of Hong Kong.

The **Sam Tung Uk Museum** (2411-2001 (9 AM to 5 PM, closed Tuesdays) on Kwu Uk Kane is a 200-year-old walled village that exhibits farming implements and highlights the daily life of the Chinese Hakka clans of the New Territories. The Hakkas migrated into southern China from the north several centuries ago. You'll see the Hakka women

---

Although Hong Kong imports most of its food from mainland China, many of the fresh market vegetables found locally are grown in the New Territories.

all over the New Territories, distinctive for their wide-brimmed and fringed black hats, and on the construction sites in the urban areas, where they've made it a tradition to work as laborers.

A short taxi ride from the MTR station will take you to **Lo Wai Village** and the **Yuen Yuen Institute** (9 AM to 5 PM daily), a temple complex dedicated to Buddhism, Daoism and Confucianism, and featuring a replica of Beijing's Temple of Heaven. Vegetarian food is available.

TUEN MUN

In the center of Tuen Mun's high-rise housing estates you'll reach two of the most interesting places of worship in Hong Kong, the **Ching Chung Koon Temple** at Tuen Mun and the **Miu Fat Monastery** at nearby Castle Peak. Ching Chung Koon, next to the Ching Chung LRT station, is a purely Daoist temple, also known as the "Temple of Green Pines" and packed with garish images and altar guardians that were carved in Beijing 300 years ago. It's dedicated to Liu Tung Bun, one of the Daoist Eight Immortals, legendary beings who have been deified as superior human spirits, or fairies, and have the power to become invisible and bring the dead back to life.

Among Ching Chung Koon's other treasures are its famous bonsai collection; a series of lanterns, more than 200 years old, which once decorated the Imperial Palace in Beijing; a 1,000-year-old jade seal; and a library of 3,872 books covering 4,000 years of Daoist history. The temple is also a sanctuary for elderly people without homes or families, who live within the complex and are supported by visitors' donations.

At Castle Peak's Miu Fat Monastery you're confronted by what could, without irreverence, be called Buddhism Inc. It's a huge, multi-storied temple, packed on most days with worshippers and visitors, and virtually lined throughout with thousands of small Buddha images and niches paid for by the faithful to gain merit and to keep the establishment in the style to which it has become accustomed. And that style, judging from its latest renovations, is considerably upmarket.

Sunrise over fish farms in the New Territories.

The New Territories

Miu Fat has many treasures, including the beautiful gilded images of the Three Precious Buddhas that decorate the altar in the main temple. The central figure of these Buddhas represents the founding Sakyamuni Buddha — he is flanked by the Healing Buddha on one side and by the Lord of the Western Paradise (which is the Chinese Buddhist version of Nirvana) on the other.

Miu Fat also boasts a large vegetarian restaurant, where the lunch menu is as good as any in Hong Kong.

Long, is a worthwhile excursion. The ancestral hall at Kun Ting is one of the largest in the New Territories, comprising three halls and two internal courtyards. The hall remains in use today. The study hall was built around 1870 mainly for education and ancestral worship. Nearby, you'll find the ancient, hexagonal **Tsui Shing Lau Pagoda**, constructed in the fourteenth century to ward off evil spirits. Somewhat diminished in size from seven stories to three, the pagoda used to rise up out of a rustic swathe of duck farms and rice paddies — today

HOW TO GET THERE

From Hong Kong Island, take the Tuen Mun hoverferry from Pier No. 5 in Central; from Kowloon, take the MTR to Tsuen Wan, then bus No. 66M, or take bus 68X from the Jordan Road terminus. From Tuen Mun the Light Rail Transit (LRT) goes to both destinations; to reach Ching Chung Koon Temple alight at Ching Chung station and to reach Miu Fat Monastery go to Lam Tei station.

YUEN LONG

For another look at traditional Chinese life, the **Kun Ting Study Hall** in Ping Shan, which is a few kilometers west of Yuen

most of the farms have disappeared and the pagoda is now dwarfed by recent high-rise development.

East of Yuen Long, **Kam Tin Walled Village**, or **Kat Hing Wai**, has all the character, sights and smells of Old China, although its inhabitants now get so many tourists they not unreasonably "request" a donation (HK$5 is reasonable; HK$1 is the least you can give) when you enter and a fee for posing for photographs. Surrounded by high brick walls and a moat, the village was built in the 1600s by the Tang clan. It was fortified as protection both against the pirates who operated from Hong Kong and Kowloon and warring factions in this, a peripheral southern area which has always lain far beyond the centers of imperial authority to the north. There was also a "walled" city in urban Kowloon, near the old Kai Tak Airport, but it was established for a far different reason. The area was left exempt from the colonial lease on the New Territories to provide a safe haven, or diplomatic quarters, where Chinese government officials could reside and conduct business as ambassadors to the colony. Until the early 1990s, when the buildings were completely demolished and the site transformed into a park, it was home to more than 50,000 people.

LAU FAU SHAN

On the edge of Deep Bay, and right next to the huge new township of Tin Shui Wai, **Lau Fau Shan** is an interesting little fishing settlement which has been the center of the oyster farming industry in Hong Kong for many years: the entire township is built on discarded oyster shells. It's a dying industry these days because of the increasing pollution in Deep Bay; previously, most of the oysters were exported or turned into oys-

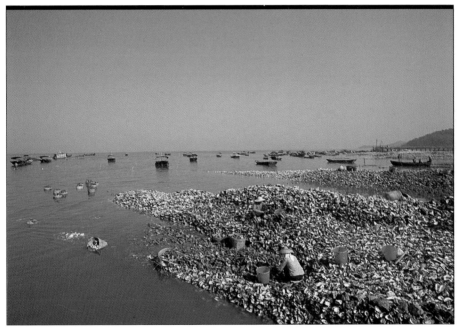

How to Get There

From Hong Kong Island, take the Tuen Mun hoverferry from Pier No. 5 in Central, then the LRT to Ping Shan station. From there the ancestral hall is a 30-minute walk along Ping Ha Road, so if you see a taxi, grab it. If you're coming from Kowloon, it would be best to take the MTR to Tsuen Wan station then bus No. 68M to Yuen Long. You can also catch bus No. 68X from the Jordan Road terminus but the journey is quite long, taking about one and a half hours. Once in Yuen Long, take the LRT to Ping Shan station, or go by taxi. To reach the walled village, take bus No. 64K from Yuen Long to Tai Po (it passes Kam Tin en route).

ter sauce. There are still some popular seafood restaurants here, though.

To get to Lau Fau Shan from Yuen Long, hop on bus No. 655, or take a taxi.

THE BORDER AREAS

Further north at San Tin are the ancestral halls, **Man Lun-Fung** and **Man Shek Tong**, along with a stately traditional Chinese official's house, **Tai Fu Tai**, which has been beautifully restored. Built in 1865 by the Man clan, the mansion is decorated with wood carvings, murals and terracotta figures. It's now the

OPPOSITE and ABOVE: Oyster shells festoon the waterfront and streets of Lau Fau Shan in the New Territories.

highlight on the HKTA Heritage Tour (see TAKING A TOUR, page 90 in YOUR CHOICE). Just beyond San Tin is **Lok Ma Chau** lookout point, which for more than three decades was the closest most foreigners were able to get to China. Along with the Lo Wu Bridge to the east, it was a point where tour groups could mount observation towers and look across rice paddies, duck farms and the Shenzhen River and boast later that they actually saw "Red China." Nowadays, of course, the ducks and paddy fields have been replaced by the towering skyscrapers of

days) is believed to have been constructed in 1525.

Po Sang Yuen Bee Farm produces the most exquisite honey and invigorating honey drinks. The farm is near the KCR station; to arrange a visit call (2669-5840.

A short taxi ride from the town center, the **Hong Kong Golf Club** has three championship courses, which are open to visitors, but on weekdays only. For more details see SPORTING SPREE, page 35 in YOUR CHOICE.

For naturalists, the **Luk Keng Bird Sanctuary** at Starling Inlet in the far northeast

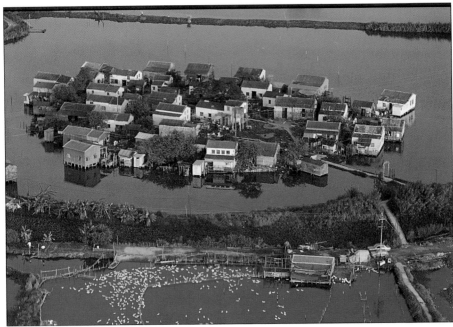

Shenzhen's Special Economic Zone. With the China door wide open to tourism, you can get a visa on the border nowadays and see the real thing.

Heading east you'll arrive at **Fanling**, on the main KCR railway line, once just a farming community but now a booming town. But despite its progress, Fanling has still managed to retain some of its past, which can be seen at **Luen Wo Market** — a traditional rural market with stalls selling dried fish and mushrooms, thousand-year-old eggs, herbal medicines, bean curd, goldfish and paper offerings; it's at its best from 10 AM to noon. The recently restored **Tang Chung Ling Ancestral Hall** (9 AM to 1 PM, 2 PM to 5 PM, closed Mondays, Tuesdays and Fri-

of the New Territories combines a study of egrets and herons, and their breeding season from March to September, with another vantage point for views of China.

To get even closer to the border, you can carry on to **Sha Tau Kok** at the mouth of the bay, but again, you can just as easily get a bus or train to the Shenzhen Special Economic Zone or the train to Guangzhou in mainland China.

HOW TO GET THERE

To get to Lok Ma Chau, take a taxi from Sheung Shui KCR station. San Tin and Tai Fu Tai are also best reached by taxi from either Sheung Shui or Yuen Long.

Luk Keng Bird Sanctuary isn't as difficult to get to as you would expect — from Fanling KCR station minibus No. 56K takes you right there.

TAI PO

Tai Po is a fast-changing "new town," though the market for which it was once renowned still remains, and remains a lively place. For railway enthusiasts, the old Tai Po Market station has been preserved and tarted up and turned into the **Hong Kong Railway Museum** (2653-3339 (9 AM to 5 PM, closed Tuesdays), featuring an exhibition gallery, old coaches and a mock-up of a modern-day electric-powered coach. Nearby, two Tin Hau temples have also been restored — one is near the Railway Museum on Fu Shin Street and the other across the river on Ting Kok Road.

At Shek Kong, west of Tai Po, is **Kadoorie Experimental Farm** (2488-1317 on the northwestern slope of Hong Kong's tallest mountain, Tai Mo Shan. Established in 1951, the farm was originally set up to teach modern agricultural techniques to refugees from over the border. The property is beautifully landscaped with steep terraces of pools, crops and trees, and the view from the top of the slope is magnificent. If you're interested in visiting, please give the farm at least two day's notice. To reach Kadoorie Experimental Farm from Tai Po Market KCR station take either bus No. 64K or 65K. Keep your eyes peeled for the farm entrance, on the left side of the road, as it's easy to miss.

PLOVER COVE

Plover Cove, north of Tolo Harbor, is an excellent destination for a day of exploring. Weekends, as is the case with all but the most remote corners of Hong Kong, sees it inundated with cars, picnickers and hikers, so try and choose a weekday.

The **Plover Cove Reservoir** was once part of the sea. In the early 1970s the inlet was closed off, the entire bay sealed, the seawater pumped out — and the monsoon rains did the rest. Now it's one of Hong Kong's main guarantees against its old summertime

agony: either too much rain, with accompanying land slips and death and injury; or not enough, with accompanying strict water rationing.

The reservoir, inevitably, has taken off as a tourist attraction, with bicycles and rowboats for rent, dozens of barbecue areas (bring your own supplies) and two short nature trails. The Country Park Visitor's Center at **Tai Mei Tuk** (head north from the bus stop for about 400 m / 440 yd and it's just off the main road) has information about these trails as well as displays on the flora, fauna and geology of the area. But to be sure of getting the detailed trail brochures in English, call in at the Country Parks Office before you go (393 Canton Road, Kowloon), or the Government Publications Center next to Pacific Place in Admiralty. The Countryside Series map for the area is No. 5.

The easiest of the trails is the one-kilometer (half-mile) **Bride's Pool Nature Trail**, which passes the 15-m-high (50-ft) Bride's Pool Waterfall, named after a bride who supposedly plunged to her death here long ago as she was being carried in her sedan chair on the slippery path above the waterfall. To get to the start of the trail, though, you'll have to walk along the main Bride's Pool Road for about an hour or hail a passing taxi (the No. 75K bus goes to Bride's Pool from the Tai Po KCR station, but only on Sundays and public holidays). The trail is well signposted.

The **Pat Sin Leng Nature Trail**, a four-kilometer (two-and-a-half-mile) hike that starts near the Visitor's Center and ends at Bride's Pool, is more demanding but more rewarding, with wonderful views of the reservoir and Pat Sin mountains. Allow about two hours for the walk, though you can always cut it short and take a side loop just after Stop No. 8, which will bring you back to the start in about half-an-hour. It's possible to combine both trails in one go.

To get to Plover Cove, take the MTR to Kowloon Tong, change to the KCR line and get off at Tai Po Market. The 75K bus at the terminal outside goes directly to Plover Cove, a 30-minute ride that ends at Tai Mei Tuk at the edge of the reservoir.

This small fishing village has been built on stilts and reclaimed land.

SAI KUNG PENINSULA

There's one other interesting place to visit on the "other side" and that's the **Hebe Haven** and **Sai Kung** area, where a cluster of old villages around the shallow bay are rapidly being transformed into marine resorts. If you feel like taking a rest from the shopping plazas and packed streets of the urban tourist districts, or feel the need to lay back and get your feet up after your New Territories tour, you'll find relative tranquility, windsurfing and other water sports, blazing sunsets, interesting fishing communities, and wonderful hiking in the country parks.

From Choi Hung MTR station in Kowloon, bus No. 92 and minibus No. 1 both go to Sai Kung town via Hebe Haven.

CLEAR WATER PENINSULA

Clear Water Bay is another quite dramatic area of beaches, country parks and fishing communities, along with the **Tin Hau temple (Ta Miu)** in **Joss House Bay**. The temple, which has been restored a number of times, is thought to have been built in the thirteenth century, toward the end of the Song (Sung) dynasty. If you happen to be in Hong Kong for the Tin Hau Festival, held each year to celebrate the birthday of Tin Hau (Goddess of the Sea), on the twenty-third day of the third lunar month, that is, April or May — then head for Joss House Bay where you'll see thousands of fisherfolk in festively decorated boats paying their respects to the goddess.

From Choi Hung MTR station take bus No. 91 to the entrance of the Clear Water Bay Golf Club. From there follow the signposts to the temple.

THE TOUR TRAIL

The simplest way to get around the dispersed sights of the New Territories is with a tour either through the HKTA or any of several private tour operators (see TAKING A TOUR, page 90 in YOUR CHOICE, for details). The HKTA Land Between Tour, for example, takes in the Bamboo Forest Monastery near Tsuen Wan, Tai Mo Shan mountain, the fish and duck farms of Shek Kong, the golf club at Fanling, Luen Wo market, the bird sanctuary at Luk Keng, Plover Cove Reservoir, a fishing village in Tolo Harbor, Tai Po, the Chinese University and Shatin.

It's an interesting tour and quite reasonably priced considering the distance it covers (HK$365 for adults and HK$315 for children). But it's also becoming increasingly difficult to promote and sustain, with the amount of new development that's going on throughout the area. In many places, especially around the gigantic "new towns," the old rustic paddy life is scarred by major construction, new roads and drainage systems, and its traditional tranquility can only be glimpsed through convoys of huge dump-trucks and their clouds of exhaust. But then, development is as much — if not more — a matter of pride in Hong Kong as tradition.

WHERE TO STAY

While the New Territories make an interesting excursion, hardly any foreign travelers stay overnight. To be honest, there is absolutely no reason to.

The luxury **Gold Coast Hotel** (2452-8888 FAX 2440-7368, 1 Castle Peak Road, Castle Peak Bay, has to be seen to be believed. For a start, it's big. Situated on the coast in 40.5 ha (100 acres) of landscaped gardens, the 18-story, 450-room resort's facilities include fine restaurants, a spa, adult and children's swimming pools, a chip and putt golf and driving range, water sports facilities, squash and tennis courts, a fitness center, a nightclub, a business center and conference facilities, and its own hoverferry service from Central and Tsimshatsui East. Rates are very reasonable at around US$140 and upwards.

The **New Beach Resort** (2791-1068 FAX 2792-7102, Tai Mong Tsui Road, Sai Kung, has its own beach, swimming pool and recreational amenities. It's more of a getaway for Hong Kong residents than for visitors from abroad. It's about one kilometer (half a mile) from Sai Kung town, and is best reached by taxi. Rates are around US$100.

Of the four hostels in the New Territories, the easiest to reach is the **Bradbury Lodge** (2662 5123, Tai Mei Tuk, Tai Po. From Tai Po KCR station, take bus 75K to Tai Mei

Tuk. It's a couple of minutes walk south of the bus terminal. Dormitory beds start at HK$35.

WHERE TO EAT

Shatin is one of the best known dining districts in the New Territories. Firmly docked on the Shing Mun River Channel, the three-decked marbled concrete **Treasure Floating Restaurant** (2637-7222, 55 Tai Chung Kiu Road, offers *dim sum* and seafood. At night the restaurant is a blaze of lights, and is a popular place to eat after a day at the races. On the same road, the **Regal Riverside Hotel** ((8852) 2649-7878 has Thai, Western and seafood restaurants along with a disco and karaoke rooms. Another good spot is the 50-year-old Lung Wah **Hotel Restaurant** (2691-1594, 22 Ha Wo Che, which is famous for its pigeon and bean curd dishes.

If you've taken time out to explore Sai Kung Country Park, its beaches and surrounding islands, the picturesque fishing port of Sai Kung is a convenient stop-off point for lunch and dinner, or even breakfast. The town has a number of street-side cafés, nothing fancy, as well as excellent Cantonese seafood restaurants such as **San Shui** (2792-1828, Ground Floor, 7-15 Siu Yat Building, Lot 941, New Town, which has some interesting dishes on its menu — barbecued fish in bamboo stems, fried clams with black beans and chilies and stuffed cuttlefish. On Fook Man Road, the **Duke of York Pub** (2792-8435 offers pub fare and cold beer, while **Susanna's** (2792-2139, 7 Man Nin Street, is a friendly place that does a brisk business in Mediterranean dishes.

Fish traps adorn the foreshores of Po Toi O Bay in the New Territories.

The Outlying Islands

USUALLY THE LAST THING ON FOREIGN VISITORS' LISTS OF THINGS TO DO, the pleasures of Hong Kong's outlying islands are generally left to Hong Kong's residents, many of whom to choose to live on them — drawn by the quieter lifestyle, lower rents and relatively stress-free water-borne commutes into the hustle and bustle of Central. Curiously, while these islands are called "outlying" they're nothing of the sort: Lamma lies not far to the south of Hong Kong Island, while Lantau, the largest, lies directly east of Hong Kong Island. But then, for the residents of Hong Kong, anywhere that is not Hong Kong is "outlying."

In many ways, the islands, in particular Lantau and Lamma, make for more pleasant getaways than the more popular New Territories, especially mid-week, when it is often possible to enjoy the leisurely lunches and ambling walks in near solitude. Offering walks and hikes as well as old temples and interesting fishing villages, the islands are an area of Hong Kong that most tourists don't even know exists.

Not that development isn't taking its toll. Cheung Chau, for example, has been transformed from a bustling fishing community with a bay packed with junks — where waterfront cafés provide rustic salons for an expatriate and Chinese community of artists, photographers and media people — into a paved residential "new town." But the biggest offshore development has taken place at Discovery Bay on the southern tip of Lantau Island — a largely undeveloped island that's actually one-and-a-half times the size of Hong Kong. Discovery Bay has been turned into a vast, constantly growing residential resort of high-rise apartment blocks and beach front condominiums, with its own shopping center, sports and social club and fire station, and a 24-hour hovercraft service linking its largely executive community with Central District.

A decade ago, the plan was to retain Lantau as Hong Kong's biggest parkland and nature reserve, but the pressure for new development, particularly in middle- and upper-class residential property — and the advent of the new airport at Chek Lap Kok off Lantau's northern coast, has put paid to that. While Lantau is still a comparative

wonderland of soaring, untouched hillsides and mountain peaks, with tremendously inspiring views and hiking trails, its days are numbered as a parkland. It is now the site of the next big property boom.

LANTAU

Lantau is, in fact, a whole new Hong Kong. It is nearly twice the size of Hong Kong Island, and despite the arrival of Chek Lap Kok International Airport remains relatively undeveloped, offering magnificent hiking,

camping, fishing and other recreational pursuits. It also features a colossal Buddha statue, monasteries, temples, a fort and even has a small tea plantation. The island broods just beyond the urban jungle of Hong Kong — dark and silent and huge and almost mysterious at night, a rustic green rolling switchback of hills in the day's sun.

Ferries from Central run to **Silvermine Bay**, also known by its Chinese name, Mui Wo, or "Five Petal," the island's major township. It's named after a silver mine which once operated north of the town. The

OPPOSITE AND ABOVE: Two faces of Lantau Island — twice the size of Hong Kong Island and only marginally settled and developed, Lantau so far has remained one of the territory's main areas of open-air recreation.

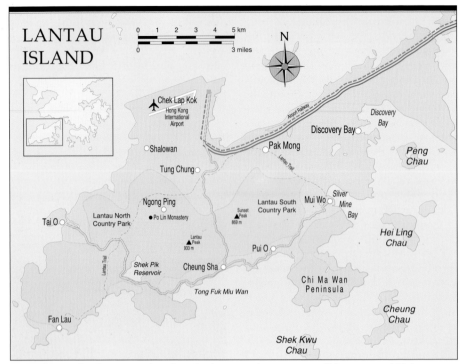

LANTAU ISLAND

0 1 2 3 4 5 km
0   3 miles

N

Chek Lap Kok
Hong Kong
International
Airport

Airport Railway

Discovery Bay

Discovery Bay

Peng Chau

Shalowan

Pak Mong

Lantau Trail

Tung Chung

Ngong Ping

Po Lin Monastery

Lantau South
Country Park

Mui Wo

Silver Mine Bay

Hei Ling Chau

Tai O

Lantau North
Country Park

Sunset Peak
869 m

Lantau Peak
933 m

Pui O

Lantau Trail

Shek Pik
Reservoir

Cheung Sha

Chi Ma Wan
Peninsula

Cheung Chau

Tong Fuk Miu Wan

Fan Lau

Shek Kwu
Chau

town has a fairly upmarket hotel, the Silvermine Beach Hotel, and also has an indoor sports center with swimming pool and squash courts.

But the prime reason for visiting Lantau is the beautiful **Po Lin (Precious Lotus) Buddhist Monastery** (10 AM to 5:45 PM daily), which lies on the high Ngong Ping plateau close to Lantau Peak. To get there take bus No. 2 from Mui Wo Pier, passing the **Shek Pik Reservoir**. Po Lin was first established in 1905 by a group of reclusive Buddhist monks, and the present temple complex dates back to 1927. It's the most important Buddhist center in Hong Kong, and once every three years it attracts hundreds of novice monks from all over Asia for special study and prayer. The main temple features three magnificent bronze Buddha images — Sakyamuni, the Healing Buddha and the Lord of the Western Paradise; and an even more spectacular one — the "world's largest" outdoor bronze Buddha statue (34 m/ 112 ft high and weighing 275 tons) which, on a clear day, can be see from as far away as Macau. Vegetarian food is available.

At the nearby **Tea Gardens (** 2985-5161 — Hong Kong's only commercial tea plan-

tation — stop off for a cup of Chinese tea, or even stay overnight in one of their (very basic) bungalows and spend the next day watching the picking and processing of several varieties of tea.

From Silvermine Bay, buses run to **Tai O**, on the northwestern shoreline of the island, a small fishing and market town which for more than a century was the center of the salt-panning industry in Hong Kong. Now, Tai O is more famous for its seafood restaurants, which cluster along the waterfront, and its fisherfolk huts on stilts above the muddy estuary.

Tai O has an eighteenth-century **Kwan Tai Temple**, dedicated to the God of War and Righteousness, a deified general who lived in the Three Kingdoms Period (AD 220–265) and who is remembered for his crusades against injustice and corruption. Two other temples have been renovated: **Han Wong**, overlooking the bay, and **Kwan Yum**, just outside the village. There's also a direct ferry service to Tai O from Central District, during the weekends and on public holidays only, which calls in at a small coastal village, Sha Lo Wan, along the way.

Another route from Silvermine Bay goes to the foot of **Sunset Peak**, a 869-m (2,851-ft) mountain which offers blissful solitude and rest for those who find the clamor of Hong Kong too much to take. It's an arduous three-hour climb to the peak, up a winding path that leads through woodlands and misty meadows, but the effort is rewarded with cool breezes, and panoramic views of Lantau Island and a great deal of the rest of the territory. Camp up here and you may awake in the mornings to the clang of cow-bells, as a herd of dairy cattle feeds on the lush hilltop grasses. The old stone huts are for the use of companies and community groups, who rent them for employees and members in need of a break from it all.

Down below, in the village of **Pui O**, a Sunset Peak expedition can be rounded off with a meal and bottle of wine in one of Hong Kong's most unusual and most popular "outlying" restaurants. Alight from the bus near the Pui O village school and walk up the hill that rises from the right-hand side of the road to **Charlie's** (see WHERE TO EAT, below, for details).

Another hoverferry and high-speed ferry service goes from Star Ferry in Central District to the **Discovery Bay** residential resort on the northeastern coastline of Lantau. It's a new executive-class dormitory of high-rise blocks and two- and three-story beachfront condominiums with a sweeping man-made beach where windsurfers and sailing dinghies can be rented for the day. It also has a 27-hole top-class golf course (see SPORTING SPREE, page 35 in YOUR CHOICE).

Behind Discovery Bay a path leads up and over the steep mountainsides to another of Lantau's main cultural attractions, the **Trappist Monastery**. Built in 1956 by Cistercian monks, the monastery supports itself through a dairy farm at Yuen Long, which provides fresh milk to some of Hong Kong's major hotels. It welcomes visitors, and offers cheap accommodation at about HK$150 a day — for inquiries call (2987-6292. Another way to reach the monastery is to take the Silvermine Bay ferry to Peng Chau Island from Central (but make sure it's the ferry that crosses via Peng Chau), and then cross by small motorized boat,

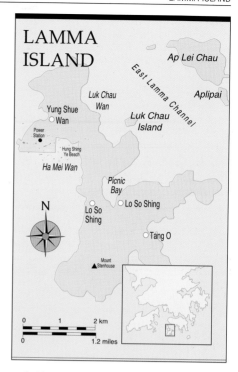

or *kaido*, to the hillside on which the monastery stands.

LAMMA ISLAND

Lamma Island is the closest of Hong Kong's other islands, and again it's largely undeveloped — except for the Hong Kong Electric Power Station on the northwest waterfront — and still nods sleepily in a rustic atmosphere of small villages and fishing havens. The ferries go to two destinations, **Yung Shue Wan**, or "Banyan Tree Bay" in the north near the power plant, and **Sok Kwu Wan**, which lies in the island's narrow central spine.

A good idea is to take the ferry to Sok Kwu Wan and walk over the spine of the island to Yung Shue Wan. It's a steep walk of around an hour, with fine views along the way. Yung Shue Wan, with its harborside seafood restaurants, is a welcome reward at the end. There are frequent ferries from here back to Central.

Lamma features several good beaches, many countryside walks, including a strenuous climb up its main peak, **Mount Stenhouse**, along with interesting village life and two Tin Hau temples, one in each major town. But it's famous above all for its seafood restaurants, which virtually line the waterfront in both Yung Shue Wan and Sok Kwu Wan. Those in Sok Kwu Wan are probably the most popular because the environment is more pleasant — a bay filled with fish-traps. On weekends, tourists and local residents flock there to pack the covered alfresco eating places, feasting off deep-fried spiced crab, prawns, mussels, oysters and prawns. Yung Shue Wan also has a lively expatriate community and many bars and restaurants.

CHEUNG CHAU

N

Radar Station
Tung Wan
Tsai Beach

Pak Tai
Temple

Cheung Chau
Harbour

Kwun Yam
Wan Beach

Hung Shing
Temple

Fa Peng

Cheung Po
Tsai Cave

Nam Tam
Wan Beach

Observatory

CHEUNG CHAU

Cheung Chau is less scenic than Lamma, but it has a popular huddle of seafood restaurants on its main waterfront, or Praya. There's also a huge fishing and trading fleet, including many junks, that sits off the promenade. At the boat-building yard next to the harbor, traditional fishing junks, elegant teak and yakal pleasure junks were once constructed, in a confusion of crowded slipways. Nowadays, the yard mostly just does repairs and the occasional building of a new fishing trawler.

Cheung Chau was once a thriving port, watering place and market town for junks plying the South China Coast to and from

Macau, and had a busy, well-developed society long before Hong Kong itself was settled. Much of that society remains — clans and trade guilds still dominate the island's industrious but carefully paced fishing and business life. For some years the island has been a place of retreat for foreign writers, photographers and other "media types" anxious for a more relaxed lifestyle than that of the urbanized main island and Kowloon. But the peace and quiet pace is blown away every April or early May for the week-long **Bun Festival**,

held to appease the spirits of victims of a plague that swept Cheung Chau in the later 1880s. As huge towers loaded with buns loom over the island's most famous cultural monument, the **Pak Tai Temple** to the east of the Praya, parades, lion dances and processions clash, bang and howl along the waterfront day after day, highlighted by children in ornate traditional costumes harnessed on tall poles so that they seem to be floating over the mêlée. An altar near the Pak Tai Temple bears giant papier-mâché effigies of the God of the Earth, God of the Mountains and the black-faced Lord of the Ghosts. Throughout the festival, no meat is eaten on the island, so the restaurant fare is strictly vegetarian.

At other times, Cheung Chau is a place for strolling, especially through the market stalls and narrow streets of the waterfront area, where you'll find small factories and workshops engaged in traditional arts and crafts. Its main temples are quite dramatic — the Pak Tai Temple, built in 1783, features images of its supreme deity, the Spirit of the North, also known as the Supreme Emperor of the Dark Heaven and Protector of all Seafarers, along with the attendant gods Ten-Thousand Mile Eye and Favorable Wind Ear.

swim, laze on the beach, eat excellent Portugese or Chinese-style seafood at one of the many restaurants along the Praya, or go windsurfing. The **Cheung Chau Windsurfing Center** (see SPORTING SPREE, PAGE 35 in YOUR CHOICE), just past the Warwick Hotel on Tung Wan Beach, is where local Cheung Chau girl, Lee Lai Shan — who won Hong Kong's first gold medal in the 1996 Olympics — first learned to windsurf. You can rent equipment here and have a go yourself, or just sit at the Center's open-air café and watch other Olympic hopefuls.

A sampan ride from the Praya to Sai Wan will take you to **Tin Hau Temple** and the **Cave of Cheung Po Tsai**, a notorious pirate who once menaced the seas from Cheung Chau. Inland from the Praya there's another small temple, the **Kwan Kung Pavilion**, dedicated to the martial god, Mo, of the Man Mo Temple on Hong Kong Island.

The **Kwun Yum Temple**, to the east of the pavilion, commemorates Guanyin, the Goddess of Mercy, and the **Kwai Yuen Monastery** is a small and remote place of worship to the south.

On weekends, especially during the summer, Cheung Chau is packed with local holiday-makers who come here to

WHERE TO STAY

While very few travelers do, staying on one of the outlying islands for the duration of a Hong Kong stay is not such a bad idea. Rates — particularly mid-week — are very affordable, the surroundings relaxing, and from most island destinations it's just half an hour to Central by ferry. It does curtail your nightlife options somewhat, however, as many ferry services stop by midnight.

OPPOSITE: Po Lin Monastery high on Ngong Ping plateau, Lantau. ABOVE: For centuries boat-building has been one of the traditional occupations for villagers in the outlying islands. OVERLEAF : Cheung Chau, a comfortable 50-minute ride by air-conditioned ferry from Hong Kong Island, is one of the most densely populated outlying islands.

Cheung Chau's **Warwick Hotel** (2981-0081 FAX 2981-9174, East Bay, Cheung Chau, is a popular weekend retreat for Hong Kong families, but with a swimming pool and other amenities it is a good place to stay for out-of-towners too. It's a 10-minute walk from the ferry pier.

Lamma Island has several places to stay, including the **Man Lai Wah Hotel** (2982-0220, near the Yung Shue Wan ferry pier, where rooms start at HK$300. Prices double on weekends, but mid-week it's extremely good value compared to Kowloon and Hong Kong. The **Concierto Inn** (2982-1688, Hung Shing Ye Beach, is a wonderful place to stay providing you don't have too much luggage — it's a good 25-minute trudge from the

Yung Shue Wan ferry pier. Rooms start at HK$300, and there's an attached restaurant. Don't think about staying here on weekends, when the beach, restaurant and hotel gets packed with day-trippers and vacationers from Hong Kong.

The **Silvermine Beach Hotel** (2984-8295 FAX 2984-1907, Silvermine Bay, Mui Wo, is the best of Lantau's hotels. It has a pleasant beachfront location, a tennis court, swimming pool and sauna, and rates from around HK$700. The **Mui Wo Inn** (2984 8295, Tung Wan Road, Mui Wo, is a cheaper option, with attractive seaside rooms from HK$300 (HK$600 on weekends). The **S G Davis Youth Hostel** (2985-5610, at Ngong Ping, near the Po Lin Monastery, is another of

Hong Kong's uniformly remote and inconvenient hostels. To get there, take a No. 2 bus from Mui Wo to Ngong Ping and follow a sign-posted track for 10 minutes. Dormitory beds start at HK$35.

WHERE TO EAT

Lamma and Cheung Chau are both famous for their seafront Cantonese seafood restaurants, and on both islands the large number of foreign residents means that there are English menus for easy ordering.

The easiest place to get to for a seafood meal is Lamma Island's main village of Yung Shue Wan, which is around 25 minutes from Central by ferry. The pick of the pack — and

there are quite a few restaurants lining the harborfront — is the **Lancombe (** 2982-0881, 47 Main Street. It has an extensive menu and a wonderful terrace that looks out onto the harbor. The **Lung Wah Sea Food (** 2982-0281, 20 Main Street, is on the left before you reach the Lancombe and has some alfresco tables, as does the nearby and slightly more up-market **Sampan Seafood Restaurant (** 2982-2388. For Western food, the **Deli Lamma (** 2982-1583, 36 Main Street, can be something of a scene, but on a quiet evening is an excellent place to eat. The menu is eclectic, covering pasta dishes and curries, and service can be slow, but it rarely disappoints once the food turns up.

On the other side of the island the small fishing village of So Kwu Wan, or Picnic Bay, is a popular destination for expatriates, who flock there in junkloads during the weekends and evenings to drink and gorge on peppered prawns, chili crab and baked lobster in the many open-air, waterfront restaurants. Recommended are the **Lamma Mandarin (** 2982-8128, **Peach Garden (** 2982-8581, and the **Rainbow Seafood Restaurant (** 2982-8100.

On Cheung Chau, the **Warwick Hotel (** 2981-0081, on the east side of the island, serves Western and Chinese food. But if you'd rather not be in an air-conditioned environment there are plenty of open-air Chinese restaurants along the waterfront promenade, including **Baccarat Restaurant (** 2981-0606, 9A Pak She Praya Street.

Charlie's Restaurant and Bar (2984-8329, 13-14 Law Uk Village, Pui O, is a welcome stop-off point for lunch for those touring around Lantau. The alfresco restaurant offers Cantonese, Indian and Western cuisine, as well as afternoon tea, and has an extensive wine list. Visa, Master Card and Amex credit cards are accepted. It's closed for lunch on Tuesday and all day Wednesday unless you make a prior booking. A little further along the coast is **The Gallery (** 2984-7645 at Tong Fuk, which serves a popular open-air barbecue on weekends and public holidays (bookings on Sundays essential).

An Outlying Islands ferry glides through lighters and fishing trawlers off the central bottleneck of Cheung Chau Island.

Macau

MACAU

ON DECEMBER 20, 1999, HONG KONG'S NEIGHBOR, MACAU, JOINED THE CHINA FOLD. While it was a far more muted affair than the Hong Kong handover two years earlier, in China it was a significant event. At last, the final reminder of China's colonial humiliations was once again Chinese soil. But in Macau China inherited a very different place from Hong Kong. Under Portuguese administration, Macau had evolved into a territory that was at once a Latin-influenced siesta zone and a freewheeling city in which casinos were the major source of wealth. For travelers and tourists it was a place both to have a whirl with the dice and to enjoy the city's equally impressive architecture and food.

Little has changed. The casinos are doing better business than ever, the city may be modernizing but many of its charms linger on, and the food is as good as it ever was. Macau is even home to a nightlife scene that seems healthier today than it ever was under the Portuguese.

All the more reason to visit. An hour from Hong Kong by jetfoil, it is a fascinating laid-back counterpoint to the go-get-it former British colony across the waters.

Macau arose as a trading port for foreigners on the South China Coast long before Hong Kong, having been established by Portuguese traders and missionaries in 1557. In the centuries that followed, though, Macau's trading power gradually gave way to that of Canton (Guangzhou) and the other treaty ports that were opened up by the British in China. Macau was eventually eclipsed by the phenomenal growth of Hong Kong — leaving this tiny mainland enclave with a lot to show in the way of culture, especially its Roman Catholic churches and cathedrals, but with not much else.

Nowadays it's a fascinating blend of Cantonese joss and often crumbling Portuguese architecture — along with the annual roar and high-octane odors of its most celebrated European contribution, the Macau Grand Prix (held on the third or fourth Sunday of November). It's a fascinating place to visit, and for those who linger a day or two, it offers superb dining and luxurious accommodation.

GENERAL INFORMATION

Macau's visa regulations are similar to those of Hong Kong. In other words, visitors from the United States, Australia, New Zealand and Britain and most other European countries are entitled to a visa-free entry for a specified period of time — more than enough to see the sights.

The local currency is the pacata, but Hong Kong dollars are accepted throughout the territory — their values are nearly identical, though the pacata is worth fractionally less.

The **Macau Government Tourist Office** (**MGTO**) ((853) 331-5566 FAX (853) 351-0104, 9 Largo do Senado, Macau, is open daily from 9 AM to 6 PM. The MGTO also has offices at the ferry terminal in Macau and at the airport, both also open daily from 9 AM to 6 PM.

In Hong Kong the MGTO (2549-8884 has an office at Room 1303, Macau Ferry Terminal, Shun Tak Center, 200 Connaught Road, as well as manning an information desk (2769-7970 at Hong Kong's international airport.

ORIENTATION

Macau is actually three fairly distinct entities. The old city is on a peninsula jutting out from mainland China. This peninsula is linked by a bridge to the island of Taipa, which is in turn linked by a bridge to a second island called Coloane.

Macau is a small place — a little over 23 sq km (about nine square miles) — and the city itself is easily explored on foot. For longer trips, taxis are easily flagged down and are very inexpensive.

WHAT TO SEE AND DO

Macau is a wonderful place to explore on foot, mostly due to the fascinating convergence of Portuguese and Chinese influences in the old city's culture and architecture. This confluence of cultural influences can be seen most markedly in the intriguing contrast of Buddhist temples and Roman Catholic churches, and in how much more

Macau

laid-back the Cantonese character is here than in nearby Hong Kong. The comparisons with "Hong Kong 20 years ago" are inevitable, but they're becoming less and less applicable as Macau rebuilds itself. Nevertheless, Macau remains a far less hectic destination than Hong Kong, and it's still possible to stumble across back-street scenes that are long gone in all but the most remote backwaters of the New Territories in Hong Kong.

A good place to start exploring the city is at its very center, where the remains of Macau's emblematic church of **São Paulo** stands. Built between 1602 and 1627, it was destroyed by fire in 1835. Today all that remains of the Portuguese church that was

once Christianity's greatest monument in the East is its façade (carved by Japanese Christians). Still, São Paulo remains a stunning sight, and is Macau's most popular postcard image. The **Museum of Sacred Art** (9 AM to 6 PM, daily), in a vault behind the São Paulo façade, houses religious reliquaries that have been collected from other, Asian churches of similar provenance as São Paulo.

Overlooking the church is the **Fortaleza do Monte**, a nearly-400-year-old fort that in its day was used to keep guard against, and fire at, Dutch ships that strayed too close to Portuguese waters. The fort has been partially renovated, though the interior buildings that were destroyed by fire

It's a pleasant walk a couple of hundred meters northwest of here to the **Luís de Camões Museum** (9:30 AM to 5:30 PM, closed weekends) and the **Camões Grotto and Gardens** (sunrise to sunset). The museum, named after a sixteenth-century Portuguese poet, is notable mostly for the structure it is housed in, a beautiful eighteenth-century villa, but it also has some interesting local history on display. The park is a favorite local gathering place, and a good spot to rest up and watch Macanese doing the same.

Be sure, too, while you are in central Macau, to visit the **Old Protestant Cemetery** (9 AM to 6 PM daily). Most of the gravestones here have been restored, and their epitaphs make fascinating, often touching reading. There are some famous names interred in the cemetery, including the grandfather of Winston Churchill.

East of the central district are a couple of interesting attractions. At the **Lou Lim Ioc Gardens** (sunrise to sunset), a leafy glade in the middle of the city, old men while away the hours playing mahjong and walking their birds. Shut out from the din of the city by a wall, the impeccably maintained gardens are laid out in the classic Chinese style, and make for a wonderful walk. Behind the gardens is the **Memorial Home of Dr. Sun Yatsen** (10 AM to 5 PM, closed Tuesdays). Considered by Chinese as the founder of modern China, Sun lived briefly in Macau during the 1890s, but then he seems to have lived almost everywhere in Asia at some point or another in his wandering, Quixotic career.

in 1835 have not been restored. The fascinating **Museum of Macau** (open 10 AM to 5.30 PM, closed Mondays) is in the base of the fort and provides a brilliant overview of Chinese and Portuguese cultural exchange over the last four centuries. It is highly recommended.

Immediately south of São Paulo are a couple of worthwhile attractions, though none of them is compelling. The **Government Palace** is an elegant colonial building that was formerly the Portuguese seat of power in Macau — it's only very rarely open to the public. Opposite the palace is the **Church of St. Lawrence** (10 AM to 4 PM daily), a beautiful structure that visitors are free to enter.

Above the gardens is the **Guía Fortress and Lighthouse**. The whitewashed lighthouse is very photogenic — built in 1865, this is the oldest lighthouse on the entire Chinese coastline. It can be reached by cable car, or on foot in around an hour, although unfortunately the lighthouse itself is not open to the public. The small white chapel on the hill dates from the early eighteenth century, and while not officially a tourist attraction is often open.

With its Portugese architecture and European lay-out — including a central fountain — the busy town square in front of the city hall in the center of Macau feels far more like Lisbon than China.

Beneath the lighthouse is the Macau Ferry Terminal, where you can find the **Grand Prix Museum** (10 AM to 6 PM daily) and the **Wine Museum** (10 AM to 6 PM).

Unless you happen to be a keen racing fan, or unless you have children in tow (who tend to enjoy the race simulators), the Grand Prix Museum is not likely to be of great interest. The Wine Museum can be more appealing, particularly as it is enlivened by free tastings.

South of the center is the **A-Ma Temple**, at Barra Point, from which Macau derives its name, A-Ma Gau or Bay of A-Ma. The temple's origins are lost in time, but it was here when the Portuguese arrived in 1533, making it the oldest building in Macau. One story has it that the temple was built for a peasant girl who miraculously survived a violent storm on her way to Guangzhou in the early sixteenth century and subsequently re-appeared in Macau as a goddess. The monastery does feature several images of a local peasant girl, along with Buddhist and Daoist statues and a model of an ancient war-junk.

A little south of A-Ma Temple along the waterfront is the **Macau Maritime Museum** (10 AM to 5:30 PM, closed Tuesdays), which concentrates on Portuguese and Chinese maritime links past and present. Excellently presented, the exhibits are a treat, incorporating some interesting examples of different types of boats and artifacts rescued from the many shipwrecks in these parts. It's even possible to take a boat tour of the harbor on a nineteenth-century vessel.

The chief attraction north of the center, which is a mostly residential district, is the **Kuan Iam Tong Temple** on the Avenida do Coronel Mesquita. It is dedicated to the Goddess of Mercy (Kuan Iam, or Guanyin) and features the deity herself costumed in embroidered silk and flanked by 18 Buddha images. There are also images of the Three Precious Buddhas in pavilions and halls placed among elaborately landscaped gardens and fountains.

Macau's two islands are not rich in sights, but they're worth exploring all the same. On Taipa Island, the **Macau Jockey Club** has room for 15,000 spectators, but unless it is a race day there are usually only a few horses, jockeys and trainers here. Of more interest is the nearby **Taipa Village** and **Taipa House Museum**.

Bikes are available for rent in Taipa Village, but it's chief draw is its shore-front restaurants, some of which serve superb quality Chinese food and make the perfect place for a leisurely lunch. The museum is minor, but it is interesting in the way it contrasts the turn-of-the-twentieth-century living styles of the Macau Chinese and Portuguese residents.

On the considerably larger Coloane Island, the **Chapel of Saint Francis Xavier** rates a special visit because of its baroque cream and white, oval-windowed architecture and its relics of the disastrous attempt to Christianize Japan — a crusade that ended with the massacre of hundreds of foreign and Japanese missionaries, priests and Christian followers in 1597 and again in 1637.

Bicycles can be rented at **Coloane Village**, and are a good way to explore the island further.

WHERE TO STAY

It's definitely worth allocating a day or two to stay in Macau, if you are not too pressed for time.

Travelers get much better value for their money in Macau than they do in Hong Kong. Granted, the best in Macau does not quite rival the best in Hong Kong, but Macau exudes an Old World charm that Hong Kong long ago swept aside. Bear in mind that prices for Macau hotels rocket on weekends, when pleasure-seekers from neighboring Hong Kong and Taiwan flock there. Reservations are a good idea, especially in Macau's better hotels. In late November too, during the Grand Prix, it is necessary to make hotel reservations as far in advance as possible.

LUXURY

The **Hotel Lisboa** ((853) 377-666 FAX (853) 567-193 E-MAIL lisboa@macau.ctm.net, 2-4 Avenida da Lisboa, simply has to head any list of luxury hotels in Macau, but not necessarily for the obvious reasons. For a start, this faintly ludicrous orange-colored cylinder is Macau's major architectural landmark. With more than 900 rooms, the Lisboa is Macau's largest hotel, and includes four restaurants and numerous stores and other services for guests and non-guests alike. And then there are the scarlet carpets, the chandeliers, the bell boys and the "ladies with rooms." Blame it on the casino. But, whatever the detractors say, there's no denying that the Lisboa is an experience like no other in China.

its excellent harborfront restaurant is a wonderfully relaxed way to retreat from the bustle of the city. Other less expected treats that make the Mandarin Oriental a perennial favorite include a reputable children's club and even a rock-climbing center. The hotel's heated outdoor pool is another nice touch.

A favorite for Hong Kong residents looking for a romantic weekend is the beautiful **Pousada de São Tiago** ((853) 378-111 FAX (853) 552-170 E-MAIL saotiago@macau .ctm.net, Avenida da República. It is unique

Standard rooms at the Hotel Lisboa, which are in the lower end of the mid-range category, really do not have a lot going for them beyond their price, but the suites — which are more extravagant than their just-over-mid-range price tag might suggest — make a luxurious retreat from the "Crazy Paris Show" and the push and shove of the casino.

A much classier downtown place to stay, though, is the **Mandarin Oriental** ((853) 567-888 FAX (853) 594-859 WEB SITE WWW .mandarin-oriental.com/macau/, 956-1110 Avenida da Amizade, which has the full complement of luxury amenities one would expect of a five-star hotel. Its waterside location is a winner, and alfresco dining in

in that guests get to stay in a seventeenth-century fort. The rooms are superbly appointed in period style and come with balconies overlooking leafy grounds.

The Pousada de São Tiago is easily one of the most atmospheric places to stay in all of China, and attached to it is the lovely Catedral de São Tiago, an eighteenth-century addition.

MID-RANGE AND INEXPENSIVE

One highly recommended mid-range hotel is the **East Asia Hotel** ((853) 922-433 FAX (853) 922-431, 1 Rua da Madeira. One

The Macau Grand Prix — a major annual event.

of Macau's oldest, it has recently undergone a thorough overhaul job and is now a modern, smart and conveniently located place to be situated. Ask for a room on the upper floors, where there are great views to be had.

The **Hotel Metropole** ((853) 388-166 FAX (853) 330-890 E-MAIL mhhotel@macau .ctm.net, 493-501 Avenida da Praia Grande, is another reliable hotel with a good location. Close to the Lisboa, it offers luxurious standards at prices slightly cheaper than the lowest of those at the latter.

Moving down in price is the excellent **Vila Universal** ((853) 573-247, 73 Rua de Felicidade. The less expensive rooms come at budget prices (around US$10), but in all price brackets the Universal gives off a spacious, breezy air that makes it a pleasure to stay in. Friendly staff keep the place spotlessly clean.

Similarly priced, the **Hotel London** ((853) 937-761, 4 Praça de Ponte e Horta, is not quite as winning a place to stay as the Universal, but it has very reasonably priced rooms that are infinitely better value than anything it's possible to find in Hong Kong.

WHERE TO EAT

Many Hong Kong residents pop over to Macau for the food alone. The reason they do so is not for the Chinese food — which is better in Hong Kong — but for the combination of small city ambiance with the great flavors of Macanese cuisine, a curious mixture of Portuguese, African and Cantonese influences.

The famous place for the total Macau dining experience is **Fernando's** ((853) 882-531, 9 Hac Sa Beach, Coloane. Chances are, if someone from Hong Kong says they're going to Macau for dinner, this is where they're going. A beachside bistro with oodles of character and some of the best Portuguese food in the territory — everybody raves about the salads — reservations are essential on the weekends.

Also on Coloane, although far less famous (which means it is generally easier to get a table) is **Cacarola** ((853) 882-226, 8 Rua de Gaivotas, Coloane, which earns

countless repeat visitors for its friendly service and excellent food. Try the squid with black bean salad. The beef with garlic and bacon is also recommended.

In Macau itself, another institution is **Alfonso III** ((853) 586-272 11A Rua Central. Reservations are essential at this intimate and popular restaurant, which serves famously authentic Portuguese fare. Restaurateur Alfonso's three daily specials are chosen according to whatever is freshest at the market, and are thus, for obvious reasons, recommended.

Restaurante Nova Caravela ((853) 356-888, 205 Avenida de Almeido Ribeiro, is a good place to escape to if the crowds are hogging Macau's more famous eating houses. Situated in a restored colonial building, it's the perfect place to sample that Macanese classic — African chicken.

Locals can argue all day over which is the best Portuguese restaurant in town, but the name that comes up most frequently is **A Lorcha** ((853) 313-193, 289 Rua do Almirante Sergio, close to the Maritime Museum. It's by no means the most atmospheric restaurant in Macau, but the food is unfailingly good.

For superb Italian cuisine — indeed possibly the best in Macau — **Pizzeria Toscana**

((853) 726-637, Grand Prix Building, Avenida da Amizade, is directly opposite the Macau Ferry Terminal. It has an excellent wine list, and can be recommended for everything from its antipasto to its delicious desserts.

For top-range Chinese cuisine, try the Hotel Lisboa, where the **Chiu Chau** ((853) 577-666, extension 83001, specializes in the cuisine of the same name. Related to Cantonese cuisine, for many Chinese this is the ultimate in dining, and is a cuisine that features famous dishes such as bird's-nest and shark-fin soup. For *dim sum*, the **Jade Garden** ((853) 710-203, 35-39 Rua do Dr. Pedro J. Lobo, is recommended.

NIGHTLIFE

For many Hong Kong and Taiwanese visitors, there is just one reason to descend on Macau: casinos. It goes without saying that all those who enter do so at their own risk. The odds are stacked in the house's favor. But providing you know exactly how much you have to lose, a quick whirl can be a lot of fun, and who knows…

The **Lisboa** is the biggest, most popular and busiest casino, and the only place in Macau where roulette is still played. There are eight other casinos, including the **Macau Palace** floating casino, the **Kam Pek**, the **Jai Alai** (near the Yaohan Department Store and ferry terminal) and deluxe casinos in the **Mandarin Oriental** and **Hyatt Regency**. You'll find the main Chinese games are roulette, *fan tan*, blackjack and big and small (*dai-siu*). The ranks of slot machines are left to the bread-and-butter punters, Japanese tour groups and other visiting foreigners. The Chinese games are only for experienced gamblers. Best to stay out of it and just watch. Watching Chinese gamble is a fascinating, if not scary, experience — the atmosphere can be very tense.

Macau's most venerable nightlife experience is the **Crazy Paris Show** ((853) 377-666 at the Hotel Lisboa. How it has lasted as long as it has is anyone's guess. Tacky in the extreme, the "naughty" semi-nude dancing modeled on a Parisian cabaret is at moments almost embarrassing, but it never fails to pull the punters in.

The waterfront area on Avenida Marginal Baia Nova has emerged as Macau's new nightlife area over the last couple of years. It's not as sophisticated as Lan Kwai Fong in Hong Kong, but the "docks," as local expats have taken to calling the area, does have some interesting spots for a drink. Oddest of these perhaps is the **MGM Café** ((853) 753-161, which has, for reasons unknown, chosen to theme its decor around the comic superhero Batman.

For something a little more sedate, expats tend to gather for convivial drinking sessions at a number of back-home-style pubs near the racecourse on Taipa Island. The most popular is the **Irish Pub** ((853) 820-708 Shop C-D, Block 6, Edifício Nam San, 116 Avenida Kwong Tung, Taipa. It's a good place to toss darts and knock back a couple of ales.

HOW TO GET THERE

From Hong Kong's Shun Tak Center in Central (access is from the Sheung Wan MTR station), jetfoils, high-speed catamarans and ferries cross the Pearl River Estuary to Macau every 15 minutes, 24 hours a day. Jetfoils are fastest, taking just under an hour and costing around US$20.

All tickets from Hong Kong include a government departure tax. On arrival in Macau, immigration takes no time at all.

An increasingly large number of flights are landing at Macau's international airport, though most of them are from regional destinations.

FROM MACAU TO MAINLAND CHINA

It's possible to cross over to Zhuhai and take a look at this Special Economic Zone without first applying for a visa. Visas are available at the border, though on weekends the queues can be horrendous. It's a short taxi ride from the Macau Ferry Terminal to the border. From Macau there are also daily ferries to Guangzhou. The land crossing to Zhuhai is virtually a hop, skip and a jump from the Macau Ferry Terminal — a five-minute taxi ride.

A mixture of colonial Portuguese and Chinese architecture gives Macau its special East-West flavor.

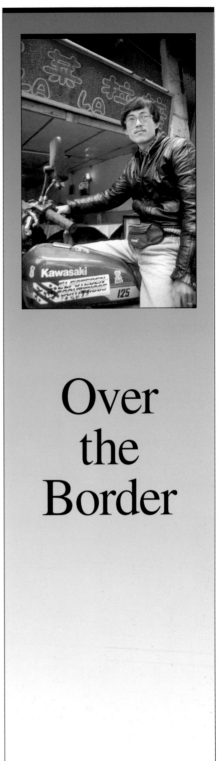

Over
the
Border

WITH EASIER VISA RULES AND GOOD TRANSPORT LINKS, a trip into China proper from Hong Kong (or from Macau) has in recent years become a relatively simple affair. Be warned though: Hong Kong and Macau may well be part of China now, but it's still a different world over the "border."

SHENZHEN

BACKGROUND

Old China hands remember Shenzhen, in the days before the Open Door policy was launched in 1979, as nothing but ricefields, a hamlet, and a border river — a popular place for tourists who were bussed to the Hong Kong side of the border for their first glimpse of the forbidden PRC. Today, Shenzhen is China's capitalist showplace, a city that sprang up overnight, taking mighty Hong Kong by surprise. It's easily China's most successful, most freewheeling Special Economic Zone (SEZ). You don't go there today to catch a glimpse of China, you go to take a look at the future — the combination of high-tech, joint-venture manufacturing and processing and rapid urban development that is being repeated, at a somewhat slower pace, in cities right across the country. Many of these Chinese have the same idea in mind, and Shenzhen has become the target of so many domestic "migrants" — people from poorer areas of China seeking work, especially the higher-than-average wages it offers — that the city has had to throw an electric fence around its export processing zone to keep unauthorized people out. As for Hong Kong, Shenzhen has become both a major business opportunity and something of a pain in the neck. While it's the center of massive cross-border investment and trade, with many Hong Kong Chinese middle-management now moving there to live closer to their factories, it's also a den of corruption and a haven for large-scale smuggling of everything from black market watches and cigarettes to stolen luxury cars — Mercedes Benzes and others — from Hong Kong.

Shenzhen is also set to take some of the infrastructural strain off Hong Kong. The city has its own international airport, which lies around 40 minutes by taxi from the Hong Kong border — flights from here to other China destinations can be as little as half the price of flights bought overseas. It's also developing a major new deep-water port and container terminal at Yantian, aimed at providing a new southern conduit for China's trade.

GETTING AROUND

Shenzhen has arguably the best public transportation system in all of China. Its bus

network is cheap and less crowded than elsewhere, as are the minibuses, which are privately operated and cheap — although the maps and destination information are all in Chinese only, so you may need help. Taxis are ubiquitous and are required to use their meters, though for long distances you will need to bargain a fare.

WHAT TO SEE AND DO

There's very little for visitors to do in central Shenzhen but to stroll around and gawk at the high-rise hotels and prosperous shopping complexes.

The western part of the Special Economic Zone is Shekou port, where hoverferries arrive from Hong Kong. In this area are Shenzhen University and Shenzhen's mind-boggling vacation resorts.

OPPOSITE: Nothing but ricefields, a hamlet, and a border river in 1979, Shenzhen today is a burgeoning city, the center of the nation's most successful, most free-wheeling Special Economic Zone.
ABOVE: Historic Zhenhai Tower now houses a cultural museum.

Two sprawling attractions at the western end of the Special Economic Zone, near Shenzhen Bay, are extremely popular with Chinese tourists but will seem tacky to most Westerners. **Splendid China** reproduces the historical sights of China in miniature; **Window of the World** does the same on a global scale. Minibuses run frequently from the Hong Kong border, or you might take a taxi. CTS and CITS have one-day tours here from Hong Kong which also call at a traditional Hakka village (see TAKING A TOUR, page 89 in YOUR CHOICE).

and restaurants. The four-story atrium features a very pleasant Mediterranean café that is a good place for lunch. Also recommended is the 553-room **Shangri-La (** (755) 233-0888 FAX (755) 233-9878 E-MAIL slz@shangri-la.com, East Side, Railway Station, Jianshe Road, which is less than five minutes from the Lo Wu customs area.

A good place for mid-range accommodation is the **Nanyang Hotel (** (755) 222-4968 FAX (755) 223-8927, Jianshe Road. The staff may not be particularly accommodating, but the rooms are large and well maintained.

Close by and similar in concept to these are 20 **re-creations of the villages** of China's minorities, this time in original size, complete with dancing and daily enactment of minority festivals. Tacky in the extreme.

WHERE TO STAY

Shenzhen has a good range of accommodation, though whether the city is worth an overnight stay is debatable. The city has no shortage of luxury hotels: among the best of them is the **Landmark Hotel (** (755) 217-2288 FAX (755) 229-0473 E-MAIL landmark@szlandmark.com.cn, 3018 Nanhu Road, which, unlike most of its rivals, actually conjures up some atmosphere in its foyer

Also recommended, and possibly the most convenient mid-range hotel in town, given that it's planted on top of the railway station, is the **Dragon Hotel (** (755) 232-9228 FAX (755) 233-7564, a massive structure with red Chinese characters down its side.

If you are looking for bargains, try Hong Kong travel agents (including CTS), which often have special package deals that would otherwise be difficult to find.

WHERE TO EAT

Dim sum breakfast and lunch is widely available and tends to be found on the second and third floors rather than the lobby. Prices are slightly lower than in Hong Kong; you'll probably have to pay in Hong Kong dollars. One recommended place that is popular with Hong Kong visitors is the Dragon Hotel's *dim sum* restaurant, located above the railway station.

The **Banxi Restaurant** ((755) 223-8076, on Jianshe Lu, has long been rated as one of Shenzhen's top places for a seafood meal.

Food Street is a small lane off Renmin Nanlu specializing in seafood and freshwater fish. Make sure you find out the price before you order here, even though prices are generally quite low. Old-timers will

The Kowloon–Canton Railway (KCR) has the fastest and most convenient transport to Shenzhen from Hong Kong. Take a train to Kowloon Tong station and change there for Lo Wu. It's possible to get a one-day visa at the border, providing you stay in the Shenzhen SEZ. Citybus (see above) has eight departures daily to Shenzhen.

There are four hoverferries daily from the China Ferry Terminal in Tsimshatsui (see above) to Shekou, a port on the west side of Shenzhen. The trip takes around 50 minutes.

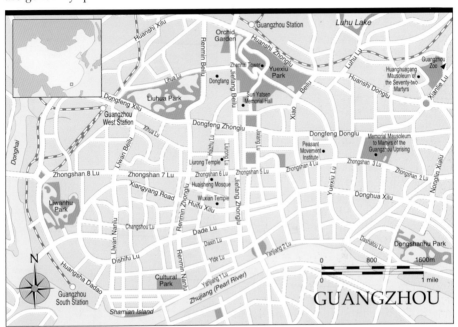

remember this street as the location of China's first McDonald's — today the hallowed site is occupied by a KFC.

HOW TO GET THERE

Shenzhen airport is around 40 minutes by taxi or an hour by minibus from the Hong Kong border. Direct hoverferry services run to the airport from the China Ferry Terminal (China Hong Kong City Building) (2736-1387, Canton Road, Tsimshatsui, Hong Kong, six times daily. The trip takes around one hour. Citybus (2736-3888 runs to Dongguan five times daily, leaving from the basement of the China Ferry Terminal, and stopping at Shenzhen airport.

GUANGZHOU (CANTON)

The capital of China's Guangdong province, Guangzhou is also the country's preeminent southern gateway. From here it's possible to strike out to almost anywhere in China, though it also makes an interesting destination in and of itself.

Guangzhou's climate, along with that of most of the southern region, is subtropical: hot and humid in summer (July and August average 29°C or 84°F), while from July to September the area is prey to heavy monsoon rains and fierce typhoons that boil

A Shenzhen seafood restaurant, where a large selection of live fish and crustaceans is displayed in front of the restaurant for customers to choose from.

up out of the Pacific south of the Philippines and dash themselves, virtually one after the other, on the China coast. The most comfortable time to visit Guangzhou is between October and March, though you should be prepared for cold weather in the height of winter.

BACKGROUND

Like Shanghai and Beijing, Guangzhou is one of China's most modern and progressive cities. Two factors have played a lot in this: first, its Cantonese-speaking population of (unofficially) more than eight million lives on the doorstep of one of the world's most prosperous cities — Hong Kong is just 111 km (69 miles) away; second, as locals like to point out, Guangzhou has some 1,500 years' history of foreign contact, starting with Arab merchant seafarers and then later with Portuguese Jesuits in Macau during the Ming dynasty, and the guns of the British "merchant princes" opening up Guangzhou as a trading port in the seventeenth century.

In the early years of the nineteenth century, Guangzhou was the main arena of the fierce test of strength between the British traders and the Qing throne over the alarming rate at which British opium exports were pouring into the society. In the two Opium Wars that followed, British warships and troops broke the back of the obsolete Qing defenses, grabbed Hong Kong as a colonial trading haven and triggered an international carving-up of Chinese territory and sovereignty that eventually led to the complete collapse of the 4,500-year-old dynastic order. As that collapse approached at the turn of the twentieth century, it was to be the sons and daughters of Chinese merchants and reformists in Guangzhou and the south — some who had been educated overseas, some of them influenced by local foreign missionaries, all of them hungry for modernization and reform — who led the first major rebellions against the Manchu rule. Sun Yatsen, the exiled "spiritual" leader of the reformist movement and the first republican president, was born in Huaxian to the northwest of Guangzhou. In 1923, Guangzhou was where Sun Yatsen gave the nationalist Guomindang Party its final form, the movement that later formed the military backbone of Chiang Kaishek's brutal campaign to exterminate the Chinese communists.

GENERAL INFORMATION

American Express ((20) 8331-1611 is in room 816 of the Guangdong International Hotel (see WHERE TO STAY, below).

Airlines represented in Guangzhou include **Air China** ((20) 8668-1319, **China**

Eastern Airlines ((20) 8668-1688, **China Northwest** ((20) 8330-8058, **China Southern** ((20) 8668-1818, **Malaysia Airlines** ((20) 8335-8828 and **Singapore Airlines** ((20) 8335-8999. **Garuda Airlines** and **Thai International** both have offices at the Garden Hotel on Huanshi East Road.

Consular offices include **Australia** ((20) 8335-0909, in the GITIC Plaza building, and the **United States** ((20) 8188-8911, on Shamian Nanjie, Shamian Island.

Chinese visas, which you will need, are easily obtained in Hong Kong, either directly through the Visa Section of the People's Republic of China **Office of the Ministry of Foreign Affairs** (2585-1794, Fifth Floor, Lower Block, China Resources Building,

26 Harbour Road, Wanchai, or through the China Travel Service (CTS) and China International Travel Service (CITS). But the simplest solution is to apply through a travel agency, almost all of which in Hong Kong offer visa services for China. Visas can be issued within one day.

In Macau, Chinese visas are issued by the **Department of Consular Affairs**, at the Office of the Commissioner of the Ministry of Foreign Affairs of the People's Republic of China ((853) 791-5106, 992 Avenida do Dr. Rodrigo Rodrigues, Macau.

Settlement in the treaty port days; the **northern commercial and tourist district**, which includes the main railway station, the Dongfang and China Hotels, the Trade Center and Yuexiu Park, and the **cultural district**, running to the east along Zhongshan Lu, and featuring the main temples and mosques and monuments to Guangzhou's more recent revolutionary history.

The easiest way to find your way around Guangzhou is by using the new metro line, which after more than six years of digging now has an 18-km (11-mile) east–west line

GETTING AROUND

Guangzhou is a flat, sprawling city, crossed from east to west by a main artery — **Zhongshan Lu** — which is over 15 km (nine miles) in length, and from north to south by two main roads, **Renmin Lu** and **Jiefang Lu**. Circling the central city area is **Huanshi Lu**; the northeast area, Huanshi Donglu, is where many of the best hotels can be found.

If Guangzhou seems at first to be too vast and populous to make sense of, these three major thoroughfares help simplify it by linking up the three principal districts that are of interest to tourists — the **waterfront and Shamian Island**, site of the International

in operation. It won't connect you with the main train station, but for trips around central Guangzhou and connections with Shamian Island it's a convenient way to get around. Essentially, it travels north from Shamian Island before traveling east along Zhongshan Lu, taking in many of the city's prime attractions. Magnetic tickets are fixed at Y6.

For destinations not served by the metro, taxi is the best alternative. Finding one is never a problem — the streets are teeming with them. Fares start at Y8 — reckon on around Y20 for trips around

The Peasant Movement Institute LEFT, and its shrine-like setting ABOVE where Mao Zedong's communist lieutenants were first trained.

town, Y40 to the airport. The only problem is communication: Few drivers speak much English.

Bicycles are available for rent on the street close to the rear entrance of the White Swan (see WHERE TO STAY, below). There's also a good trolley-bus service running between the three districts, but like public buses all over China they're overcrowded, slow-moving and distinctly uncomfortable in the Guangzhou humidity and heat. There's a good English-language tourist map in circulation that can be found at the desks of any of the top hotels.

WHAT TO SEE AND DO

Guangzhou and most of the entire south of China were isolated for many centuries from the imperial seats of power, and therefore are not exactly overloaded with great cultural attractions. However, Guangzhou does have the Guangxiao Temple, dating back to the third century BC, and to this it has added the relics of its foreign trading contacts, its monuments to latter-day rebellion and its special present-day social character to offer itself as a city well worth strolling about and touring.

Being as big and spread out as it is, covering about 60 sq km (36 sq miles), it's also difficult to get around in the space of a few days unless you approach it from the point of view of its three distinct tourist districts — Shamian Island and environs; the northern commercial area around the train station; and the tourist district that includes Yuexiu Park and the complex of temples, and monuments spreading to the east off Zhongshan Lu.

Shamian Island and Environs

Flat and partly reclaimed, Shamian Island is linked by two bridges to the Pearl River waterfront, and is where the "foreign devil" British and French traders and taipans built their warehouses, homes, banks and business headquarters after the British victory in the Opium Wars. The buildings are still there, providing a time warp of sedate, sometimes slightly pompous Victorian architecture. Efforts have been made to renovate some of the old buildings, and some

boutiques and cafés have arrived, giving the area something of a facelift. Gentrification continues to proceed at a snail's pace, though, and for the moment Shamian remains a winning mix of new and old, cafés and bars rubbing shoulders with busy *dim sum* restaurants.

With the entirety of Guangzhou bustling so prosperously it's difficult to believe now how "revolutionary" this area was back when market reforms were tentatively introduced at the tail end of the 1970s. Back then tourists were advised that **Qingping Market**, on Qingping Lu just to the north of Shamian Island, heralded a new era, as they gawked at the caged animals and piles of vegetable produce. Nowadays it's just another market, though a particularly busy one. To the east, across the bridge and along the waterfront, **Renmin Nanlu** was another pioneering commercial district. It has retained that emphasis and is a fascinating district to explore on foot.

Qingping Market in particular is a raucous, friendly, crowded bazaar in which every step and turn of the head is living proof of the Cantonese taste for all things bright and beautiful, all creatures great and small: sugarcane, vegetables and fruit (look for succulent lychees in June and pineapples in October); live catfish and carp; eels, snakes and tortoises in netted bowls, and big fish tanks sprayed continuously from hoses to keep the water aerated; baskets full of chickens and pigeons; caged monkeys, dogs and raccoons; racks hanging with roast dog and a confusing array of butchered furry flesh and offal, all of it bound to be cooked up in the wok. Of course, some animals end up here that shouldn't, and locals can sometimes get irate with shutter-happy tourists. The Guangdong government is stepping up its efforts to stop locals eating endangered species, but is finding it very difficult to enforce. Monkeys are seen less often in Qingping Market, but all this means is that prospective customers now have to ask for "behind the counter" service.

Directly north of the market, along Dishipu Lu, is the **Yuexiu District**, a newly restored collection of old store fronts that now house family restaurants and souvenir operations.

From the market area you can wander north along Haizhu Zhonglu which runs parallel to Renmin Lu, turn right on Huifu Xilu and find the Daoist **Wuxian (Five Immortals) Temple**. It's said to be the spot where more than 2,000 years ago five rams appeared carrying ears of rice in their mouths and ridden by five gods. The gods vanished, but the rams stayed and turned to stone, whereupon the local people began planting rice.

The Wuxian Temple has a large rock in its courtyard bearing a hollow that is said

to be the footprint of one of the gods. It also sports a huge Ming dynasty bell, three meters (10 ft) high and weighing five tons. The bell has no clapper and is believed would warn of impending disaster for the city should it ever make a sound.

North of Wuxian Temple on Guangta Lu, the **Huaisheng Mosque** represents the centuries of Islamic culture brought to Guangzhou by Arab traders. Like most Islamic places of worship, it's quite severely free of ornamentation and idolatry, but its arched gateways and main hall of prayer are an interesting contrast of Moslem and Chinese architecture. It has a minaret that looms over the sweeping, tiled Chinese-style roofs and looks as though it's been rendered

with concrete; but it's said to take its name, Guangta (Smooth Minaret) from this apparently unique surfacing. The mosque dates back to the year AD 627 in the Tang dynasty and commemorates the Arab missionary Saud Ibn Abu Waggas, who was the first to bring the Koran to China.

Further north, on the other side of the main east–west artery Zhongshan Lu, stand the two most interesting Buddhist temples in Guangzhou, the **Guangxiao Temple** and the **Liurong (Six Banyan Trees) Temple** with its towering nine-story **Hua Ta (Flower**

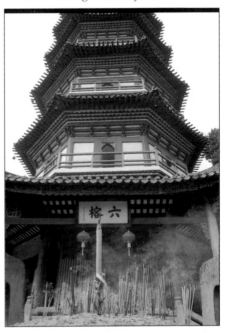

Pagoda). You can't miss the elegant pagoda, which can be reached by walking north along either Haizhu Beilu or Liurong Lu from Zhongshan Lu.

The Liurong Temple was given its name by the renowned poet Su Dongpo, who visited it some seven centuries ago and was captivated by the banyan trees (long since gone) in its grounds. Both Liurong and the nearby Guangxiao Temple were built in honor of Hui Neng, the sixth patriarch of Chan (Zen) Buddhism, and in the grounds of the Guangxiao complex there's an open

Religion re-emerges in the post-revolutionary age —
a worshipper LEFT and joss and towering pagoda
RIGHT at Liurong (Six Banyan Trees) Temple,
Guangzhou.

pavilion featuring frescoes of Hui Neng preaching to the monks and of the Indian monk, Bodhidharma, who is said to have visited Liurong at one stage.

Both temples attract large crowds of Cantonese sightseers and worshippers. Religion is coming back in Guangzhou, and none are happier about it than the elderly men and women who can be seen teaching their grandchildren how to light the joss stick, place it in the incense altars and kowtow to the images.

These two temples are about as far as you can comfortably go in one day's walking, and mark the boundary of Shamian Island and environs exploration.

At night, there's another treat in the Shamian Island district that definitely should not be missed — the **Cultural Park**. This large playground off Liu'ersan Lu and Renmin Nanlu just north of Shsamian Island is where the Cantonese go at night to have fun. It's just as much fun watching them enjoying themselves. In the eerie, ill-lit tropical darkness you come across a fairground and Ferris wheel, a roller-skating rink packed with teenagers, an early Buck Rogers rocket ship space simulator, a shooting gallery with pneumatic "bazookas" that fire tennis balls, a pool hall and the very latest in modernized leisure in Guangzhou — a video arcade.

Meanwhile, at an auditorium near the stage, the high-pitched singsong shriek and clash of gongs announces another act in the continuing story of Cantonese Opera, with its regal and lavishly-costumed princesses, kings and mandarins gliding and flapping about the stage.

Pet Birds and Pagodas

The district from the Dongfang to the China Hotel between Renmin Beilu and Jiefang Beilu places you within close strolling proximity of a number of scenic and cultural attractions. To the north, heading toward the railway station, there's the **Orchid Garden** where, in a landscaped setting, you can view more than 10,000 orchids from 100 species, and visit the seventh-century **Mohammedan Tomb**, claimed to be the burial place of the same Moslem missionary Waggas to whom the Huaisheng Mosque is dedicated.

Directly south of the Mohammedan Tomb, and far more worthy of an hour or so of your time, is the **Nanyue Tomb**. Discovered in 1983, this 2,000-year-old archeological site is home to the tomb of Zhao Mo, the grandson of Zhao Tuo, a Qin dynasty general sent to subjugate the southern tribes, and who, on hearing of the collapse of the Qin dynasty, promptly established his own independent southern kingdom here in Guangzhou.

Liuhua Park, to the west of the Dongfang Hotel, is a pleasant garden set among artificial lakes, but the much larger **Yuexiu Park** on the eastern side of Jiefang Beilu is of more interest for its cultural and social attractions. Take a stroll through Yuexiu Park and inevitably you will find yourself at the **Zhenhai Tower**, the solitary remnant of the old city wall of Guangzhou, and now home to the **Municipal Museum**, which provides a fascinating journey through 2,000 years of local history culminating in a top-floor tea shop with views over the city. West of the tower is the **Five Rams** statue, remarkable only insofar as they celebrate the founding of Guangzhou (nicknamed in Chinese *yangcheng* — "the city of the rams"), which according to legend is owed to the arrival of five immortals riding rams.

Close to Zhenhai Tower there's a monument to Guangzhou's favorite son, Sun Yatsen, but it's a drab concrete monstrosity and could well be given a miss — except on Sundays, when it's a venue for hundreds of bird lovers showing off their caged warblers. On other days of the week a more interesting park diversion is the **Journey to the West Theme Park (Xiyouji Leyuan)**, a tacky but enjoyable tribute to one of China's best-loved tales.

For candid photography in which you run little risk of offending anyone's sensibilities, the **Children's Park** to the southeast of the Sun Yatsen Memorial Hall is a good place to go. You get there by going directly south from the memorial on Jixiang Lu and turning left on Zhongshan Lu.

The Revolutionary Tour

The third main tourist venue of Guangzhou begins roughly at the Children's Park and continues east along Zhongshan Lu. There you'll find the city's contemporary monuments, the **Original Site of the Peasant Movement Institute (Nongmin Yundong Jiangxisuo)**, where in 1926 Mao Zedong trained the cadres, including Zhou Enlai, who were to spearhead his communist revolution. Nearby is the **Memorial Mausoleum to the Martyrs of the Guangzhou Uprising (Qishier Lieshi Mu)**, where, only a year later, these same cadres headed a startling communist takeover of most of Guangzhou, only to be crushed by the ruling Guomindang forces.

To the south of here, and close to the Nongjing Suo metro stop, set back from Yuexiu Lu, is the **Guangzhou City Museum**. Don't be put off by the first-floor exhibition of Guangzhou's industrial products; head upstairs to a fine natural history exhibit and some good selections of Chinese fine arts.

Farther to the northeast along Xi'anlie Nanlu, you can view the **Huanghuagang Mausoleum of the 72 Martyrs**, the monument to a similar, earlier uprising — and a similar reprisal — that took place in April 1911, during the final days of the Manchu Qing rule. Beyond that there's only one major attraction left, **Guangzhou Zoo**, which, like most Chinese zoos, is best passed up unless you're keen on watching pandas and other wildlife in old-fashioned, dank and quite dispirited captivity.

WHERE TO STAY

Guangzhou has a good range of accommodation. However, watch out for the Guangzhou Trade Fair, which is held for a week twice annually, in mid-April and in mid-October. During these periods rooms are almost impossible to secure, and it's not unusual for rates to double.

Luxury

By Chinese standards, Guangzhou has a large number of luxury hotels, and you get better value here than in Hong Kong. Expect to pay from US$170 upwards for a double in the luxury bracket.

With 843 rooms, the **White Swan Hotel** ((20) 8188-6968 FAX (20) 8186-1188 E-MAIL

landmark@szlandmark.com.cn, was one of China's earliest luxury hotels, and it remains top-class by any standards. Its tastefully decorated riverside coffee lounge and vast atrium feature a traditionally styled pavilion and waterfall and a viewing deck on to which visiting Chinese groups are allowed each day to take photos of each other. But the White Swan's main selling point is its location on Shamian Island, the peaceful former foreign concession.

For first-class international standards, the **Furama Hotel Guangzhou** ((20) 8186-

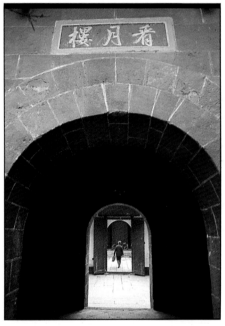

3288 FAX (20) 8186-3388 E-MAIL fhgz@furama -hotels.com, 316 Changdi Lu, is recommended. It has 360 rooms and suites, and the full complement of business and recreational facilities.

The **Garden Hotel** ((20) 8333-8989 FAX (20) 8335-0467 E-MAIL gzgarden@public .guangzhou.gd.cn, 368 Huanshi Dong Lu, is a long-running luxury hotel in Guangzhou with a good location. With its elaborate chandeliered lobby, bowling alley, swimming pool, roof restaurants, disco, coffee lounge, sun decks, bars, boutiques and beauty salons, some travelers claim it is the best in Guangzhou.

The main entrance to Huaisheng Mosque in Guangzhou.

Mid-range

One of Guangzhou's outstanding mid-range options is the renovated **Guangdong Victory Hotel** ((20) 8186-2622 FAX (20) 8186-2413, 53 Shamian Beijie. The location, on charming Shamian Island, is a great plus, but the tastefully appointed rooms with rates from around US$60 are also hard to beat. There's an excellent Cantonese-style restaurant with *dim sum* breakfasts on the ground floor.

The somewhat institutional **Aiqun Hotel** ((20) 8186-6668 FAX (20) 8188-3519, 113 Yanjiang Xilu, (the name means "love the masses") is a massive, refurbished structure that overlooks the Pearl River. Foreign guests rarely stay here, and beyond the front desk English is rarely spoken, but rooms are reasonably priced and a discount of around 20 percent is generally available upon request. Not far from here, the **Guangzhou Hotel** ((20) 8333-8168 FAX (20) 8333-0791, Haizhu Square, is a more upmarket option, where English is spoken and hotel amenities include shopping, hairdressers, restaurants and so on.

Inexpensive

For as long as anyone can remember, the **Guangzhou Youth Hostel** ((20) 8188-4298, on Shamian Island, has had a monopoly on Guangzhou's foreign budget travelers. In the past it was a grim place, where the staff were known to steal from the guests. It has cleaned up its act, renovated, and now has rooms (complete with satellite television) from around US$15.

Nowadays, however, the Shamian Island youth hostel has a rival — a real youth hostel that is recognized by the World Youth Hostel Federation. The **Guangzhou City Youth Hostel** ((20) 8666-6889 extension 3812 FAX (20) 8667-0787, 179 Huanshi Xilu, has basic but clean rooms with private bathrooms for less than US$10 — a real bargain in Guangzhou.

If you don't mind spending slightly more, a superb choice is the **Guangdong Shamian Hotel** ((20) 8188-8359 FAX (20) 8191-1628, 52 Shamian Nanjie, just around the corner. It may have little in the way of the amenities available in better hotels, but its rooms are clean and the staff are friendly.

The hotel's one drawback is that so many of the cheaper rooms lack windows — ask to see your room before you check in.

WHERE TO EAT

For the Chinese, a visit to Guangzhou is a culinary pilgrimage. Some of the famous "old houses" have been serving customers for over 100 years. As was the case elsewhere in China, the fortunes of many of Guangzhou's best restaurants took a turn for a worse during the dark days of the Cultural Revolution, although nowadays Guangzhou's reputation as one of the best cities in China to eat out in is right back on track.

Starting with the best, *dim sum* aficionados should head over to the **Taotaoju Restaurant** ((20) 8181-6111, 20 Dishipu Lu, an atmospheric place that was an academy of learning in the seventeenth century and is now one of Guangzhou's most celebrated restaurants.

The **North Garden Restaurant (Beiyuan Fanguan)** ((20) 8333-0087, 202 Xiaobei Road, is a series of rooms laid out around a Chinese garden where fish swim in a miniature lake crossed by a miniature bridge. Prices are close to those of Hong Kong. It gets packed early in the evening and has an extensive menu. The new annex next door is something of an eyesore, but business is business, and few Chinese guests are likely to complain.

West of the city, the **Panxi Restaurant** ((20) 8181-5718, 151 Longjing Xilu, is one of Guangzhou's busiest restaurants, and its dining rooms and pavilions are scattered through a romantic landscape of gardens, pools and ornamental bridges. Like the North Garden, its menu is upmarket and gourmet — stewed turtle in its individual terracotta casserole dish, swallow's nest and crabmeat soup, white fungus (which only grows on stone) and bamboo pith with chicken slices in consommé, fried sea slug with chicken, perch, kidney, shrimp and vegetables. But the Panxi also offers fried prawns, fried frog and chicken slices, chicken with spicy sauce, fried noodles, and chicken slices in soup, with beer, at quite a reasonable price for a one-night blowout in a restaurant that, more than any other in contemporary China, recalls the splendor of the dynastic past.

It's worth sampling some Chinese vegetarian dishes while in Guangzhou. Most of the classic vegetarian dishes are Buddhist in origin, and often use products like tofu to ingeniously duplicate the tastes and textures of various meats. The revered **Tsai Ken Hsiang Restaurant** ((20) 8334-4363, 167 Zhongshan 6-Lu, is a famous vegetarian restaurant, sometimes spelled in the tourist literature Caigenxiang.

Ask a local where to eat and chances are they'll direct you to the Dashatou wharf on Yanjiang Lu, next to the Pearl River. A string of neon-strung seafood restaurants have sprung up along the wharf, catering to the Cantonese passion for expensive seafood. If you can get a group of people together — with preferably one Chinese speaker — they can be a lot of fun.

With so many top-notch hotels around town, as you might expect there are also countless hotel restaurants to choose from. A couple of favorites are **Le Grill** ((20) 8331-1888, at the Guangdong International Hotel, and **La Casa** ((20) 8333-8989, at the Garden Hotel. In the China Hotel is the **Hard Rock Café** ((20) 8666-6888, where you can find that internationally tried-and-tested formula of loud rock music and overpriced treats such as hamburgers and French fries — don't forget to buy the T-shirt.

For inexpensive dining there are any number of good choices around town. Guangzhou has the full complement of fast-food barns these days — **KFC**, **McDonald's** and **Pizza Hut** are just a few of the big names that have set up shop here. Popular Hong Kong chains like **Café de Coral** have also had considerable success. For inexpensive local dining, take a stroll around Shamian Island, where almost all the restaurants (including the excellent *dim sum* restaurant in the **Victory Hotel**) sport English menus these days.

NIGHTLIFE

Guangzhou has a lively nightlife, but like many other Chinese cities places come and go in popularity much faster than the lifespan of a guidebook. The best place to get an idea of where is currently in is the free giveaway magazine *Clueless in Guangzhou*, which is available in most big hotels.

A reliable and friendly place for reasonable pub food and a few casual drinks is the **Elephant and Castle** ((20) 8359-3309, 363 Huanshi Donglu, which seems to have taken over from the nearby and once popular **Hill Bar** ((20) 8333-3998 extension 3913, 367 Huanshi Donglu, as the bar where Guangzhou's expatriate community choose to rub shoulders.

The more adventurous might want to try a late-night excursion to **L'Africain**, on the junction of Dongfeng Donglu and Nonglinxia Lu, a rave venue that packs in sweaty bodies on Friday and Saturday nights until late.

HOW TO GET THERE

See GETTING THERE, page 230 in TRAVELERS' TIPS, for detailed information on how to get to Guangzhou from Hong Kong. From Guangzhou, trains and planes, and even buses, fan out to nearly every corner of China.

A Guangzhou street scene and mural.

AROUND GUANGZHOU: FOSHAN AND SHUNDE

Getting to the sights around Guangzhou under your own steam can be tiresome, especially in the hot summer months. A good alternative is to take a tour. The tour offices in the major hotels run coach tours to cultural locations around the city, and their itineraries include visits to carving and other crafts factories. They also operate tours of Foshan, the famous ceramics and

of Shamian Island. It's a one-hour bus ride to Foshan, where you can find reasonably-priced accommodation at the relatively upmarket **Golden City Hotel ℓ** (757) 335-7228 FAX (757) 335-3924, 48 Fengjiang Nanlu, or the cheaper **Foshan Huaqiao Hotel ℓ** (757) 222-3828 FAX (757) 222-7702, 14 Zumiao Lu, if you want to stay overnight.

Shunde is a small town — approximately 45 km (27 miles) away — famous among gourmets as the home of Cantonese cuisine. The place to sample the cuisine is the **Qinghui Yuan**, a two-in-one treat — a Qing

crafts city 28 km (17 miles) southwest of Guangzhou, where you have the opportunity to watch artists at the **Foshan Folk Art Research Society** making traditional lanterns, paper-cuttings and brick carvings, weavers producing silk in the city's mills and ceramic miniatures being painted in their thousands at the **Shiwan Artistic Pottery and Porcelain Factory**.

Tours of Foshan also include a visit to the 900-year-old Song dynasty **Ancestral Temple**, whose remarkable architecture features dozens of ceramic figures and animals lining the crests of its roofs. It's possible to go on your own from the Guangzhou–Foshan (Guangfo) Bus Terminal, which you will find just off Daxin Zhonglu to the east

dynasty garden and a restaurant that is rated as one of the best Cantonese restaurants in the province. Should you want to savor the flavors a little longer, opposite the garden and restaurant is the 384-room **Courtyard New World Hotel ℓ** (765) 221-8333 FAX (765) 221-4773, a top-notch member of the Marriott chain. Shunde can be reached by train from Guangzhou.

ABOVE: Traditional herbal medicine shops offer tonics and cures that call upon thousands of years of medical research. OPPOSITE: The herbal teas contained in these ornate brass urns are taken as much for restorative as preventive effects.

Over the Border

Travelers' Tips

GETTING THERE

Unless you are traveling from China, the only way to get to Hong Kong is by air. The thrill-a-minute landings in the heart of Kowloon are now a thing of the past, and all flights touch down at the vast, ultra-modern Chek Lap Kok Hong Kong International Airport at Lantau Island. Despite some initial teething problems, about the only complaint that could be leveled against the new airport today is its sprawling dimensions — if you have a tight connection, don't dally in duty free.

FROM THE UNITED STATES AND CANADA

Almost all major airlines out of the United States and Canada have Hong Kong flights, with airlines such as Singapore, Cathay and United offering non-stop flights. Vancouver is the best-served Canadian city, with direct flights offered by both Canadian and Cathay. Cheaper airlines out of the United States will involve connections in Seoul or Taipei, among other places.

If you are trying to save money on your flight, avoid traveling in the peak summer months of July and August, Christmas and New Year period, and Chinese New Year (late January to late February, varying year to year). The best deals are usually Apex tickets, which require you book and pay at least three weeks in advance, stay at your destination at least seven days (but no longer than three months). Scheduled changes (while sometimes possible) are frowned upon, and will sometimes involve further payments, or "penalties."

FROM EUROPE

There is a choice of at least four or five daily flights from Britain and continental Europe direct to Hong Kong, though the cheaper tickets will involve a layover of varying length somewhere en-route. Peak seasons, which mean higher prices, are Christmas and New Year, Chinese New Year (late January to late February, varying year to year) and the entirety of summer, from June through September. It's usually possible,

depending on the airline, to find tickets that allow a stopover in Asia or the Middle East, depending on the airline. Local newspapers are the best place to check for bargains. British travelers looking for bargains might look at **www.cheapflights.co.uk**, which offers a staggering selection of discounted tickets to Hong Kong and every other conceivable destination.

FROM AUSTRALIA AND NEW ZEALAND

Australia and New Zealand have a good range of flights to Hong Kong, many offering the possibility of stopovers in other Asian destinations en-route. Garuda, for example, which is one of the cheaper airlines flying this route, offers stopovers in Bali or in Jakarta. Royal Brunei has some very good deals, but Brunei — one of Asia's smallest and most expensive countries — is perhaps one of the least appealing stopovers in the region. Perth is the least expensive Australian location to fly from. Finding bargains out of New Zealand, on the other hand, is a challenge.

FROM CHINA

For many travelers, Hong Kong is the gateway to China. There may be direct international flights to a host of Chinese destinations nowadays, but Hong Kong is still the regional hub and is likely to remain so for the foreseeable future. Travelers making their way from China to Hong Kong, or vice versa, have a number of transportation options open to them.

By Air

China Air (CAAC) (2840-1199 (reservations) flies from Hong Kong directly to most cities in China, and covers virtually the entire country from Guangzhou. You'll find them at two locations: Ticketing, Ground Floor, Gloucester Tower, The Landmark, 17 Queen's Road, Central; or 34th Floor, United Center, Queensway, Central.

Dragonair (3193-3888 (reservations) or 2868-6777 (ticketing) FAX 2810-0370 (for reservations and reconfirmation) has direct services to Beijing, Changsha, Chengdu, Chongqing, Dalian, Fuzhou, Guilin, Haikou, Hangzhou, Kunming, Nanjing, Qingdao,

Sanya, Shanghai, Wuhan, Xiamen and Xi'an. **Dragonair** are located in Room 4609-4611, 46th Floor, COSCO Tower, 183 Queen's Road, Central.

By Train

The main route from China to Hong Kong is by rail from Guangzhou to the Kowloon–Canton Railway's (KCR) Hung Hom terminus next to the Cross Harbor Tunnel's Kowloon exit. Trains run to and from Lo Wu at the Hong Kong–China border from around 6 AM until 10 PM, every six to 12 minutes. From Shenzhen customs you can connect directly with Lo Wu trains. From Guangzhou, the Hong Kong–Canton Express leaves five times a day between approximately 8:30 AM and 5 PM. It is now also possible to travel directly from Beijing, Shanghai and other destinations such as Hangzhou to Kowloon. While these services are frequent enough, they are often booked up weeks in advance.

By Bus

Air-conditioned buses leave daily from Shenzhen and Guangzhou (these are separate services) to the Admiralty bus terminus on Queensway, and to the basement of China Hong Kong City, 33 Canton Road, Kowloon. For more information contact **CityBus** (2873-0818. The **CTS Express Bus** (2764-9803, only runs from Guangzhou, but does so 15 times a day to various Hong Kong locations. Ticket arrangements can be made at virtually any Guangzhou or Shenzhen hotel.

By Boat

From Shekou, a China–Hong Kong trading and manufacturing enclave west of Shenzhen, hoverferries make frequent daily passages to the China Ferry Terminal, China Hong Kong City, 33 Canton Road, Kowloon. There are also four daily ferries from Shenzhen International Airport, though they require a connecting bus journey from the airport, a somewhat chaotic affair.

There are regular sea services, many of them daily, from a variety of cities in Southern China such as Guangzhou, Nanhai, Haikou, Xiamen and Wuzhou.

The China Ferry Terminal also has hydrofoils to Macau across the mouth of the Pearl River, one hour away. Boats leave every half hour and can be booked through travel agents, CTS, CITS or along Hong Kong Island's waterfront at the Macau Ferry Terminal, which is in the Shun Tak Center at 200 Connaught Road Central — next to the Victoria Hotel. (Hydrofoils also leave from the China Ferry Terminal.)

From Macau you can take a bus across the border to Gongbei in the Zhuhai Special Economic Zone and from there, buses or minibuses to Guangzhou or elsewhere in Guangdong province.

OVERLAND ROUTES

There are some interesting, though usually arduous, alternatives to flying into Hong Kong, though for almost everyone taking such routes, Hong Kong is more an interesting stopover than a destination in itself.

The most famous overland route is the so-called **Trans-Siberian Express**, which is in fact two separate rail routes: the **Trans-Manchurian**, which runs almost the length of Siberia before cutting south through Manchuria to Beijing; and the **Trans-Mongolian**, which travels through Mongolia to Beijing after leaving Siberia. Neither of these long journeys offers much in the way of creature comforts, and both involve navigating a minefield of bureaucratic paperwork — in the form of visas — before the journey can be embarked upon either from Beijing or from Europe. The Manchurian train is slightly slower, taking around six days to complete the journey; the Mongolian takes around five.

Decorative lanterns in a Buddhist temple.

Even more difficult, though undoubtedly tempting to latter-day world explorers, is the route so recently opened up through **Central Asia** to China's western Xinjiang province. Nevertheless, if you can get to the capitals of either Kazakhstan (Almaty) or Kyrgystan (Bishkek) — both of which are accessible from Moscow by rail and air — and you have a valid Chinese visa in hand, it is possible to continue on to China. The easier route is from Almaty, which is connected to Ürümqi, in Xinjiang province, by a twice-weekly rail service.

From the **Indian Subcontinent**, it is possible to travel to China either via Pakistan and the **Karakorum Highway** or via Nepal to Tibet via the **Friendship Highway**. Both are grueling routes, and in the case of the Karakorum slightly dangerous. To travel onwards from Nepal to Tibet you will have had to have obtained your visa somewhere other than Nepal — do not indicate your intention to travel this route when applying for the visa.

An increasingly popular overland route into China with budget travelers is that from **Vietnam**, which also has overland connections with Laos — this route now allows overlanders to travel all the way from Indonesia into China. Crossings from Vietnam to China are a straightforward affair these days, and can be undertaken either at Dong Dang (for China's Guangxi province) or at Lao Cai (for Yunnan).

All such trips will require extensive overland travel across China to Hong Kong, for which a China travel guide such as the *Traveler's China Companion* will be essential.

ARRIVING AND LEAVING

CUSTOMS

Hong Kong is a free port, but that doesn't mean you can bring in anything you like. The usual strict restrictions on firearms, dangerous items, drugs and what-have-you apply here as elsewhere, and as far as duty-free goods are concerned you can carry in a one-liter bottle of alcohol, 200 cigarettes (or 50 cigars or 250 gm of tobacco), 60 milliliters of perfume, and 250 milliliters of eau-de-Cologne.

VISAS

For nationals of most countries, all that is required to qualify for a visa-free 90-day stay in Hong Kong is a passport with six months validity and (in theory, though seldom requested) onward tickets. This no longer qualifies Commonwealth citizens to work in Hong Kong, for which it is necessary to apply for the relevant working visa. All residents of Hong Kong are required to carry an identity card, and visitors are advised to carry their passport or some other identification with a photo at all times.

DEPARTURE TAXES

Hong Kong International Airport levies an extremely reasonable, by regional standards, HK$50 departure tax. This is included in the cost of air tickets, so there is no messing about with last-minute payments at the airport: an extremely civilized set-up that one can only hope catches on elsewhere around the region.

EMBASSIES AND CONSULATES

Almost every country in the world has official representation in one way or another in Hong Kong.
Australia (2827-8881 FAX 2585-4121 E-MAIL acghkadm@netvigator.com, 21st to 24th floors, Harbor Center, 25 Harbor Road, Wanchai.
Belgium (2524-3111 FAX 2868-5997 E-MAIL consulhk@netvigator.com, Ninth Floor, St. John's Building 33 Garden Road, Central.
Canada (2810-4321 FAX 2810-6736, 11th to 14th floors, One Exchange Square, 8 Connaught Place, Central.
Denmark (2827-8101 FAX 2827-4555 E-MAIL danconhk@netvigator.com, Room 2402B, Great Eagle Center, 23 Harbor Road, Wanchai.
Finland (2525-5385 FAX 2810-1232, Room 1818, Hutchison House, 10 Harcourt Road, Central.
France (2529-4351 FAX 2866-9693 E-MAIL consinfo@france.com.hk, 25F, Tower II, Admiralty Center, 18 Harcourt Road, Admiralty.

The entrance of the first Cross-Harbor Tunnel emerges amid a network of highways at the Causeway Bay waterfront. The second Cross-Harbor Tunnel links Kowloon Bay with Quarry Bay while the third connects western Kowloon to Kennedy Town on Hong Kong's western harbor.

Germany (2529-8855, 8856 FAX 2865-2033, 21st Floor, United Center, 95 Queensway, Admiralty.

Italy (2522-0033 FAX 2845-9678 E-MAIL itconshk@netvigator.com, 805-810 Hutchison House, 10 Harcourt Road, Central.

Netherlands (2522-5127 FAX 2868-5388, 5702 Cheung Kong Center, Queen's Road, Central.

New Zealand (2877-4488 FAX 2845-2915, Room 6508, 65th Floor, Central Plaza, 18 Harbor Road, Wanchai.

South Africa (2577-3279 FAX 2845-5784,

27/F Sunning Place, 10 Hyson Avenue, Causeway Bay.

Spain (2525-3041 FAX 2877-2407, Eighth Floor, Printing House, 18 Ice House Street, Central.

Sweden (2521-1212 FAX 2596-0308, Eighth Floor, Hong Kong Club Building, 3A Chater Road, Central.

Switzerland (2522-7147 FAX 2845-2619, Room 3703, Gloucester Tower, 11 Pedder Street, Central.

United Kingdom (2901-3000 FAX 2901-3066 E-MAIL information@britishconsulate.org.hk, 1 Supreme Court Road, Central.

United States (2523-9011 FAX 2845-1598 WEB SITE www.usconsulate.org.hk, 26 Garden Road, Central.

TOURIST INFORMATION

The Hong Kong Tourist Association (HKTA) is one of Asia's most efficient tourist organizations. Their multilingual **Visitor Hotline** (2508-1234 takes care of telephone inquiries from 8 AM to 6 PM daily except Sundays, and they also operate a very useful 24-hour **INFOFAX Facsimile Information Service** ((900) 6077-1128.

Most visitors' first contact with the HKTA is at **Hong Kong International Airport**, where there are offices in the arrival halls and in the transfer area. Both of these desks are staffed daily from 7 AM to 11 PM, and provide tourist brochures and access to the tourist authority's Intranet service — i-Cyberlink — 24 hours daily.

The main **HKTA office**, Ground Floor, The Center, 99 Queen's Road, Central, is open 8 AM to 6 PM daily. On the **Kowloon** side, the HKTA office is at the Star Ferry Concourse, Tsimshatsui, and is open the same hours. HKTA has 16 offices worldwide, including:

Beijing ((10) 6465-1603 FAX 6465-1605, C211A Office Building, Beijing Lufthansa Center, 50 Liangmaqiao Road, Chaoyang District, Beijing 100016, People's Republic of China.

Australia ((02) 9283-3083 FAX (02) 9283-3383 E-MAIL hktasyd@hkta.org, Level 4, Hong Kong House, 80 Druitt Street, Sydney, NSW 2000.

Canada ((416) 366-2389 FAX (416) 366-1098 E-MAIL hktayyz@hkta.org, 3/F Hong Kong Trade Center, 9 Temperance Street, Toronto, Ontario M5H 1Y6.

France ((01) 4265-6664 FAX (01) 4265-6600 E-MAIL hktapar@hkta.org, 37 rue de Caumartin, 75009 Paris.

Germany ((069) 959-1290 FAX (069) 597-8050 E-MAIL hktafra@hkta.org, Humboldt Strasse 94, D-60318 Frankfurt/Main.

Italy ((011) 669-0238 FAX (011) 668-0785 E-MAIL hktaita@hkta.org, Corso Marconi 33, 10125 Turin.

Singapore (336-5800, 5801 FAX 336-5811 E-MAIL hktasin@hkta.org, 9 Temasek Boulevard, 34-03 Suntec Tower Two, Singapore 038989.

Spain ((93) 414-1794 FAX (93) 201-8657 E-MAIL hktabcn@hkta.org, Pau Casals 4, 08021 Barcelona.
United Kingdom ((020) 7533-7100 FAX (020) 7533-7111 E-MAIL hktalon@hkta.org, 6 Grafton Street, London W1S 4EQ.
United States of America ((212) 421-3382 FAX (212) 421-8428 E-MAIL hktanyc@hkta.org, 5/F, 115 East 54th Street, New York, New York; and ((310) 208-4582 FAX (310) 208-1869 E-MAIL hktalax@hkta.org, 10940 Wilshire Boulevard, Suite 2050, Los Angeles, California 90024-3915.

The Airbus is a cheaper alternative but is considerably slower than the train service, and can get snarled up in traffic, particularly during peak morning and evening hours. It does, however, offer the convenience of stopping at most major hotels in both Kowloon and Hong Kong.

BY TRAIN

MTR (Underground)

The Mass Transit Railway (MTR) operates four lines (including the Airport Express).

GETTING AROUND

Compact and small, Hong Kong is rivaled only by Singapore as Asia's most convenient destination for ease of getting around. Trains, trams, buses and boats make every corner of the region accessible.

FROM THE AIRPORT

The simplest way to get into town from the international airport is via an Airport Express train. The service leaves every 10 minutes and takes 23 minutes to Hong Kong Central station. The Free Airport Express Shuttle bus service leaves from Kowloon and Hong Kong stations to major hotels every 20 minutes.

The Island Line runs east–west across Hong Kong Island, between Sheung Wan in Western District and Chai Wan in the east, passing through Central, Wanchai, Causeway Bay, North Point, Quarry Bay, Taikoo, and Shau Kei Wan. The Tsuen Wan Line shoots across the harbor to Tsimshatsui, though Yau Ma Tei, Mongkok, Sham Shui Po and Lai Chi Kok to as far as Tsuen Wan in western Kowloon. The Kwun Tong Line connects eastern Hong Kong with eastern Kowloon, and from Quarry Bay crosses the harbor to Lam Tin, continuing northwest through Kwun Tong,

OPPOSITE: Garish pavilions, sculptures and other attractions at Aw Boon Haw (formerly Tiger Balm) Gardens in Causeway Bay. ABOVE: The on-course crowd at Shatin racetrack.

Choi Hung, Wong Tai Sin and Kowloon Tong and then south to Mongkok and Yau Ma Tei.

MTR trains run from 6 AM to 1 AM, every two minutes during rush hour. For more information call (2881-8888, or you can collect an MTR handbook, free of charge, from any MTR ticket office.

KCR (Overground)

From Hung Hom, the Kowloon–Canton Railway (KCR) runs through Kowloon and the New Territories, with access to such places as Mongkok, Shatin, Taipo, Fanling

BY TAXI

Taxis are plentiful, and reasonably cheap, on both sides of the harbor, with urban taxis operating on a HK$15 flagfall for the first two kilometers (one mile) and HK$1.40 for each 200 m (about 220 yd) thereafter and rural taxis on a HK$12.50 flagfall and HK$1.20 for each 200 m thereafter. Lantau Island has a separate pricing structure of HK$12 flagfall and HK$1.20 for each 200 m thereafter.

and Sheung Shui, to Lo Wu at the Chinese border. But unless you have a Chinese visa, Sheung Shui is the last stop as Lo Wu is a restricted area. MTR tickets can be used on the KCR, which connects with the MTR at Kowloon Tong. Trains run from 5:30 AM to 12:20 AM about every six minutes. For inquiries, call (2602-7799.

LRT (Overground)

The Light Rail (LRT) operates in the western New Territories between Tuen Mun ferry pier and Yuen Long. The LR has a number of lines, which can be a bit confusing, so be sure to study the route map before getting on any train. It runs from 5:40 AM to 12:30 AM. For information call (2468-7788.

Despite the abundance of taxis, at peak hours they can be hard to flag down. The best bet is to head to the nearest big hotel — there always seems to be one near by — where taxi ranks can always be found.

The worst times to try to get a cab are around 4 PM each day, when the fleets change drivers, and on race days. If you cross the harbor you must pay an extra HK$20 for the Cross-Harbor Tunnel fee — it's actually HK$10 each way, the driver gets to keep the extra HK$10 for his return toll. The Western Harbor Tunnel has a toll of HK$20. The toll for the new Lantau Link is HK$30.

Aside from the occasional young hot-rodder, Hong Kong taxi drivers are quite expert drivers, and most speak at least a little

English. If you're not happy with their service, there's a police hotline that you can call — (2527-7177 — but remember to note the taxi number or your complaint cannot be investigated.

BY BUS

Public buses are also plentiful, both on the island and in Kowloon, and the HKTA provides timetables and information on routes. The main bus terminals are just west of Exchange Square on the island and the Star Ferry in Tsimshatsui. Fares are cheap, but you must have exact change. There are also mini-buses that dart in and out of the mainstream transport, picking passengers up wherever they're hailed, rather like taxis, and feeding awkward or distant destinations. Maxi-cabs, a green and yellow version of these "service" vehicles, provide direct access to distinct points — the Star Ferry terminal in Central to the Mid-Levels, Aberdeen and Ocean Park, for example.

For more information on routes, fares and other inquiries, call **Kowloon Motor Bus Company** (KMB) (2745-4466 or, for Hong Kong Island, **China Motor Bus Company (CMB)** (2565-8556 and Citybus (2736-3888.

BY TRAM

For the cheapest scenic land transport, nothing beats the near century-old (started in 1904) tram service that runs from Kennedy Town in Western District right through the heart of Central, Wanchai and Causeway Bay and then heads east into North Point, Quarry Bay and Shau Kei Wan. The fare is HK$2. But don't use them if you're trying to get somewhere in a hurry — they're slow. During peak hours they get very crowded. Trams run down from 6 AM to 1 AM. For inquiries call (2118-6338.

Peak Tram

On Hong Kong Island, the Peak Tram runs every 10 minutes from 10 AM to 11:45 PM from its lower terminus on Garden Road in Central, taking about 10 minutes to the Peak Terminus up Victoria Peak. The fare for adults is HK$20 one-way, HK$30 for the round trip. Children under 12 pay HK$6 one-way, HK$9 round trip, and there's a seniors' fare for those over 60 of HK$7 one-way, HK$14 round trip. From Star Ferry a free, open-air double-decker shuttle-bus service runs to the Peak Tram, though it's not very far to walk.

BY FERRY

The **Star Ferry** (2366-2576 shuttles back and forth from 6:30 AM to 11:30 PM between Central District and Tsimshatsui for HK$2.20 first class (upper deck) and HK$1.70 for the lower

deck. There is also a service between Central District and Hung Hom via Whampoa Gardens and another between Central District and Wanchai.

If you want to reach the outlying islands and Tuen Mun in the New Territories, the **Hong Kong Ferry Company** (2542-3081 operates from a group of piers in Central district on Hong Kong Island, just west of the General Post Office and Star Ferry. There's also a hoverferry service between Central and Tsimshatsui East, departing from Queen's Pier, in front of City Hall.

OPPOSITE: Hong Kong's beaches provide a contrast to the urban clamor and thrusting skyline of its fast-paced cities. ABOVE: Buddhist statues at Repulse Bay.

BY RICKSHAW

Once the cheapest form of travel in Hong Kong, the rickshaw is now one of the most expensive. Now all but phased out, they're there mainly for tourist snapshots, and for a short run around the block. Negotiate first — if you're lucky, you just might be able to get a photo for HK$50 and a ride for HK$100. But be warned: these drivers are aggressive and greedy.

BY HELICOPTER

Helicopters can be chartered for sightseeing — for more details and prices contact **Heliservices (** 2802-0200, Fenwick Street Pier Heliport, Central. For flights to Macau, try **East Asia Helicopters (** 2859-3359.

CAR RENTAL

Chauffeur-driven cars are widely used in Hong Kong. Most major hotels have limousines available for guests, or you can call **Avis Rent-a-Car (** 2576-6831. Car rental is not a good idea in congested Hong Kong. Drivers, particularly those not familiar with the lay of the land, spend most of their time searching for somewhere to park.

ACCOMMODATION

Freewheeling Hong Kong has accommodation to suit all budgets and tastes. Luxury travelers will find some of Asia's, indeed the world's, best hotels on either side of the harbor, while budget travelers can find inexpensive digs in Kowloon's Tsimshatsui and in several youth hostels, which offer inexpensive accommodation in remote locations — wonderful if you are not a lover of the big city; less wonderful if you plan to do some sightseeing in the center.

Travelers looking for good-value mid-range accommodation, on the other hand, may find Hong Kong frustrating. Bargains are rare unless you organize something with a travel agent before you arrive. The Hotel Reservations Center at Hong Kong International Airport is a worthwhile stop if you have arrived in Hong Kong with no accommodation booked — it has enormous folders with pictures of hotels, their rooms and amenities, and the rates quoted are often considerably lower than the walk-in rates would be.

Most of Hong Kong's **luxury** hotels are on the harborfront, either in Central or in Tsimshatsui. Both are ideal areas from which to explore the city and outlying islands and territories. Tsimshatsui has arguably more character, but it is also something of a mad house at street level. Rates in the best hotels in either of these areas start at around US$300 and higher.

It is possible to find **mid-range** accommodation (US$100 and up) in these areas too, although Tsimshatsui has a wider range of places to choose from. Obviously, the farther you travel from either of these tourist centers, the more likely it is you'll find something that starts to represent value for money.

Tsimshatsui is the **inexpensive** accommodation center of Hong Kong. Much maligned, Chungking Mansions may be a backpacker ghetto, but somewhere amid its 17 floors of hotels, guesthouses and inexpensive restaurants, scattered across four blocks, even the most fastidious of budget travelers usually manage to find somewhere to flop for the night. A big clean-up in the late 1990s closed down some of Chungking's most notorious dives and made the structure less of a firetrap — today most of the guesthouses here are at least clean and tidy. Mirador Mansions is a nearby rival to Chungking, and slightly smarter. The cheapest accommodation in either is dormitory style, for around HK$70 per bed. Private rooms range from around HK$200.

EATING OUT

Along with Tokyo, Hong Kong is the dining capital of Asia. This is a city obsessed with food, and as a result you are never very far from somewhere to eat, whether it be a quick sandwich and an espresso or a multicourse extravaganza of Chaozhou cuisine — thought by Hong Kong Chinese to be China's best.

Prices vary enormously depending on where you eat, but a meal at most of the restaurants recommended in this book will cost at least US$20 per person, more with drinks. Cheaper restaurants are noted accordingly, as are those which are notably more expensive — and there is no shortage of these.

One of Hong Kong's great treats, of course, is trying the various regional Chinese cuisines at their best, but it is worth sampling other cuisines too. Hong Kong has fabulous Indian and Thai restaurants, and plenty of restaurants serving home-away meals for those who cannot face another tray of dim sum or another plate of steamed fish.

While luxury travelers will find no end of opportunities to indulge themselves in Hong Kong, it is not all bad news for budget travelers either. Hong Kong's armies of office workers and students almost all eat out once a day, and the city is thick with restaurants offering budget bowls of noodles, stir-fries and steamed dumplings. Fast-food restaurants are also plentiful, and some, such as the Oliver's chain, are extremely good places for a quick, healthy lunch.

BASICS

BUSINESS AND BANKING HOURS

Hong Kong follows business and banking hours that will be familiar to all Westerners. Most offices are open 9 AM to 5 PM weekdays, and 9 AM to 1 PM on Saturdays. Banks follow almost the same hours, closing at 4:30 PM weekdays, 12:30 PM Saturdays.

CURRENCY

The Hong Kong dollar is linked to the American dollar and its banknotes come in denominations of $1,000, 500, 100, 50, 20 and 10. Don't be confused by the different designs — they are issued by the three major banks: the Hongkong Bank, the Standard Chartered and the Bank of China. There are also silver coins in $5, $2 and $1 denominations, and bronze coins for 50 cents, 20 cents and 10 cents. Most banks are open Monday to Friday from around 9 AM to 4:30 PM, and generally on Saturdays untill 12:30 PM.

Generally speaking, banks give the best rates. Whatever you do, don't change more than you absolutely need at the Hong Kong International Airport bureaux de change, as extortionate commissions are charged.

Exchange rates at the time of publication were as follows:

US$1 = HK$7.77
1 euro = HK$6.74
£1 = HK$11.02
AUS$1 = HK$4.06
Can$1 = HK$5.14
NZ$1 = HK$3.26

ELECTRICITY

All electrical appliances in Hong Kong work on 200/220 volts, 50 cycles. American appliances generally need transformers as well as plug adapters. Most hotels provide 110 volt adapters for shavers and hairdryers, and some can also provide extra adapters for portable computers.

NATIONAL HOLIDAYS

As in China and Taiwan, Hong Kong's biggest holiday is **Chinese New Year**, or Spring Festival, which usually falls some time at

A wealth of printed media floods Hong Kong's newsstands daily the end of January or beginning of February. Officially, businesses close for three days over Chinese New Year, but it can end up being longer than that if a weekend is loaded on either side. Some travelers think of Chinese New Year as an exciting place to be in Hong Kong, perhaps imagining the city comes to life with dragon dances and the like. It's actually a rather uninteresting time to visit — everything shuts down, and transportation in and out of the city (especially into China) becomes a nightmare.

The following days of the year are public holidays:

January 1 New Year
Late January to mid-February
   Chinese New Year (three days)
Early April
   Ching Ming (Tomb-Sweeping Day)
Mid-April
   Good Friday and Easter Monday
Late April to early May
   Lord Buddha's Birthday
May 1 Labor Day
June Dragon Boat Festival
July 2 Hong Kong Special Administrative
   Region Establishment Day
Mid-September to early October
   Mid-Autumn Festival
October 1 National Day
October Chung Yeung Festival
December 25 Christmas
December 26 Boxing Day

TIME

Hong Kong is eight hours ahead of Greenwich Mean Time, which is 13 hours ahead of United States' Eastern Standard Time, and 16 hours ahead of Vancouver or Los Angeles. It is on the same time zone as all of China, as well as Taiwan.

TIPPING

Most major restaurants include a 10-percent service charge in the check — and expect to keep some of the change too. Elsewhere, feel free to tip everyone from bellhops to toilet attendants if they offer a genuine service, but not more than HK$5. Also, add a dollar to the meter fare to keep the taxi drivers happy.

COMMUNICATION AND MEDIA

Hong Kong has highly developed communications, and its English-language media is the best in Asia.

POST

Every district in Hong Kong has a post office where English is spoken. Poste Restante will be held at the GPO in central, near the Star Ferry terminal unless otherwise directed. Air mail from Hong Kong to Europe or the United States usually takes from three to five days.

Hong Kong's main post offices in Central and Tsimshatsui are open from 8 AM to 6 PM from Monday to Saturday, and until 2 PM on Sunday.

TELEPHONE

Hong Kong has a very efficient telephone system, and local calls are free if they're made from a private phone. Some hotels charge for local calls, however, and some public phones cost HK$1 a call. Most hotel rooms have telephones with International Direct Dialing (IDD) facilities.

Cardphones for both local and IDD calls are located at some 500 sites and operate on stored-value phonecards available at most Telecom CSL shops, Hong Kong Telecom Service Centers and HKTA and other public locations in three denominations: HK$50, HK$100 and HK$250.

There are also credit card telephones and coin telephones for local and IDD calls. For more details, call International Customer Services on 10013. If you want to connect directly with your country's operator you can use the Home Direct service by using the relevant dial access number from any phone, or at the touch of a button from dedicated Home Direct phones at the airport, Ocean Terminal and other major tourist areas.

The country code for Hong Kong is (852). The country code for China is (86). For directory inquiries dial (1081.

GSM single- and dual-band mobile phones can be used in Hong Kong and in China.

FAXES AND E-MAIL

Almost all Hong Kong hotels nowadays provide fax and e-mail and Internet services — even some of the budget hostels in Tsimshatsui, though in the latter you are more likely to find e-mail services than fax. Internet cafés are to be found at every turn, especially in shopping arcades and areas popular with budget travelers. They can be surprisingly inexpensive, and many of Hong Kong's cafés now have free Internet terminals.

Television

Unless you are booked into rock-bottom digs, your hotel will probably supplement the somewhat pedestrian fare delivered by Hong Kong's two terrestrial English-language television stations with satellite and cable television. Among the many channels available are: Star TV's Star Plus, MTV, and Prime Sports, ESPN1 (an American sports network), BBC, CNN1 and CNBC Asia. Some hotels feature HKTA's Explore Hong Kong and The Hongkong Channel's video guides.

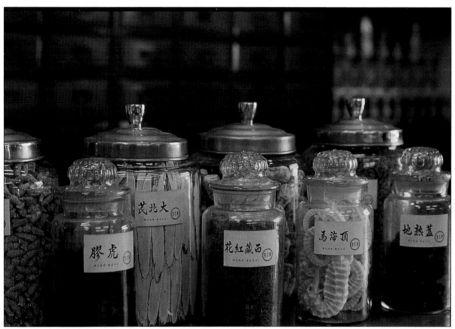

MEDIA

For local news and good coverage of China, the daily *South China Morning Post* is the best bet. The *Hong Kong iMail* was formerly known as the *Hong Kong Standard*, but despite a major makeover and a trendy change of name is still a less stimulating read than its rival. International dailies printed in Hong Kong include *USA Today International*, *Asian Wall Street Journal* and the *International Herald Tribune*.

The usual weekly news magazines such as *Time* and *Newsweek* are widely available in Asian editions, though for more comprehensive Asian coverage it's better to turn to the new-look *Far Eastern Economic Review*, or the more populist *Asiaweek*.

Radio

The main English-language radio stations are Radio Television Hong Kong's (RTHK) British-style Radio 3 AM/FM; Radio 4 AM/FM (classical music); Radio 6 AM (BBC World Service Relay); Commercial Radio's Quote AM, which sounds like a British Station trying to go West Coast; and Metro Plus AM and FM Select.

ETIQUETTE

Hong Kong can seem a particularly rude and aggressive place. Limited space and push-and-shove crowds can translate into

Dried sea-horses feature among the range of traditional products sold in herbal medicine stores.

considerable competition for limited resources. That said, there has been a move in Hong Kong to raise levels of politeness, and it does seem to have worked to a certain extent. The famous surliness of shop clerks and waiting staff has lost some of its abrasive edge in recent years, and it is even possible to encounter the occasional smile and thank you nowadays.

This is not the place for an analysis of Hong Kong's legendary unfriendliness, which most visitors encounter at some point or another, but it is worth noting that what many foreigners perceive as unfriendliness is most definitely not perceived as such by Hong Kong people themselves.

As for etiquette, Hong Kong's long colonial experience makes it Asia's most accessible destination for foreigners. Providing you act with standard good manners, you are unlikely to offend anyone.

HEALTH

Hong Kong has very high health and hygiene standards — you can safely drink the water — but the high summer temperatures and humidity can cause skin and fungal problems, called "Hong Kong Foot," if you stay for any length of time. On a short visit, with your tolerance for tropical germs quite low, it's advisable to stay away from street-stall restaurants. Unless you've been in an infected area in the previous 14 days you won't need a cholera certificate, or any other vaccination stamp.

SECURITY

Hong Kong is one of the world's safest cities, by day or by night. Obviously, as is the case anywhere, it is not a good idea to carry vast sums in cash about on your person, but many locals do. Women can feel safe in Hong Kong, but going about town late at night alone is, of course, not a good idea.

WHEN TO GO

Autumn, from September to early December, is the most pleasant season in Hong Kong, though drizzly overcast weather can sometimes mar this time of year. At its best,

autumn has low humidity, moderate temperatures and sunny weather. Spring, from March to mid-May, is also a good season to be in Hong Kong. Although later in the season the weather can turn muggy, for the most part it is a temperate time of year like autumn. Winters are variable, but can turn quite chill at times, a situation that is compounded by damp and drizzly conditions. Winter sees a high proportion of overcast days. Summer, from May to mid-September, is for the most part downright unpleasant. Humidity tends to be extremely high, making even the shortest walk outside a very sweaty experience. Late in the season, typhoons sweep through, drenching the city in torrential rains and often shutting everything (including flights in and out) down for a day or two.

It is a good idea to avoid Chinese New Year, which falls between late January and mid-February.

WHAT TO TAKE

It is difficult to imagine arriving in Hong Kong without anything that could not be replaced there. Hong Kong is Asia's most international city, and almost anything you could conceivably need is for sale.

LANGUAGE

The language of 98 percent of Hong Kong's population is Cantonese. While related to Mandarin — Cantonese is officially a "dialect" — it's as different from the latter as, say, Dutch is from English. It has a considerably more complex tonal system than Mandarin, making it a bad choice of language for tonal novices.

Mandarin is spoken more widely in Hong Kong today than it was in the pre-handover days, but — if you speak China's national tongue — do not expect everyone you meet to speak it, and do not expect those that do to speak it gladly. If you like, learn a few Cantonese phrases, but you will find English is spoken widely in Hong Kong. In the streets, there are special English-speaking Chinese police officers, identified by a red flash under the numbers on their shoulders.

Cantonese do not expect foreigners to learn their language, and are generally surprised by those that do. Unfortunately the colonial experience — very few Brits bothered to make an effort linguistically — means that the Cantonese are rarely all that encouraging to beginners: don't expect the smiles and gasps of astonishment you might get in, say, Japan, Taiwan or Thailand, when you trot out a carefully memorized Cantonese phrase.

Some basic expressions are as follows:
Hello   *Gay ho*
How are you?   *Gay ho ma*?
Have you eaten? (common greeting)   *Sik jaw fan may a?*
Good morning   *Jaw san*
Good night   *Jaw tao*
Goodbye   *Joy geen*
Thank you   *Daw dze*
I   *Ngo*
You   *Lay* (or *Nay*)
He   *Koey*
My name is …   *Ngo gyew …*
What is your name?   *Lay gyew mut yeh meng?*
Do you speak English?   *Lay sik m sik gong Yingmun?*
Here   *Ni doh*
There   *Go doh*
Where?   *Bin doh?*
1   *yat*
2   *yi*
3   *sam*
4   *see*
5   *ng*
6   *lok*
7   *chat*
8   *bat*
9   *gao*
10   *sap*
How much?   *Gay daw tseen?*

WEB SITES

Probably due to the Internet fever that took Hong Kong by storm in late 1999 and early 2000, there are a large number of web sites devoted to Hong Kong, though some of them are now starting to fall by the wayside. Be aware that some of the web sites listed here may cease to exist during the lifespan of this book, though every effort has been made to ensure that only stable sites have been selected.

www.info.gov.hk/index_e.htm
Practical information about Hong Kong provided by the Hong Kong government, with news, community announcements, information about publications, lists of government organizations and the like.

www.lcsd.gov.hk/tindexe.html
The Hong Kong government **Leisure & Cultural Services Department** offers this

useful site on Hong Kong's leisure and cultural attractions.

www.pbs.org/pov/hongkong/
The *Hong Kong 1997: Lives in Transition* is an interesting document that illuminates with transition of power with diaries from the period.

www.scmp.com
Hong Kong's top English-language daily, the *South China Morning Post*, in full, with news, features, business, technology and classifieds, among other things.

A shop in Western District specializing in ancestor-worship necessities — altars, a variety of incenses and all sorts of paper replicas.

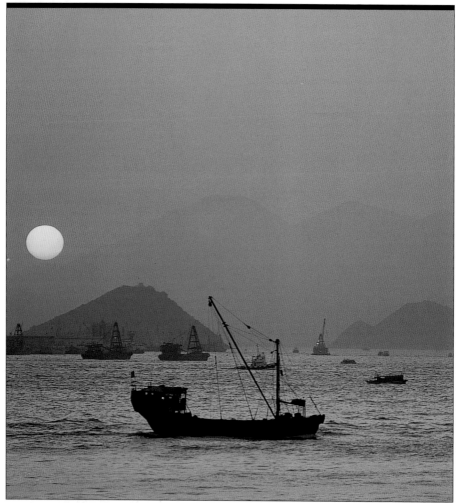

http://hk-imail.singtao.com
Formerly the *Standard*, the *Hong Kong iMail* is the *South China Morning Post*'s main rival and has a more tabloidy approach to daily news.

http://english.hongkong.com
A Hong Kong community magazine with news, entertainment, features and many other quirky odds and ends.

www.planetexpat.com/english/index.html
Planet Expat has sections on a host of destinations around the world, but the Hong Kong section is particularly worth taking a look at. It includes up-to-date information on the entire Special Administrative Region (HKSAR).

www.totallyhk.com
Features, listings and reviews on this expat and tourist-oriented site — well worth a look if you are going to Hong Kong.

www.asiagateway.com
Asia Gateway has an excellent Hong Kong section, with travel recommendations, good hotel and restaurant reviews, and feature stories.

http://www.wwf.org.hk/eng/index.html
The Internet site of World Wide Fund For Nature Hong Kong (WWFHK) has realms of information on endangered species in Honk Kong and its waters, and on local wildlife-watching, birdwatching and conservation activites.

Recommended Reading

Bilingual Hong Kong Guide Book (Hong Kong street map). Universal Publications.

BORDWELL, DAVID. *Planet Hong Kong: Popular Cinema and the Art of Entertainment.* Harvard University Press, 2000. More academic than *Sex and Zen & A Bullet In the Head* (see below), but a valuable resource for anyone with more than a passing interest in Hong Kong cinema.

CLAVELL, JAMES. *Taipan.* Dell, 1966. The classic blockbuster set in nineteenth-century Hong Kong and China.

CLAVELL, JAMES. *Noble House.* Dell, 1981. More high drama, this time in Hong Kong during the 1950s.

COONTS, STEPHEN. *Hong Kong: A Jake Grafton Novel.* St. Martins, 2000. A thriller set against the backdrop of a Hong Kong about to explode.

FENBY, JONATHON. *Dealing with the Dragon: A Year in the New Hong Kong.* Arcade, 2001. A racy, well written snapshot of Hong Kong three years after the transition to Chinese rule.

HAMMOND, STEFAN, (et al). *Sex and Zen & A Bullet in the Head.* Fireside, 1996. A fun guide to cult classics, both popular and obscure, in Hong Kong cinema.

MASON, JAMES. *The World of Suzie Wong.* Reprinted by Annereon, 1999. Evocation of Hong Kong in the 1950s that has achieved iconic status in the SAR.

MAUGHAM W. SOMERSET. *The Painted Veil.* 1925. Maugham ventures into the territory for which he is famed — expatriates in the Far East — in this, one of his lesser known works.

MORRIS, JAN. *Hong Kong: Epilogue to an Empire.* Vintage, 1997. A fine piece of travel writing about Hong Kong past, present and future.

JAMES O'REILLY, editor. *Travelers' Tales Hong Kong.* Travelers' Tales Inc., 1996. A collection of stories from the former colony.

PATTEN, CHRISTOPHER. *East and West: China, Power and the Future of Asia.* Times Books, 1998. No-holds-barred account of Hong Kong's transition from colony to semi-autonomous region, by the man who oversaw the transition. Well written and insightful.

STOKES, EDWARD. *Hong Kong's Wild Places: An Environmental Exploration.* Oxford University Press, 1996. Photographs and text by a hiker who has explored the nooks and crannies of Hong Kong's natural environment and produced a compelling book about it.

SUYIN, HAN. *A Many Splendored Thing.* Little, Brown & Co, 1952. Han Suyin's autobiography set in Hong Kong and made famous by the movie nearly of the same name, *Love is a Many Splendored Thing.*

THEROUX, PAUL. *Kowloon Tong.* Houghton Mifflin, 1998. Much maligned by local critics, Theroux's novel about the collision between British expatriate culture and the new China in Hong Kong still outshines other recent English-language novels set in the former territory.

TSUKIYAMA, GAIL. *Night of Many Dreams.* St. Martins, 1999. A family saga from the years 1940 to 1960 against the backdrop of ever-changing Hong Kong.

VINE, STEPHEN. *Hong Kong: China's New Colony.* 1998. A somewhat pessimistic and personal look at the transition of power and the prospects for Hong Kong written by a resident journalist.

WELSH, FRANK. *A Borrowed Place: The History of Hong Kong.* Kodansha, 1993. The most comprehensive history available, well written and eminently readable.

Hong Kong's harbors provide overnight shelter for thousands of small fishing boats.

Quick Reference A–Z Guide
to Places and Topics of Interest

Photo Credits

All Photos by **Nik Wheeler** except those listed below.

Adina Amsel: pages 10, 50, 54–55, 143, 197, 209.

Holzbachová Bénet: pages 26–27, 29, 206–207.

Adrian Bradshaw : pages 212–213, 213, 218, 219, 225.

Peter Danford: pages 12–13, 15, 16, 30, 31, 37, 93, 105, 116–117, 122–123, 132–133, 190-191, 243.

Alain Evrard: pages 7 *right*, 34, 35, 48–49, 56–57, 67, 71, 72, 79, 85, 118, 173 *right*, 156, 171, 177, 181, 193, 200–201, 202–203, 210.

Yann Layma: page 214.

Derek Maitland: page 191.

Chris Stowers: page 216.

Graham Uden: pages 70, 100–101, 102–103, 141, 163.

HKTA: pages 14, 73, 89, 144, 152, 173 *left*, 203.

Hong Kong Museum of History, Urban Council: page 104.

Profile Photo Library — Rex A. Butcher: 149; **Niel Farrin**: 58–59, 112; **Hans Lindberg**: 119; **A. M. MacKillop**: 52–53, 106–107; **Paul Thompson**: 62–63; **Airphoto International LTD**: 90–91.

The Public Records Office of Hong Kong: pages 120, 121.

The Stock House — Robin Moyer: page 129.